Mastering GeoServer

A holistic guide to implementing a robust, scalable, and secure Enterprise Geospatial Data Hosting System by leveraging the power of GeoServer

Colin Henderson

PUBLISHING

BIRMINGHAM - MUMBAI

Mastering GeoServer

First published: November 2014

Production reference: 1181114

Published by Packt Publishing Ltd.
Livery Place
35 Livery Street
Birmingham B3 2PB, UK.

ISBN 978-1-78328-769-7

www.packtpub.com

Cover image by Adam Plezer (bitangkajla@gmail.com)

Credits

Author
Colin Henderson

Reviewers
Luca De Felice
Stefano Iacovella
Roy A. Justo
Antonio Santiago Pérez
Richard Zijlstra

Acquisition Editor
Vinay Argekar

Content Development Editor
Poonam Jain

Technical Editor
Tanvi Bhatt

Copy Editors
Sayanee Mukherjee
Karuna Narayanan

Project Coordinator
Mary Alex

Proofreaders
Ameesha Green
Samantha Lyon
Jonathan Todd

Indexers
Hemangini Bari
Monica Ajmera Mehta
Tejal Soni

Graphics
Ronak Dhruv
Valentina D'silva
Abhinash Sahu

Production Coordinator
Nitesh Thakur

Cover Work
Nitesh Thakur

About the Author

Colin Henderson is a spatial solutions architect with 14 years of experience working on solutions to complex spatial problems. He is currently the Geospatial Systems Capability Lead for Atkins, one of the world's leading design, engineering, and project management consultancies. Although experienced in a wide range of proprietary GIS software, his current focus is on specializing in the integration of open source software in complex enterprise environments. His most recent projects involve the integration of GeoServer with FME Server from Safe Software and the delivery of spatial web-mapping applications through Esri's ArcGIS for the Server platform and Latitude Geographics' Geocortex framework. Colin is the Technical Architect and Lead Developer of Atkins' open source-based spatial integration platform, CIRRUSmaps™, a solution built on the best breed of open source spatial software, including PostGIS and OpenLayers, with GeoServer at its heart, and designed from the ground-up for deployment in cloud environments.

A self-confessed techie, Colin enjoys digging deeper to understand technology and software, and then applying this learning to create innovative solutions to problems. When possible, he likes to "pay it forward" by helping others with their problems, through contributions on GIS Stack Exchange, in particular.

I would like to dedicate this book to the memory of my grandfather, John Denis Stevens, who sadly passed away while I was writing and never got to see the finished product. He often liked to say "these computer things will never catch on!"

I would like to thank my parents for buying me my first computer, I really enjoyed breaking it and then trying to get it working again. Without the introduction, my curiosity of all things computers would never have happened.

Finally, I would like to thank my wife, Amy, and children, Evie and Max, for their patience during the writing process; I love you all very much.

About the Reviewers

Luca De Felice is a keen and passionate GIS software engineer. His educational background and working experience are in environmental sciences, with particular emphasis in the field of GIS techniques applied to risk and hazard management and monitoring. During his university studies, he started developing models for the evaluation of flood hazards. This activity continued after his graduation, with his design of GIS to build hydrologic models being applied to sample basins within a European project. For several years, he worked for a public office to contribute to the development of a hydro-geological GIS-based early warning system at the regional/national level. In this context, he learned GIS, IT environment development, database, and web mapping, applied to any kind of environmental data. Moreover, he contributed to several articles and workshops intended to disseminate novel approaches towards the development of GIS-based early warning systems.

He has been working for more than 10 years as a GIS scientific consultant in different technical contexts, where he applies his deep knowledge of GIS and IT computation in practical cases concerning the design and development of GIS-based environmental monitoring systems.

Stefano Iacovella is a longtime GIS developer and consultant living in Rome, Italy. He also routinely works as a GIS course instructor. He has a PhD in Geology. Being very curious, he developed a deep knowledge of IT technologies, mainly focusing on GIS software and related standards. Starting his career as an ESRI employee, he was exposed to, and became confident with proprietary GIS software, mainly the ESRI suite of products.

Over the last 14 years, he became more and more involved with open source software, also integrating it with proprietary software. He loves the open source approach, and really trusts in collaboration and sharing of knowledge. He strongly believes in the open source idea and constantly manages to spread it out, not only in the GIS sector. He has been using GeoServer since release 1.5, configuring, deploying, and hacking it in several projects. Other GFOSS projects he uses and likes are GDAL/OGR, PostGIS, QGIS, and OpenLayers.

He authored two books on GeoServer with Packt Publishing, *GeoServer Cookbook*, a practical set of recipes to get the most out of the software, and *GeoServer Beginner's Guide*, a first approach to GeoServer features.

When not playing with maps and geometric shapes, he loves reading about Science, mainly Physics and Maths, riding his bike, and having fun with his wife and his two daughters, Alice and Luisa.

You can contact him at stefano.iacovella@gmail.com or follow him on his Twitter handle @iacovellas.

Roy A. Justo is a geospatial application developer. He was born and raised in Havana, Cuba, and obtained a Bachelor of Science degree in Geography with Honors from the University of Havana. He also earned a Master's degree in Geographic Information Technologies from the Autonomous University of Barcelona. Roy has worked in this field as a teacher and researcher. He also worked in the private sector, creating geospatial solutions for diverse markets. His work has taken him to Munich, Barcelona, Boston, and most recently, New York City. He is currently working at one of the world's largest privately held software firms, where he integrates geospatial functionalities into BI development environments.

Roy is the coauthor and coeditor on *Environmental system research and sustainability in urbanized watersheds*, José Mateo Rodriguez, Editorial Felix Varela, the original title of which is *Estructura geográfico-ambiental y sostenibilidad de cuencas hidrográficas urbanizadas*.

Antonio Santiago Pérez is a Computer Science graduate with more than 10 years of experience in designing and implementing systems. Since the beginning of his professional life, his experience has always been related to the world of meteorology, working for different companies as an employee and freelancer. He's experienced in the development of systems to collect, store, transform, analyze, and visualize data, and is actively interested in any GIS-related technology, with preference for data visualization.

As a restless mind, which is mainly experienced in the Java ecosystem, Antonio has worked actively with many related web technologies, always looking to improve the client side of web applications.

A firm believer of software engineering practices, he is an enthusiast of Agile methodologies, involving customers as the main key for a project's success.

First, I would like to dedicate this book to my wife for understanding my passion for programming and the world of computers.

Second, I would like to dedicate this book to all the restless people that make possible great open source projects, such as OpenLayers, for the simple pleasure to create something one step better.

Richard Zijlstra is educated as a civil engineer. He has used his engineering degree in the Netherlands on water management, infrastructure planning, and geographical information management, in combination with earthquakes in Greece (Patras), on all environmental and social human aspects. He collaborates on system architecture, requirement management, and development of geographical information technology. Richard has worked on a lot of projects on geo architecture in the Netherlands. He has collaborated on www.pdok.nl across several organizations and companies.

At the moment (2014), Richard is developing Enterprise Geo Data Architecture to store data about earthquakes in the Groningen province in the northern part of the Netherlands. Gas extraction in this area produces earthquakes that damage buildings and infrastructure. The application will be a geo data storage to collaborate with all kinds of data about the problems in this area. Also, interactivity in social media will be possible. His future vision is based on Geographical Intelligence in all contexts of life and earth.

Richard is the founder and owner of the company Geoneer, which
is a pioneer in geography and information technology. From this vision and
point of view, Geoneer helps and collaborates on all aspects of geographical
information technology worldwide. You can find Geoneer on Twitter and
http://www.linkedin.com/in/geoneer/ on LinkedIn.

He has written a lot of documents on the system architecture and usage
of geographical information technology. The book *OpenLayers Cookbook*,
Packt Publishing, was reviewed by him for text and JavaScript code accuracy.

My vision and mission:

Everybody uses and shares their own geographical information to share and update
each other's knowledge about the physical and social environment.

What, where, when, and why... that's the question!

I want to thank my parents for my healthy brain and childhood
environment in the Frisian countryside. Also, I thank the people
from the town of Groningen who inspired me to do my thing. I'm
also very thankful to the people who know how I think, what I do,
and what I wish to do in future. My greatest thanks go out to my
son, Alessio Mori Zijlstra, my greatest inspiration in life!

www.PacktPub.com

Support files, eBooks, discount offers, and more

For support files and downloads related to your book, please visit www.PacktPub.com.

Did you know that Packt offers eBook versions of every book published, with PDF and ePub files available? You can upgrade to the eBook version at www.PacktPub.com and as a print book customer, you are entitled to a discount on the eBook copy. Get in touch with us at service@packtpub.com for more details.

At www.PacktPub.com, you can also read a collection of free technical articles, sign up for a range of free newsletters and receive exclusive discounts and offers on Packt books and eBooks.

https://www2.packtpub.com/books/subscription/packtlib

Do you need instant solutions to your IT questions? PacktLib is Packt's online digital book library. Here, you can search, access, and read Packt's entire library of books.

Why subscribe?

- Fully searchable across every book published by Packt
- Copy and paste, print, and bookmark content
- On demand and accessible via a web browser

Free access for Packt account holders

If you have an account with Packt at www.PacktPub.com, you can use this to access PacktLib today and view 9 entirely free books. Simply use your login credentials for immediate access.

Table of Contents

Preface **1**

Chapter 1: Installing GeoServer for Production **7**

 Java requirements **8**

  Installing Java on CentOS 6.3 8

  Installing Java on Windows Server 2008 R2 SP1 11

 Installing Apache Tomcat **14**

  Installing Apache Tomcat 7 on CentOS 6.3 15

   Running Apache Tomcat as a service 16

   Securing Apache Tomcat 20

  Installing Apache Tomcat 7 on Windows Server 2008 R2 SP1 21

   Controlling the Tomcat service 24

   Configuring the Tomcat service 25

 Deploying GeoServer to Apache Tomcat **27**

  Deploying on CentOS 6.3 28

  Deploying on Windows Server 2008 R2 SP1 29

  Checking GeoServer deployment 30

 Configuring GeoServer for maximum performance and availability **30**

  Scaling vertically 31

  Scaling horizontally 32

  Getting the best of both 33

 Configuring multiple GeoServer instances on a single server **34**

  Configuring on CentOS 6.3 34

  Configuring on Windows Server 2008 R2 SP1 37

 Summary **40**

Chapter 2: Working with Raster Data **41**

 Increasing the raster formats supported by GeoServer **42**

  Installing the GDAL binary libraries 43

   Installing on CentOS Linux 6.3 44

   Installing on Windows Server 2008 R2 SP1 45

  Installing the GeoServer GDAL plugin 49

How to optimize raster data for better performance	**51**
Understanding your source data	51
Single file versus multifile	53
GeoTIFF overviews and tiling	55
GeoTIFF overviews	55
GeoTIFF tiles	56
Converting raster formats to GeoTIFF	57
How to serve very large raster datasets	**58**
Using the ImageMosaic format	59
Creating ImageMosaic automatically	60
Creating ImageMosaic manually	62
How to use the ImageMosaic JDBC extension	67
Installing the extension	67
Configuring the extension	68
Summary	**76**
Chapter 3: Working with Vector Data in Spatial Databases	**77**
Database connection pooling	**78**
Understanding database connection pools	78
Configuring a database connection pool	79
JNDI connection or JDBC	**82**
Configuring JNDI at the servlet container	83
General database connection parameters	**87**
The primary key metadata table	87
The database session startup SQL	88
The database session close-up SQL	89
The geometry metadata table	89
Serving data from PostGIS	**90**
Publishing a PostGIS table as a layer	90
Serving data from Oracle	**93**
Installing the Oracle extension	94
Validating the installation	95
Publishing an Oracle table as a layer	96
Serving data from Microsoft SQL Server and SQL Azure	**97**
Installing the Microsoft SQL Server extension	97
Installing Microsoft JDBC drivers on Linux	98
Installing Microsoft JDBC drivers on Windows Server 2008 R2	100
Validating the installation	102
Publishing a Microsoft SQL Server table as a layer	103
Creating SQL View layers	**105**
GeoServer SQL Views versus database views	105
Creating a SQL View layer	106
Summary	**116**

Chapter 4: Using GeoServer to Serve Complex Features   **117**

The difference between simple and complex features   **117**

  Simple features – GeoServer's default   118

  Complex features   119

Using GeoServer application schemas   **121**

  Installing and configuring the extension   121

    Configuring the WFS service   123

  Application schema mapping file   125

Publishing data with an application schema   **128**

  Source data preparation   129

  The application schema mapping file   132

  Data store and feature type configuration   139

Summary   **141**

Chapter 5: Using GeoServer as a Proxy   **143**

Defining cascaded services   **143**

Using cascaded services   **144**

  Extending the capabilities of another WMS server   144

  WMS enabling a WFS-only server   145

  Using GeoServer as a reverse proxy   146

Creating a cascaded WMS connection   **147**

  Creating the data store   148

  Publishing a cascaded WMS layer   151

Connecting to a cascaded WFS   **155**

  Creating the data store   155

  Connecting through a proxy   162

Extending server capabilities   **162**

Summary   **165**

Chapter 6: Controlling the Output of GeoServer   **167**

Styling data with Styled Layer Descriptor   **168**

  Creating SLDs visually   168

  Taking SLD further – render transformations   170

Styling data using Cascaded Style Sheets   **176**

  Installing the extension   176

  The basics of CSS styles   180

  Putting it all together   182

Per-request styling of map features   **188**

Per-request filtering of data   **193**

Using Freemarker templates to change WMS responses   **195**

Summary   **201**

Chapter 7: Using GeoServer to Print Maps — 203

The GeoServer print extension — 204
Installing the print extension — 204
  Verifying the print extension installed — 205
Configuring the print extension — 207
  The dpis section — 208
  The formats section — 209
  The scales section — 209
  The fonts section — 210
  The hosts whitelist section — 211
  The layouts section — 212
Defining print layouts — 212
  Defining the layout metaData element — 215
  Defining layout pages — 216
Making print requests — 222
  The REST API — 223
    Getting the print server capabilities — 224
    Specifying print requests — 226
An example OpenLayers application — 230
  Initializing the application — 232
  Generating the print SPEC to POST — 234
  Sending the print request — 236
Summary — 237

Chapter 8: Integrating GeoServer in a Spatial Data Infrastructure — 239

Definition of a spatial data infrastructure — 240
  The technology platform of a spatial data infrastructure — 241
User perspective – editing data through WFS-T — 244
  Using a Desktop GIS — 244
    Connecting QGIS to GeoServer's WFS-T service — 245
    Using the QGIS Topology Checker tool — 249
    Using the WFS-T service to save results — 255
User perspective – consuming data — 256
  Launching Google Earth from GeoServer — 256
  Using the KML reflector to load data — 258
  Using Google Earth network links — 259
Summary — 261

Chapter 9: GeoServer as a Spatial Analysis Platform — 263

Understanding Web Processing Services — 264
  A WPS process — 264
  WPS process chaining — 265

Installing the WPS extension   **265**
  Checking whether the extension is installed correctly   267
  Configuring the extension   269
    The workspace configuration section   269
    The Service Metadata configuration section   270
    The Execution Settings configuration section   272
    The Process groups configuration section   273
Using WPS to perform spatial analysis   **274**
  Executing a WPS process   275
  Executing chained WPS processes   280
    Selecting the crime type   282
    Selecting the Police Force territory   284
    Executing the WPS process chain   286
Understanding GeoScript   **287**
  GeoScript integration with GeoServer   288
Installing the GeoScript extension   **290**
  Checking whether the extension has been installed correctly   291
Scripting GeoServer   **291**
  Creating a WPS process   292
    Defining the WPS process   292
    Creating the WPS process run method   295
    Testing the Python WPS process   297
  Creating a RESTful service   297
Summary   **303**
Chapter 10: Enterprise Security and GeoServer   **305**
Authentication and authorization   **306**
  User authentication methods   307
  User authorization methods   309
Using Active Directory for user authentication and authorization   **309**
  Configuring Active Directory for authentication   310
  Configuring Active Directory for authorization   312
Using Digest for user authentication   **316**
  Setting up an HTTP Digest authentication   317
  Testing an HTTP Digest authentication   319
Using HTTP Header for user authentication   **321**
  Setting up an HTTP Header authentication   322
  Testing the HTTP Header authentication   325
Summary   **328**

Chapter 11: Monitoring the Performance and Health of GeoServer — 329

The importance of monitoring GeoServer — 329
The GeoServer monitor extension — 330
  Installing the monitor extension — 331
  Configuring the monitor extension — 332
    The db.properties file — 333
    The filter.properties file — 333
    The hibernate.properties file — 334
    The monitor.properties file — 334
  Checking whether the monitor extension is installed correctly — 335
  Viewing the monitor extension activity and reports — 336
  Going further with the request data — 337
Stress testing GeoServer — 339
  Generating test WMS bounding boxes — 340
  Creating an Apache JMeter™ test workbench — 342
  Choosing where to execute tests — 349
  Executing the test profile — 350
Analyzing the results of the stress test — 351
Summary — 353

Chapter 12: Optimizing GeoServer for Production — 355

Deploying GeoServer in a cluster — 355
  Sharing a data directory in Windows 2008 R2 — 359
Optimizing GeoServer — 366
  Native JAI and JAI image I/O extensions — 366
  Optimizing Java Virtual Machine — 367
  Disabling unused GeoServer services — 369
  Managing request handling with the control-flow extension — 370
    Installing the control flow module — 371
    The control-flow module rules configuration — 372
Automatic recovery from service failures — 374
  Creating a Windows Watchdog script — 375
    Scheduling the Watchdog script — 378
  Creating a Linux Watchdog script — 384
    Scheduling the Watchdog script using cron — 387
Summary — 388

Index — 389

Preface

Since its release in March 2002, GeoServer continued to mature and develop into a sophisticated open source web mapping server. It has a feature set that puts it on par with (some will argue that it even beats) the most popular commercial off-the-shelf web mapping servers. The key to a successful open source software project is to have a strong and talented group of developers and a vibrant community of active and engaged users. GeoServer has both of these key ingredients, which is why it is one of the most popular open source web mapping solutions available today. From large organizations such as Great Britain's national mapping agency (Ordnance Survey) handling large volumes of data to simple small-scale community websites, GeoServer can handle it all.

This book is intended as a natural follow-on from *GeoServer Beginner's Guide* by Stefano Lacovella and Brian Youngblood, also published by Packt Publishing. It is meant as an advanced guide to GeoServer, and is ideal for when you want to take GeoServer beyond the simple delivery of web maps into advanced uses such as spatial analysis. The book covers a variety of concepts such as installing production-ready and optimized servers, loading and managing spatial data, running complex spatial analysis, and manipulating the output.

What this book covers

Chapter 1, Installing GeoServer for Production, examines how GeoServer can be deployed in a production environment. Installation of GeoServer in Apache Tomcat on both Windows and Linux platforms is covered. The chapter ends by looking at different production-deployment architectures for failover and high availability.

Chapter 2, Working with Raster Data, addresses the different types of raster data that can be served by GeoServer and how to optimize them to serve at performance. Increasing the number of raster formats that can be served by implementing the GDAL extension is covered along with an approach to storing and serving very large coverage.

Chapter 3, Working with Vector Data in Spatial Databases, concentrates on storage and serving of vector data from spatial databases. PostGIS, Oracle, and Microsoft SQL Server databases are covered along with the use of SQL Views as layers.

Chapter 4, Using GeoServer to Serve Complex Features, describes how GeoServer can be used to deliver complex-featured schemas as a WFS service. In this chapter, we take a look at the concepts involved in complex schemas, discussing the difference between simple and complex features. To illustrate the concepts, we will take the Open Street Map data and publish it as an INSPIRE Annex I Road Transport Network schema.

Chapter 5, Using GeoServer as a Proxy, takes a look at using GeoServer's cascaded services to act as a proxy to another WMS and/or WFS server. This capability is a little gem and often underutilized in production. We take a closer look and explore the different reasons why we might like to do it.

Chapter 6, Controlling the Output of GeoServer, takes a closer look at the technologies available to allow us to set styling for our layers. The chapter introduces us to the CSS styling extension that allows people familiar with this standard web technology to create gorgeous-looking maps. In addition to looking at how layers can be styled, we will also explore other areas where we can control GeoServer's output, such as responses to WMS GetFeatureInformation requests.

Chapter 7, Using GeoServer to Print Maps, tells us that no web mapping server will be complete without the capability to generate printed output. In this chapter, we take a look at the community print extension that adds the capability to generate output to print through a flexible and powerful template capability. We learn how to install and configure the extension as well as create a print template and exploit the capability with an example using OpenLayers.

Chapter 8, Integrating GeoServer in a Spatial Data Infrastructure, explores the concepts behind SDI. This chapter shows us how GeoServer can be integrated within a complete production system to provide more than just a means of delivering styled maps for a web application.

Chapter 9, GeoServer as a Spatial Analysis Platform, explores the technologies available in GeoServer that allow us to perform server-side spatial analysis. GeoServer, in production, does not have to simply deliver maps for use in web applications. It is a powerful spatial analysis platform in its own right. First, the chapter explores the use of Web Processing Services (WPS), and it then moves on to show us how we can create our own services using GeoScript.

Chapter 10, Enterprise Security and GeoServer, demonstrates how GeoServer can be secured within a corporate environment utilizing standard corporate security technologies such as LDAP and Active Directory. Other options to secure GeoServer are also covered to show us how easy it is to lock down our web mapping servers.

Chapter 11, Monitoring the Performance and Health of GeoServer, is an important chapter because it shows us the tools available to monitor the health of our GeoServer instances. Maintaining a healthy GeoServer instance is crucial for a good user experience of applications using maps and the data served. This chapter will help us to understand when our servers perform sub optimally.

Chapter 12, Optimizing GeoServer for Production, is the final chapter of the book, and this is where we take a last look at the configuration of our server. The chapter goes about providing strategies and options to optimize the configuration of our servers. It also introduces us to some special considerations when running a cluster of GeoServers.

What you need for this book

In order to implement what you will be learning in this book, you just need the following:

- Java 1.7
- GeoServer

Who this book is for

This book is for a GIS professional who intends to explore advanced techniques and get more out of GeoServer deployment other than simply delivering good-looking maps. This book will teach you advanced topics to enable you to provide a platform for server-side spatial analysis and deploy GeoServer in enterprise deployments. Familiarity with GIS and concepts of web mapping servers will be helpful, but is not essential.

Conventions

In this book, you will find a number of text styles that distinguish between different kinds of information. Here are some examples of these styles and an explanation of their meaning.

Code words in text, database table names, folder names, filenames, file extensions, pathnames, dummy URLs, user input, and Twitter handles are shown as follows: "Our `crime_type` parameter has been recognized and added to the table."

A block of code is set as follows:

```
SELECT
    ID,
    REPORTED_BY,
    CRIME_TYPE,
    LAST_OUTCOME_CATEGORY,
    GEOM
FROM
    STREET_LEVEL_CRIME
WHERE
    CRIME_TYPE = '%crime_type%'
    AND
    LAST_OUTCOME_CATEGORY = 'Under investigation'
```

When we wish to draw your attention to a particular part of a code block, the relevant lines or items are set in bold:

```
- !columns
    widths: [709, 113]
    width: 822
    absoluteX: 10
    absoluteY: 585
    items:
      - !text
        text: '${mapTitle}'
        font: Arial Bold
        fontSize: 28
        vertAlign: middle
      - !image
```

Any command-line input or output is written as follows:

```
$ sudo service tomcat-1 restart
$ sudo service tomcat-2 restart
```

New terms and **important words** are shown in bold. Words that you see on the screen, for example, in menus or dialog boxes, appear in the text like this: "To the right of the map, there is a **Print Settings** box that contains controls that can be used to set the content for print."

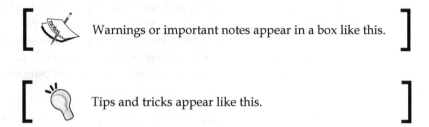

Warnings or important notes appear in a box like this.

Tips and tricks appear like this.

Reader feedback

Feedback from our readers is always welcome. Let us know what you think about this book—what you liked or disliked. Reader feedback is important for us as it helps us develop titles that you will really get the most out of.

To send us general feedback, simply e-mail feedback@packtpub.com, and mention the book's title in the subject of your message.

If there is a topic that you have expertise in and you are interested in either writing or contributing to a book, see our author guide at www.packtpub.com/authors.

Customer support

Now that you are the proud owner of a Packt book, we have a number of things to help you to get the most from your purchase.

Downloading the example code

You can download the example code files from your account at http://www.packtpub.com for all the Packt Publishing books you have purchased. If you purchased this book elsewhere, you can visit http://www.packtpub.com/support and register to have the files e-mailed directly to you.

Errata

Although we have taken every care to ensure the accuracy of our content, mistakes do happen. If you find a mistake in one of our books—maybe a mistake in the text or the code—we would be grateful if you could report this to us. By doing so, you can save other readers from frustration and help us improve subsequent versions of this book. If you find any errata, please report them by visiting http://www.packtpub.com/submit-errata, selecting your book, clicking on the **Errata Submission Form** link, and entering the details of your errata. Once your errata are verified, your submission will be accepted and the errata will be uploaded to our website or added to any list of existing errata under the Errata section of that title.

To view the previously submitted errata, go to https://www.packtpub.com/books/content/support and enter the name of the book in the search field. The required information will appear under the **Errata** section.

Piracy

Piracy of copyrighted material on the Internet is an ongoing problem across all media. At Packt, we take the protection of our copyright and licenses very seriously. If you come across any illegal copies of our works in any form on the Internet, please provide us with the location address or website name immediately so that we can pursue a remedy.

Please contact us at copyright@packtpub.com with a link to the suspected pirated material.

We appreciate your help in protecting our authors and our ability to bring you valuable content.

Questions

If you have a problem with any aspect of this book, you can contact us at questions@packtpub.com, and we will do our best to address the problem.

1

Installing GeoServer for Production

So, you decided to use GeoServer to deliver your business' critical spatial information across the enterprise and out on the web? This is a wise choice that many other like-minded GeoServer users will agree with.

Now, it's time for us to roll up our sleeves and get into the nitty-gritty of getting GeoServer up and running so that we can unlock the potential of our spatial information.

By the end of this chapter, we will have a better understanding of the following topics:

- Choosing the right version of Java to run GeoServer
- Installing and configuring Java for Linux and Windows
- Installing and configuring Apache Tomcat for the Linux and Windows platforms
- Configuring the Java VM's memory for GeoServer
- Deploying GeoServer into the Apache Tomcat servlet container
- Understanding the concepts of scalability and high availability and how to configure GeoServer for both

Java requirements

GeoServer is a software server written in Java, and as such it requires Java to be present in our environment. The process to install Java will differ according to our target server's architecture. However, in all cases, the first decision we must make is what version of Java to install and with which package. This is because Java is available in two main packages: **Java Development Kit (JDK)** and **Java Runtime Environment (JRE)**. JDK, as the name suggests, is used to develop Java applications, while JRE is generally used to run Java applications (though JDK also contains JRE).

There are a number of different versions of Java available. However, the GeoServer project only supports the use of Java 6 (also known as Java™ 1.6) or newer. The most recent version is Java 7 (also known as Java 1.7), and GeoServer can be run against this version of Java. The choice of whether to use Java 6 or 7 will largely be down to either personal preference or specific system limitations such as other software that have dependency on a version. For example, Tomcat 8.0 now requires the use of Java 7 as a minimum. The GeoServer documentation states that Java 7 offers the best performance, and so this is the version we will use.

 The upcoming GeoServer 2.6 release will require JRE7 (1.7) as a minimum. At the time of writing, GeoServer 2.6 is at Release Candidate 1.

Prior to Version 2, GeoServer required JDK to be installed in order to work; however, since Version 2, this is no longer a requirement, and GeoServer can run perfectly well using just JRE. The key to manage a successful production environment is to make sure there are no unnecessary software or components installed that might introduce vulnerabilities or increase the management overhead. For these reasons, JRE should be used to run GeoServer. The following sections will describe how to install Java to the Linux and Windows environments.

Installing Java on CentOS 6.3

A well-designed production environment will be as lean as possible in terms of the resources consumed and the overall system footprint; one way to achieve this is to ensure that servers do not contain any more software than is absolutely necessary to deliver its intended function. So, in the case of a server being deployed to deliver mapping services, it should only contain the software necessary to deliver maps.

There are many different flavors of Linux available and all of them are capable of running GeoServer without any issues, after all, Java is cross-platform! The choice of Linux distribution is often either a personal one or a company policy-enforced one. There is a great deal of information available to install GeoServer on a Ubuntu distribution, but very little on installing on a CentOS distribution. CentOS is an enterprise-class distribution that closely follows the development of Red Hat Enterprise Linux, and it is a common installation in organizations. We will use CentOS 6.3, and in keeping with the philosophy of making sure that the server is lean, we will only use the minimal server installation.

By default, CentOS 6.3 comes preinstalled with OpenJDK 1.6 as a result of potential licensing conflicts with the distributing Oracle Java that's preinstalled. The GeoServer documentation states that OpenJDK will work with GeoServer, but there might be issues, particularly with respect to 2D rendering performances. While OpenJDK can be used to run GeoServer, it is worth noting that the project does not run tests of GeoServer against OpenJDK, which means that there is a potential risk of failure if it is used in production.

As mentioned previously, Oracle Java is not packaged for the CentOS platform, and thus we will need to install it ourselves using a generic package direct from Oracle. To download Java, visit the Oracle Technology Network website:

`http://www.oracle.com/technetwork/java/javase/downloads/index.html`

Perform the following steps:

1. Download the current version of JRE 7 for the Linux platform, choosing the `*.rpm` file from the download list. At the time of writing, this file is `jre-7u51-linux-x64.rpm`.

> The eagle-eyed amongst you might spot that this file is for a 64-bit flavor of Linux. GeoServer can be installed on both 32-bit and 64-bit architectures; however, installing to a 32-bit Linux architecture will require downloading the 32-bit version of the file, which at the time of writing is `jre-7u51-linux-i586.rpm`.

2. Once we download the package to our server, we need to install it.

3. Change to the directory where the package is downloaded and execute the following command:

```
$ sudo rpm -Uvh jre-7u51-linux-x64.rpm
```

This will result in JRE being unpacked and installed to the /usr/java directory. Within this directory, there is a symbolic link called latest, which links to the actual JRE install folder. This symbolic link can be used in place of the lengthier JRE directory name. It is best practice to use the latest link so that the future upgrades of JRE does not cause Java-based software to stop working due to broken references.

4. Next, we need to tell CentOS that we want it to use Oracle JRE instead of the preinstalled OpenJDK. To do this, we make use of the alternatives command to specify the flavor of Java to use:

```
$ alternatives -install /usr/bin/java java /usr/java/latest/bin/
java 20000
```

This tells CentOS that any time the java command is used, it actually refers to the binary contained within the Oracle JRE directory and not the OpenJDK binary. The flavor of Java used by the system can be changed any time running the following command:

```
$ alternatives --config java
```

The alternatives command should present you with the following prompt:

```
There are 2 programs which provide 'java'.

  Selection     Command
-----------------------------------------------
    1           /usr/lib/jvm/jre-1.6.0-openjdk.x86_64/bin/java
*+ 2           /usr/java/latest/bin/java

Enter to keep the current selection[+], or type selection number:
```

Downloading the example code

You can download the example code files from your account at http://www.packtpub.com for all the Packt Publishing books you have purchased. If you purchased this book elsewhere, you can visit http://www.packtpub.com/support and register to have the files e-mailed directly to you.

Depending on the number of programs configured to provide the java command, you will be presented with a list. The program that is currently responding to java is indicated by an asterisk.

In this case, Oracle JRE, which we just installed, is shown to be the active one. If Oracle JRE is not currently selected, then simply enter the number matching the /usr/java/latest/bin/java entry in your list.

 An important thing to note here is the command entry for Oracle JRE. Notice how it matches the path that we used for the alternatives --install command. This is important as it means that we can now install future versions or updates of Oracle JRE without having to run the alternatives command again. Where possible, you should use the /usr/java/latest/bin/java path to reference Java, for example, the JAVA_HOME environment variable.

We can now test whether our system is using Oracle JRE issuing the following command:

```
$ java -version
```

If all goes well, we should see the following response:

```
java version "1.7.0_51"
Java(TM) SE Runtime Environment (build 1.7.0_51-b13)
Java HotSpot(TM) 64-Bit Server VM (build 24.51-b03, mixed mode)
```

Your version numbers might differ, but the rest should be the same; most importantly, we do not want to see the word *OpenJDK* anywhere.

Installing Java on Windows Server 2008 R2 SP1

If you target Windows Server in your production environment, life is a little simpler than it is for the users of Linux. For the purposes of this book, we will use Windows Server 2008 R2 SP1 Standard Edition, however other versions of Windows Server that can have Java installed should also work fine.

Once again, we will adopt the best practice to use Oracle JRE, and again we will use Version 1.7. Go ahead and download the Windows package for JRE from Oracle's Technology Network website:

http://www.oracle.com/technetwork/java/javase/downloads/index.html

At this point, we have a decision to make about which JRE installer to download, 32-bit or 64-bit. Making the right decision now is important as the choice of 32-bit versus 64-bit will have consequences later when configuring GeoServer. In the next section, we will discuss the installation of Apache Tomcat, which has a dependency on Java, in order to run GeoServer.

In the Windows environment, the Apache Tomcat installer will automatically install a 32-bit or 64-bit Windows Service based on the installed Java. So, a 64-bit installation of Java will mean that the Apache Tomcat service will also be installed as 64-bit.

The three factors influencing the choice of a 32-bit or 64-bit Java are:

- The architecture on which you run Windows
- Java VM memory configuration considerations
- The use of native JAI and JAI Image I/O extensions

Hopefully, the first reason is self-explanatory. If you have a 32-bit version of Windows installed, you can only install a 32-bit version of Java. If you have a 64-bit Windows installation, then you can choose between the two versions. We install to Windows Server 2008 R2 SP1, which is only available in 64-bit; this means that the processor architecture or Windows is not a limitation. In this case, the decision now comes down to the memory configuration and use of native JAI and JAI Image I/O extensions.

The memory consideration is an important decision since a 32-bit process, irrespective of whether it runs on a 32-bit or 64-bit processor architecture, can only address a maximum of 2 GB memory. Therefore, if we want to maximize the available server memory, we will need to consider using the 64-bit version of Java. However, the JAI and JAI Image I/O extensions are only available on the Windows platform as 32-bit binaries. If we choose the 64-bit Java, then we will not be able to use the extensions, which can be an issue if we plan on using our server to provide predominantly raster datasets. The native JAI and JAI Image I/O extensions can provide a significant performance increase when performing raster operations, in other words, responding to WMS requests.

Getting the most out of a production environment is as much about maximizing resource utilization as anything else. If we have a server with lots of memory, we can use the 64-bit Java and allocate it a large chunk of memory, but then the only real advantage this provides is that it will allow us to do more concurrent raster operations. The maximum number of concurrent requests will still be limited by other factors, which might not be the most efficient use of server resources. An alternative approach is to scale-up by running multiple instances of GeoServer on the server. This is discussed in more detail later in this chapter. Scaling-up means that we can maximize the usage of server resources (memory) without compromising on our ability to utilize the native JAI and JAI Image I/O extensions.

To install the 32-bit version of Java, perform the following steps:

1. From the Oracle download page, choose the 32-bit Java installer, which at the time of writing is `jre-7u51-windows-i586.exe`, and save it to a local disk.

2. Open the folder where you saved the file, right-click on the file, and choose the **Run as administrator** menu item:

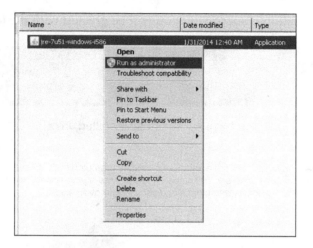

3. Accept all Windows UAC prompts that appear and wait for the Java installation wizard to open.

4. The installer will want to install Java to a default location, usually `C:\Program Files (x86)\Java\jre7`, but if you want to install it to a different folder, make sure to tick the **Change destination folder** checkbox placed at the bottom of the dialog:

5. Click on the **Install** button. If you did not tick the box to change the destination folder, then the installation will start.

6. If the changed destination checkbox was ticked, clicking on the **Install** button will prompt for the location to install to.

7. Specify the location you want to install to, and then click on the **Next** button; the installation starts.

8. If the installation is successful, you will be greeted with the following screen:

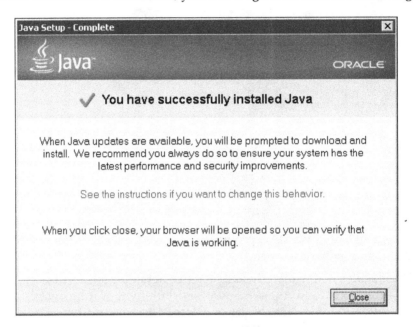

Closing the installation wizard will launch a web browser where the installation of Java can be verified by the steps given on the page loaded after Java installation.

Installing Apache Tomcat

At the time of writing this book, the most recent version of Apache Tomcat is 8. At the moment, there is limited testing of GeoServer running inside Apache Tomcat 8, which means that we should avoid using it, at least for now. Instead, we will use the latest version of Apache Tomcat 7, which is currently 7.0.50. The download page for this version is `http://tomcat.apache.org/download-70.cgi#7.0.50`.

Installing Apache Tomcat 7 on CentOS 6.3

As with all the Linux variants, CentOS has a package management system that can be used to install software, including Apache Tomcat. However, quite often, the packaged software is several versions behind the current version. Unlike other software running on Linux, Tomcat does not actually require compiling, and so installing it directly from Apache is not much of a challenge. Perform the following steps to install Apache Tomcat on CentOS:

1. First, we need to download the Tomcat package to our system. Go to the download page (`http://tomcat.apache.org/download-70.cgi#7.0.50`) and find the download link for the `tar.gz` package under the **Core** entry. With the location of the link, we can download the file with the following command:

    ```
    $ wget http://www.mirrorservice.org/sites/ftp.apache.org/tomcat/
    tomcat-7/v7.0.50/bin/apache-tomcat-7.0.50.tar.gz
    ```

2. Once the download is complete, we need to think about where we want to place the installation on the system. The most common location seems to be `/opt`, which seems as good a place as any. Extract the Tomcat files using the following command:

    ```
    $ sudo tar -xvzf apache-tomcat-7.0.50.tar.gz -C /opt
    ```

3. The contents of the tarball will be extracted to `/opt/apache-tomcat-7.0.50/`, which will now become our Tomcat home directory. These are the bare minimum steps required to get Tomcat installed, so you can now issue the following command and Tomcat will happily start:

    ```
    $ sudo ./opt/apache-tomcat-7.0.50/bin/startup.sh
    ```

4. Replace `startup.sh` with `shutdown.sh` on the last command to shut Tomcat down if you just started it.

This is interesting, but actually not particularly useful in the context of a production environment. In a production environment, we need to be able to set memory parameters for JVM, have Tomcat run as a service on startup, and run the Tomcat service using a user with limited privileges.

Running Apache Tomcat as a service

Security is a key consideration for any production environment, and wherever possible, the applications and services should run using user accounts with just the right level of privileges for them to perform their functions. To adopt this best practice, we will now create a user account under which we can run the Tomcat service:

1. At your command line, enter the following:

    ```
    $ sudo groupadd tomcat
    $ sudo useradd -s /bin/bash -g tomcat tomcat
    ```

    The first command creates a new user group called tomcat. The second command creates a new user called tomcat, adds this user to the tomcat group, and sets its shell to bash.

2. Now that we have a tomcat user, we need to set the ownership of the Tomcat installation folder to this user:

    ```
    $ sudo chown -Rf tomcat:tomcat /opt/apache-tomcat-7.0.50/
    ```

3. Now we are ready to create a service control script that will allow us to start, stop, and reload the Tomcat application. To do this, we need to create a service controller script and then register this script with an appropriate run level so that CentOS will start the service on boot:

    ```
    $ cd /etc/init.d
    $ sudo vi tomcat-1
    ```

    The preceding commands will enter the services directory on CentOS and create a blank script called tomcat-1. The name of the script is not important. However, as we will see later when scaling Tomcat in production, we might want to instantiate multiple services, and so should come up with a suitable naming convention to keep track of them. In this case, we use the convention, tomcat-n, where n will be an incremented number. The vi command will start the vim text editor with an empty file; replace this with whatever your favorite Linux text editor is.

4. In the text editor, enter the following script:

    ```
    #!/bin/bash
    # description: Tomcat 1 Start Stop Restart
    # processname: tomcat-1
    # chkconfig: 234 20 80
    JAVA_HOME=/usr/java/latest
    ```

```
export JAVA_HOME
PATH=$JAVA_HOME/bin:$PATH
export PATH
CATALINA_HOME=/opt/apache-tomcat-7.0.50
JAVA_OPTS="-server -Xmx1024m -Xms512m -XX:MaxPermSize=128m"
export JAVA_OPTS

case $1 in
start)
/bin/su tomcat $CATALINA_HOME/bin/startup.sh
;;
stop)
/bin/su tomcat $CATALINA_HOME/bin/shutdown.sh
;;
restart)
/bin/su tomcat $CATALINA_HOME/bin/shutdown.sh
/bin/su tomcat $CATALINA_HOME/bin/startup.sh
;;
esac
exit 0
```

There is quite a lot going on in this script, so let's break it down a little. The first four lines beginning with a hash (#) are settings for how the script is run. The last line in this group indicates the run levels that this service will operate under (234) and the stop and start priorities (20 and 80). This information tells the chkconfig command how to run the service.

Next, the script will set environment variables to tell the system where to find Java (JAVA_HOME), making the java command accessible on the command line (PATH) and setting the Tomcat directory (CATALINA_HOME). Next, we set an environment variable called JAVA_OPTS, which provides parameters to run JVM. This is where we can specify the memory configuration for our GeoServer instance. There is a discussion on how to determine the most appropriate memory settings for your server later in this book; for now, we will use settings that are good for an all-rounder instance of GeoServer.

The following table describes what each of these parameters are and why they are set:

Parameter	Description
-server	This parameter tells JVM to run in the server mode, which enables it to compile the optimized byte code early. Initial calls will be slow because of longer **Just-In-Time (JIT)** compiling, but subsequent calls will be faster.
-Xmx1024m	This parameter tells JVM the maximum amount of heap memory it can allocate. In this case, JVM will allocate a maximum of 1 GB of memory.
-Xms512m	This parameter tells JVM how much heap memory to allocate on startup. This will ensure that memory management is more stable. In this case, we tell JVM to allocate 512 MB heap on startup.
-XX:MaxPermSize=128m	This parameter sets the maximum size of the permanent generation (also known as permgen) allocated for GeoServer. Permgen is where the class byte code is stored. In applications that use a lot of classes, such as GeoServer, it will exhaust the default JVM allocation quickly, leading to permgen memory errors.

The final section of the script is a case statement that will perform different actions according to the first parameter (case $1) passed to the script. This can be one of start, stop, or restart. In each case, the Tomcat startup.sh and/or shutdown.sh scripts are executed.

Now we have our service script created, we need to set appropriate permissions on it, using the following command:

```
$ sudo chmod 755 tomcat-1
```

Once the script is executed, we can register it in CentOS as a service. The chkconfig utility is used to register the script as a service:

```
$ sudo chkconfig --add tomcat-1
$ sudo chkconfig --level 234 tomcat-1 on
```

The first line adds our script, and the second line sets the runtime levels for it. We can check the configuration to make sure it is registered correctly:

```
$ sudo chkconfig --list tomcat-1
tomcat-1          0:off   1:off   2:on    3:on    4:on    5:off   6:off
```

If all goes well, levels 2, 3, and 4 will be marked as on, with all other levels marked off. From this point onward, every time our server restarts, it will automatically run the tomcat-1 service, thereby giving us Tomcat on each boot.

We should now check that the script works as expected, trying each of the following commands in turn:

```
$ sudo service tomcat-1 start
Using CATALINA_BASE:     /opt/apache-tomcat-7.0.50
Using CATALINA_HOME:     /opt/apache-tomcat-7.0.50
Using CATALINA_TMPDIR: /opt/apache-tomcat-7.0.50/temp
Using JRE_HOME:          /usr/java/latest
Using CLASSPATH:         /opt/apache-tomcat-7.0.50/bin/bootstrap.jar:/opt/
apache-tomcat-7.0.50/bin/tomcat-juli.jar


$ sudo service tomcat-1 restart
Using CATALINA_BASE:     /opt/apache-tomcat-7.0.50
Using CATALINA_HOME:     /opt/apache-tomcat-7.0.50
Using CATALINA_TMPDIR: /opt/apache-tomcat-7.0.50/temp
Using JRE_HOME:          /usr/java/latest
Using CLASSPATH:         /opt/apache-tomcat-7.0.50/bin/bootstrap.jar:/opt/
apache-tomcat-7.0.50/bin/tomcat-juli.jar
Using CATALINA_BASE:     /opt/apache-tomcat-7.0.50
Using CATALINA_HOME:     /opt/apache-tomcat-7.0.50
Using CATALINA_TMPDIR: /opt/apache-tomcat-7.0.50/temp
Using JRE_HOME:          /usr/java/latest
Using CLASSPATH:         /opt/apache-tomcat-7.0.50/bin/bootstrap.jar:/opt/
apache-tomcat-7.0.50/bin/tomcat-juli.jar


$ sudo service tomcat-1 stop
Using CATALINA_BASE:     /opt/apache-tomcat-7.0.50
Using CATALINA_HOME:     /opt/apache-tomcat-7.0.50
Using CATALINA_TMPDIR: /opt/apache-tomcat-7.0.50/temp
Using JRE_HOME:          /usr/java/latest
Using CLASSPATH:         /opt/apache-tomcat-7.0.50/bin/bootstrap.jar:/opt/
apache-tomcat-7.0.50/bin/tomcat-juli.jar
```

If everything works as expected, we will see a similar output. Start the Tomcat service again if it is not already running, and then navigate to the server's IP address or the URL. We should get the Tomcat web page like the one shown in the following screenshot:

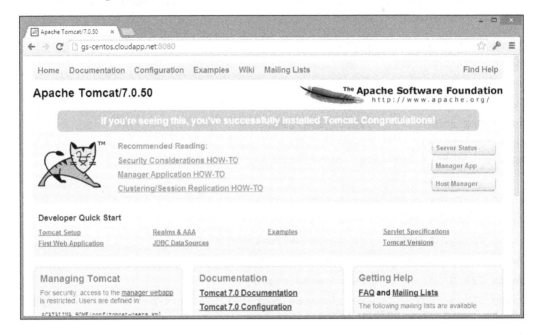

Congratulations! We now have CentOS 6.3 running Java and Apache Tomcat with the Tomcat service automatically, starting each time the server boots. Go ahead and restart the server to check that the Tomcat service starts automatically.

Securing Apache Tomcat

The default configuration of Apache Tomcat does not have any user configured for access to the web management portal. If you want to have the ability to manage your instance of Tomcat using the web management application, then you will need to configure access.

Tomcat maintains a simple user access database in the form of an XML configuration file in the `conf` directory. To enable access to the manager web application, you must edit the user database or create one if it does not already exist. The file is called `tomcat-users.xml` and has a very simple structure. Here is a very basic example of a `tomcat-users.xml` file:

```
<?xml version="1.0" encoding="utf-8">
<tomcat-users>
  <role rolename="manager-gui" />
  <user username="r2d2" password="5t4rW4r5" roles="manager-gui" />
</tomcat-users>
```

The structure of this file is very simple. First, you define the name of a role; in this case, the role name is specific to the web manager application as it expects one called `manager-gui`. Next, you create a `<user>` element and specify a username, password, and comma-separated list of roles that the user belongs to. Once you create the necessary entries for all the users, you want to grant access to the web manager application, and then you will need to restart the Tomcat service:

`$ sudo service tomcat-1 restart`

Once the Tomcat service has restarted, you should be able to access the manager web application at the `http://[your server address]/manager/html` URL. Enter your username and password when prompted.

> Bear in mind that we run GeoServer in a production environment, and as such, security must be upmost in our considerations. Think carefully about the username and password you use. Make sure the password is strong and try to avoid using common usernames such as `tomcat`, `admin`, or `manager`.

Installing Apache Tomcat 7 on Windows Server 2008 R2 SP1

Once again, Windows users get the convenience of an installation wizard to take care of installing Tomcat. For the Windows installation package, choose the **32bit/64bit Windows Service Installer** option. Download the installation file to a directory on your local hard drive.

To install Tomcat, perform the following steps:

1. For Tomcat 7.0.50, the downloaded installation file should be
   `apache-tomcat-7.0.50.exe`.

2. Open the folder where you saved the file, right-click on the file,
   and choose the **Run as administrator** menu item:

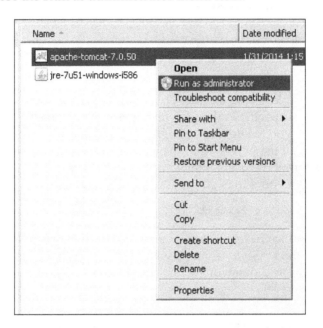

3. Use the **Next** button to move through the installation wizard until you reach
   the **Choose Components** page. For a production system, we want to avoid any
   unnecessary installation, so make sure that the **Documentation** and **Examples**
   boxes are not ticked. Under the **Tomcat** branch in the components list, we
   want to make sure the **Service Startup** box is ticked. This will ensure that the
   Tomcat service starts when Windows starts, which is very useful in cases when
   the server has to be rebooted. Finally, we need to tick the box for **Native**, which
   will make use of the native APR for better performance and scalability.

> The APR is the **Apache Portable Runtime**, which is a library
> that provides Tomcat with better scalability, performance,
> and integration with other native web technologies.

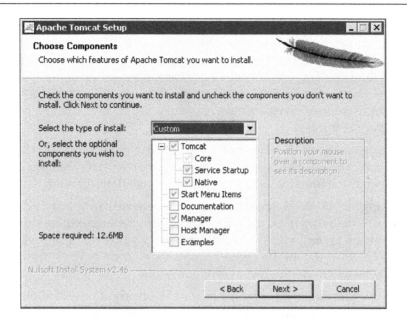

4. Click on the **Next** button to move on to the configuration page. This page is where we will set the configuration for Tomcat and Windows Service. For the first installation, we can leave the default settings for ports as they are. Enter a username and password for the web administration pages:

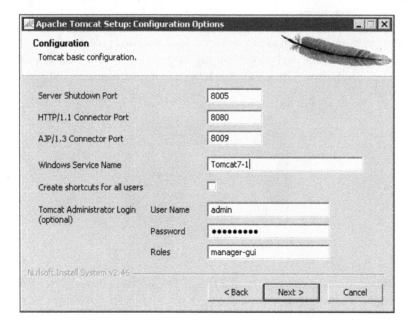

5. Before moving on to the next step, an important change to the default configuration is the name of the Windows service. If we want to maximize server resources, then we will want to scale-up on the server by running more than one Tomcat service. In this case, we need to have a naming convention to distinguish between them, so we will use **Tomcat7-1** and adopt a naming convention of Tomcat7-n, where n is an incremented number to identify the instance.

6. Clicking on **Next** will move to the Java environment page that should have automatically selected the installation of Java we performed earlier. If it did not, you can manually browse to your JRE installation folder.

7. Clicking on **Next** will move to the page where we can specify the installation folder. A default will be provided, which will be the combination of a default installation folder, with the Windows Service name set in step 5 appended. You can either accept the default or specify your own. For simplicity, we will set the installation folder to C:\Tomcat7-1.

8. Once the installation is complete, the final wizard page will allow us the choice to start Tomcat. Uncheck the box marked **Start Tomcat Service** so that Tomcat does not start when we exit the installer.

Tomcat is now installed as Windows Service, which we can control like any other service.

Controlling the Tomcat service

The Windows version of Tomcat comes with an application called *Monitor Tomcat*, which starts automatically each time you log on to Windows. It is a System Tray application that allows quick access to monitor and manage the running Tomcat service.

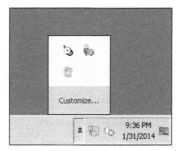

Notice the icon in the top-left corner of System Tray; this is the *Monitor Tomcat* application and its icon tells us that Tomcat is not currently running (indicated by the red square in the middle).

If the Tomcat service runs, it displays a green triangle on its side, like a "play" symbol. If we right-click on the Monitor Tomcat application icon, we get a context menu as shown in the following screenshot:

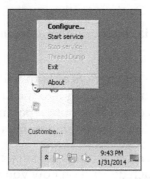

The context menu provides us with the ability to access the Tomcat service configuration and allows us to stop and start the service without the need to go through the normal Windows service applet. Of course, Tomcat still runs as a normal Windows service, so there is nothing stopping us to manage it in the normal way; the Monitor Tomcat application is just a convenience tool.

Configuring the Tomcat service

Before we start the Tomcat service to check our installation is alright, we must configure the memory settings that Tomcat will use for Java VM. Right-click on the Monitor Tomcat application icon and select the **Configure...** menu item to open the Tomcat service configuration dialog. Once it is open, click on the **Java** tab at the top:

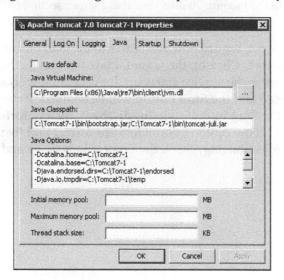

The **Java** tab allows us to set options that control the way Tomcat starts Java VM; the most important of these, from our perspective, is the memory configuration. Memory settings can be specified in one of the following two ways:

- Parameters in the **Java Options** textbox
- Entering values in **Initial memory pool**, **Maximum memory pool**, and **Thread stack size**

The choice is merely one of the preferences as both will achieve the same effect. My personal preference is to put everything into the **Java Options** textbox as it is good to remind oneself of the correct Java option parameter names, especially if you have a mixed Linux/Windows server environment.

The actual values to use for memory settings are subjects that we will cover later in this book, and we will very much depend on how you intend to use your GeoServer in production. For example, if you only intend serving vector data (through WFS), then GeoServer requires very little by way of memory allocation. For now, we will set the memory to some good defaults for an all-rounder GeoServer. Click on the **Java Options** textbox and scroll to the last parameter, press *Enter* to start a new line, and then enter the following parameters:

```
-Dserver
-Xmx1024m
-Xms512m
-XX:MaxPermSize=128m
```

 These parameters and what their values mean are described in the table given in the *Running Apache Tomcat as a service* section of this chapter.

With the Java options set, we are now ready to fire up the Tomcat service and check everything as is expected. Click on the **General** tab, then on the big **Start** button, and cross your fingers as the service starts up. If everything works, then the **Start** button will be disabled and the **Stop** button will be enabled. If the **Start** button is enabled again, and the **Stop** button remains disabled, then unfortunately something is wrong. Check that all the option parameters are correct and then try again. If you still don't get the service starting, check the Tomcat logs to try and figure out why.

If all goes well, we should be able to open a browser window, navigate to
`http://localhost:8080/`, and get the Tomcat 7 web page, as shown in the
following screenshot:

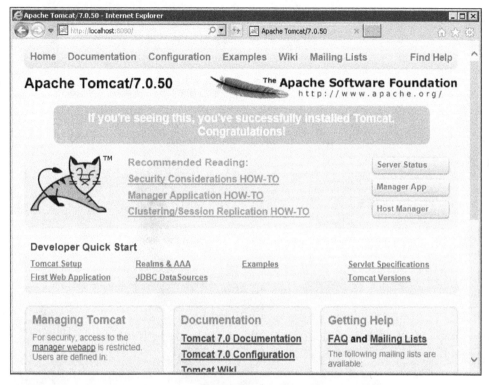

Tomcat 7 web page

That's it! Java and Tomcat are now both configured on your Windows Server,
and it is now ready to take the GeoServer application.

Deploying GeoServer to Apache Tomcat

We are getting there for a basic configuration of GeoServer, which we can use as a
basis to architect our production environment for high-availability, failover, and
scalability. Now we need to deploy GeoServer into Apache Tomcat, which is happily
a straightforward process.

We will utilize Apache Tomcat's auto-deploy feature that allows us to copy the
GeoServer **WAR (Web Archive)** file directly to `appBase` of a running Tomcat
instance. Tomcat will detect the presence of the WAR file, and then deploy it
ready for use.

First, we need to download the WAR file from the GeoServer download page at `http://geoserver.org/release/Stable`. At the time of writing, the current stable version of GeoServer is 2.5.2:

Click on the **Web Archive** link and save the downloaded ZIP file somewhere it is accessible.

Deploying on CentOS 6.3

Deployment of GeoServer on CentOS is a very straightforward process, thanks to the way Tomcat is architected. WAR files can automatically be deployed by copying them to a specific location in the Tomcat home directory.

Download the WAR file to a location on your system, for example, your home directory:

```
$ cd ~
$ wget http://sourceforge.net/projects/geoserver/files/GeoServer/2.5.2/
geoserver-2.5.2-war.zip
```

The WAR file that we want to deploy to GeoServer is contained within the downloaded ZIP file, so we need to extract this from the Tomcat `appBase` directory:

```
$ sudo unzip geoserver-2.5.2-war.zip *.war -d $CATALINA_HOME/webapps/
```

This command will only extract the `geoserver.war` file from the ZIP file and place it in the Tomcat `appBase` directory. Tomcat will then autodeploy the WAR file, and you should see a `geoserver` directory appear.

Deploying on Windows Server 2008 R2 SP1

Deploying the GeoServer WAR file on Windows follows the same process as that of Linux. The WAR file is copied in the Tomcat home directory, where it is unpacked and the GeoServer context started.

The following steps are required to deploy the GeoServer WAR file in Tomcat:

1. Download the WAR file to a location on your system, for example, the `Downloads` folder within your home directory.

2. Double-click on the `geoserver-2.5.2-war.zip` file to open it in Windows Explorer (assuming you do not have another ZIP application installed).

3. Drag and drop the `geoserver.war` file from the ZIP folder to the `webapps` folder in your Tomcat service home directory. If you followed the steps to install Tomcat on Windows, then this directory will be `C:\Tomcat7-1\webapps`:

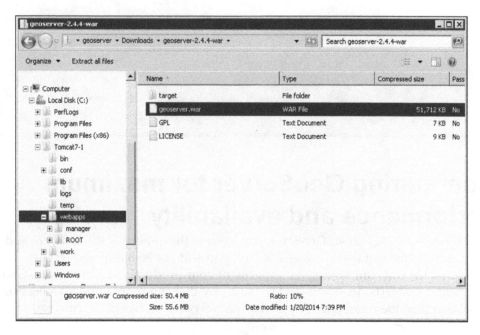

4. After dropping the file into the folder, Tomcat will autodeploy it and a directory called `geoserver` will appear.

Checking GeoServer deployment

We should now have a basic configuration of GeoServer deployed inside an Apache Tomcat instance. Test that GeoServer was successfully deployed by opening a web browser and navigating to the GeoServer administration interface:

```
http://[your server address]:8080/geoserver
```

If everything worked as expected, then we should be presented with the GeoServer administration interface's front page:

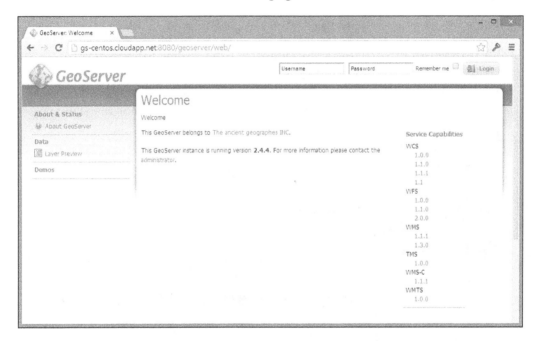

Configuring GeoServer for maximum performance and availability

One of the best things about GeoServer, apart from the quality of the software and community, is the fact that because it is free, you will not be hampered by cost considerations when increasing the capacity of your production environment. Unlike the **Commercial-Off-The-Shelf (COTS)** software that commonly utilizes a licensing model based on the number of physical or virtual cores, the software runs on.

Since there is no financial implication (in terms of software licensing) on running multiple instances of GeoServer, the only limitation will be the amount of infrastructure you can afford to implement. With the growth in cloud computing and **Infrastructure as a Service (IaaS)** providers such as Microsoft (Windows Azure) and Amazon (EC3), the costs of implementing large infrastructures is becoming more reasonable.

Performance can be gained by maximizing the usage of resources within your production environment and/or by increasing the capacity through additional nodes. Load balancing traffic across the environment to spread the load will also aid in ensuring that the environment performs well. Increasing the number of nodes within the environment will present an opportunity to set up for high availability. This is when one or more nodes in the environment are reserved to take over if the primary nodes fail. Usually, this can be handled by the load balancer by intelligently switching traffic to a reserved node when it detects that one or more primary nodes failed.

Scaling vertically

Scaling vertically, also known as scaling up, is when additional resources are added to a single (physical or virtual) node. In other words, this is when you create more than one instance of GeoServer to run on the same physical or virtual server. The following diagram depicts scaling vertically:

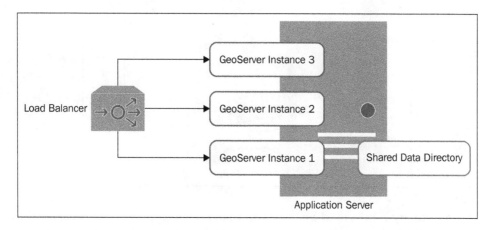

The available resources on the server are maximized by running multiple instances of GeoServer. Consistency of data is maintained across each of the instances by all of them sharing a common data directory, either located on the node itself or elsewhere on the network.

Traffic is managed across the GeoServer instances by a load balancer that can be a physical one in the network or even a software-based one.

Scaling horizontally

Scaling horizontally, also known as scaling out, is when you add additional nodes (physical or virtual) to your environment. Each additional node can have an instance of GeoServer running on it. The following diagram depicts scaling horizontally:

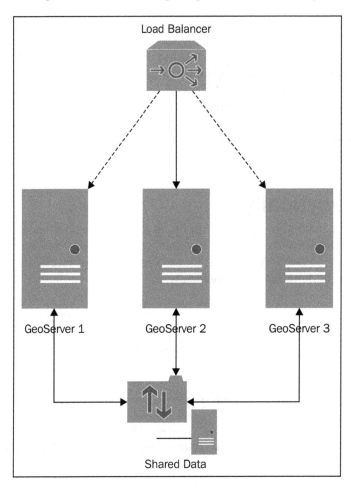

Increased capacity is provided by the additional nodes running GeoServer, and the traffic across them is managed through a physical load balancer in the network.

In a scaled-out architecture, the data directory for GeoServer is shared across the additional nodes to ensure consistency of the configurations. With this approach, you can choose to place the shared data directory on one of the nodes and allow access to the additional nodes, or you can choose to have a separate server to hold shared data such as a **Network Attached Storage (NAS)** device.

If you configure multiple instances of GeoServer to provide resilience to your infrastructure, high availability, or failover, then best practice is not to place your shared data directory on one of the nodes running GeoServer. If this node fails, then all other nodes will lose their data connections. For proper resilience, the shared data server should also be replicated.

Getting the best of both

To really get the best performance from your production environment, it is worth considering scaling GeoServer both vertically and horizontally. Increase the capacity of your environment through additional nodes, and then maximize the resources on each node by running multiple instances of GeoServer. The following diagram depicts scaling vertically as well as horizontally:

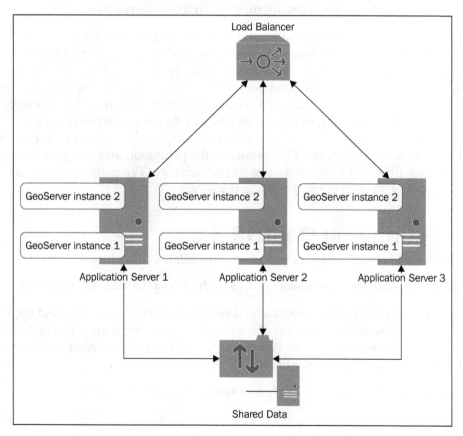

In this architecture, traffic to each of the GeoServer instances running on each node is managed through a physical load balancer on the network. The load balancer can be configured to register one of the GeoServer nodes as the failover node, ensuring continuity of service should one or more of the primary nodes fail.

Once again, a shared data directory is used across the nodes to ensure consistency, but in this case, it will definitely make sense to keep the directory on a separate server instance.

Configuring multiple GeoServer instances on a single server

You might have spotted a common thread running through each of the scenarios outlined. In all cases, multiple instances of GeoServer are implemented, and in the case of scaling up, these instances are running on the same node.

Setting up multiple GeoServer instances on a single node is actually quite straightforward and will involve you creating several instances of the Tomcat installation. In the following examples, we will configure an additional instance of GeoServer for CentOS and Windows Server 2008. However, you can apply the same principle to create as many instances as you want, but bear in mind the memory configuration of your server, making sure that you do not add more instances than your resources will allow. Also, bear in mind the number of processing cores available; too many instances will overburden the processor, and any gain in adding the instance will be lost through decreased performance. Typically, you should not consider adding more than *four* instances per server.

Configuring on CentOS 6.3

First, we need to create a copy of our Tomcat installation directory:

```
$ sudo cp -R /opt/apache-tomcat-7.0.50/ /opt/apache-tomcat-7.0.50-2
```

This command will copy our installation directory to the same location and append 2 to the end. The name and location of the directory does not matter; just ensure that it has a different name so that you can distinguish it from others. Next, we need to make the tomcat user the owner of the new directory:

```
$ sudo chown -Rf tomcat:tomcat /opt/apache-tomcat-7.0.50-2/
```

Then we need to configure the Tomcat instance so that it can co-exist with other instances. This involves altering the `server.xml` file stored in the `conf` folder of the copied installation. Edit the file with your favorite text editor, and look for the line containing the following:

```
<Server port="8005" shutdown="SHUTDOWN">
```

Change the value of the port attribute to `8006` by incrementing it by 1. Further down the file, look for the line containing:

```
<Connector port="8080" protocol="HTTP/1.1" connectionTimeout="20000"
redirectPort="8443" />
```

Change the value of the `port` attribute to `8081` by incrementing it by 1, save the file, and exit the text editor. We also need to change the value of `redirectPort`, again incrementing it by 1 to make it `8444`. What we just did has changed the ports on which the Tomcat service will listen for connections. Failing to do this will generate an error when we try to start the Tomcat service. If we want to add more Tomcat instances, we just need to follow the same process; increment each value by 1 again.

Next, we need to copy our data directory out to a location where each instance can share it. For this, we will make a new directory:

```
$ sudo mkdir /mnt/share
$ sudo cp -R /opt/apache-tomcat-7.0.50/webapps/geoserver/data/ /mnt/
share/geoserver-data
$ sudo chown -Rf tomcat:tomcat /mnt/share/geoserver-data/
```

Now, we created a directory to share amongst our instances, copied our original GeoServer data directory into it, and then made the `tomcat` user the owner of the directory.

You might be wondering why we just copied the data directory out to a different location. This is an important step for two reasons:

- It is necessary to ensure that both instances of GeoServer deliver the same data and services
- It makes upgrading GeoServer much simpler

The last point is an important one. Even if we only run a single instance of GeoServer, it is a good practice to place the data directory outside of the GeoServer installation. When we decide to upgrade, we can do so by simply deploying a new WAR file without having to back up and restore the original data directory.

Now we can make a new service for our newly configured instance:

```
$ sudo cp /etc/init.d/tomcat-1 /etc/init.d/tomcat-2
```

Next, we need to make some changes to the service script to tell each GeoServer instance where the data directory is located, and we will also control the name and location of the default logfile for GeoServer. Edit the `tomcat-1` and `tomcat-2` script files in your favorite text editor, and add the following lines near the start:

```
GEOSERVER_DATA_DIR=/mnt/share/geoserver-data
export GEOSERVER_DATA_DIR
```

This line sets an environment variable for our external data directory. Next, add the following lines:

```
GEOSERVER_LOG_LOCATION=$GEOSERVER_DATA_DIR/logs/geoserver-1.log
export GEOSERVER_LOG_LOCATION
```

This sets another environment variable, but this time it tells GeoServer what to call the logfile that will be generated. This is another important aspect of running multiple instances of GeoServer, and it is essential to avoid clashes on the logging.

Do the same for both the service scripts, but change the name of the logfile to suit each instance. Now we just need to register the second service script so that it can be controlled:

```
$ sudo chkconfig --add tomcat-2
$ sudo chkconfig --level 234 tomcat-2 on
$ sudo service tomcat-1 restart
$ sudo service tomcat-2 start
```

That's it! Now, we have two instances of GeoServer running on our server and sharing a common data directory. You can test it by opening a web browser and visiting the following:

- **GeoServer instance 1**: http://[your server address]:8080/geoserver
- **GeoServer instance 2**: http://[your server address]:8081/geoserver

Configuring on Windows Server 2008 R2 SP1

Once again, life is a little simpler in the world of Windows. All we need to do is configure some environment variables to set the location of the shared data directory and the name and location of the logfile, and then create a new service instance. First, copy the current GeoServer data directory (`C:\Tomcat7-1\webapps\geoserver\data`) to a location outside of the container, for example, `D:\Data\geoserver-data`. Then, click on the Windows **Start** button, right-click on **Computer**, and choose the **Properties** menu option:

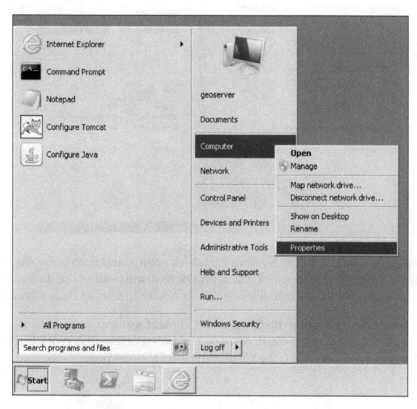

In the **System Properties** dialog that opens, click on the link at the left-hand side labelled **Advanced system settings**, and in the dialog box that opens, click on the **Advanced** tab. Click on the button labelled **Environment Variables…** to open a new properties dialog:

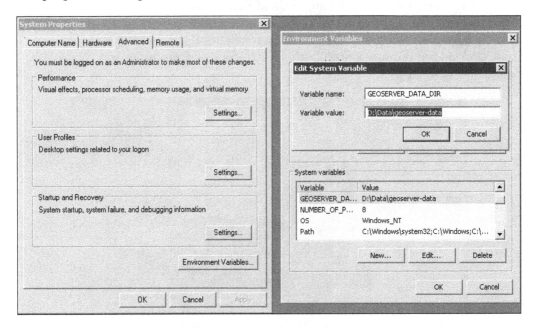

Click on the **New** button in the **System variables** group, and then enter the details shown in the preceding screenshot. Click on **Ok** to dismiss all of the dialogs. We now have an environment variable to tell GeoServer where to find its data directory.

Next, we need to create a new instance of the Tomcat service. To do this, we just need to rerun the installation file that we downloaded originally. Work through all of the pages until you reach the **Configuration Options** page:

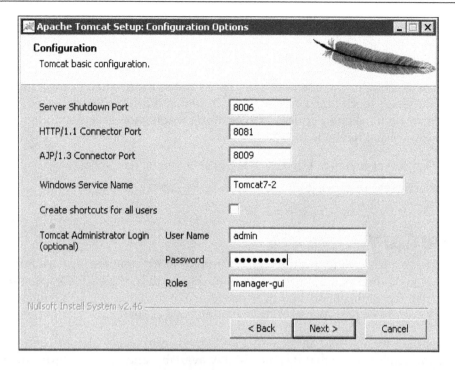

On this page, we need to change the settings for the ports by incrementing the default values by 1, for example, **HTTP/1.1 Connector Port** will be 8081 instead of 8080. We also need to change the default value of **Windows Service Name**, in this case, we continue with our naming convention of incrementing each instance by 1. Click on **Next** to check whether the Java installation directory is correct, and then click on **Next** again to specify where we want to install the files. Change the installation location so that it points to C:\Tomcat7-2.

Now we need to use the Tomcat Monitor application to control the new service. Copy the same values for the Java options, but also include an additional parameter to tell GeoServer where to create its logfile this time:

```
-DGEOSERVER_LOG_LOCATION=D:\Data\geoserver-data\logs\geoserver-2.log
```

Wee created a second instance of Tomcat, so we just need to deploy the `geoserver`. `war` file to it by copying it into the `C:\Tomcat7-2\webapps` folder and letting Tomcat perform autodeploy when it starts up.

Remember to include `-DGEOSERVER_LOG_LOCATION` in the original Tomcat instance Java options, and specify the name of a logfile so that it can be distinguished. Then, restart both the new services. If everything works as expected, you can open a browser and navigate to:

- **GeoServer instance 1**: `http://localhost:8080/geoserver`
- **GeoServer instance 2**: `http://localhost:8081/geoserver`

Summary

We now have a basic configuration of GeoServer that we can take forward into a production environment. This basic configuration will be the basis for exercises in the remainder of this book, and over the course of the book, we will build a well-configured and high-performing instance(s) of GeoServer.

In this chapter, we also had an introduction to the concepts of scalability and configuring GeoServer so that it can be highly available and/or high performing. These basic concepts will give you a good understanding of the concepts and enable you to start to consider and design the implementation of a GeoServer cluster within an enterprise environment. With the barrier of software licensing costs removed through the use of GeoServer, the only limitation on the power of your production environment will be how much you can afford to spend on infrastructure.

Creating a high-performing installation of GeoServer is as much about data optimization as it is about Java VM configuration and clever architecture. In the next chapter, we will look at how we can optimize raster data for high-performance rendering.

2
Working with Raster Data

In the first chapter, we looked at setting up one or more instances of GeoServer in a way that will make them perform well in a production environment. However, configuring instances so that they run well is only a part of the performance equation. Loading well-structured and optimized data for GeoServer to serve is another part.

In this chapter, we will focus on how raster data can be prepared and stored so that GeoServer can serve it efficiently, and in doing so, we will maximize the benefit of the effort that we put in setting up GeoServer. This chapter assumes a basic knowledge of how raster datasets are served by GeoServer and how to use the web administration interface, configure stores, and publish layers.

We will address a range of topics, from looking at how we can increase the types of raster data we can serve to how we can serve vast coverage of raster data efficiently. By the end of this chapter, you will have a better understanding of the following topics:

- Increasing the range of raster formats supported using GDAL
- Optimizing raster datasets for better performance
- Converting raster formats to GeoTIFF
- Processing GeoTIFF to get maximum performance
- Understanding the concept of image mosaicking
- Serving very large coverages using the ImageMosaic format

Increasing the raster formats supported by GeoServer

Out of the box, GeoServer supports a good range of raster formats, and for the majority of use cases, the standard supported formats are, most likely, all you will need. The standard formats supported by GeoServer Version 2.5.2 are:

- **ArcGrid**: The ArcGrid coverage format
  (http://en.wikipedia.org/wiki/Esri_grid)

- **GeoTIFF**: A tagged image file format with geographic information
  (http://en.wikipedia.org/wiki/GeoTIFF)

- **Gtopo30**: The gtopo30 coverage format
  (http://en.wikipedia.org/wiki/GTOPO30)

- **ImageMosaic**: An image-mosaicking plugin

- **WorldImage**: A raster file accompanied by a file that contains geo-reference information

It is likely that the vast majority of raster data that you will use with GeoServer will be in GeoTIFF and/or WorldImage (for example, **TIFF** files with an accompanying TIFF world file). However, there might come a time when you need to serve a *nonstandard* raster format through GeoServer, for example, **MrSID**. Luckily for us, these fringe cases are considered by the GeoServer developers and they implement a plugin that utilizes the **Geospatial Data Abstraction Library (GDAL)**.

GDAL is an open source library designed to process and transform raster data. The clever thing about GDAL is that it provides an abstract data model as a single reference point for a calling application. The calling application only needs to concern itself with understanding one data model. GDAL performs the magic to turn the supplied features into their respective underlying format. In addition to the abstract data model, GDAL also supplies a number of command-line utilities that can be used to process and translate raster data.

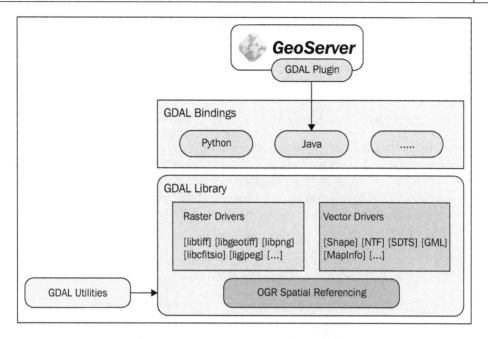

The GDAL library is written in C++, and binaries are available for a range of operating systems and architectures, including Windows and Linux. There are also a number of bindings available so that the GDAL library can be called from different programming languages such as Python and Java.

Adding GDAL support to GeoServer is a two-stage process:

1. Installing the GDAL binary libraries for your platform.
2. Installing the GeoServer GDAL plugin.

Installing the GDAL binary libraries

Before we can install and use the GeoServer GDAL plugin, we must make sure that our system includes the GDAL binary libraries. The GDAL plugin requires the binary libraries to be installed as it utilizes Java bindings to perform raster processing and transformation. In the following sections, we will look at how to prepare our system with the GDAL binary libraries.

Installing on CentOS Linux 6.3

There are a couple of options to install GDAL libraries on CentOS, or for that matter, on any other Linux distribution:

- Compiling from the source
- Using a package management system such as YUM or APT

For those of you that are well-versed in the world of compiling Linux applications and libraries from source, or for the adventurous among you, there is nothing better than the satisfaction arising from a Linux compilation without any dependency issues. If, on the other hand, you do not know how to compile the source code on Linux, or are looking to save time, then nothing can beat using a package management system.

There are a range of options for packaged distributions of the GDAL library; some of the more popular ones are listed in the following table:

Repository	GDAL version	Web address
PostgreSQL PGDG 9.3	1.9.2	`http://yum.postgresql.org/repopackages.php`
Enterprise Linux GIS	1.9.2	`http://elgis.argeo.org/`
Boundless Geo	1.9.2	`http://www.boundlessgeo.com`

Ultimately, it doesn't matter which repository you choose, the process will be the same; so if you have a favorite, use it. For this example, we will use the repository at Boundless Geo to install GDAL. Perform the following steps to install GDAL on Linux:

1. Create a repository (`.repo`) file in the `/etc/yum.repos.d/` directory by issuing the following command:

   ```
   $ sudo vi /etc/yum.repos.d/OpenGeo.repo
   ```

2. This will create a blank repository file that we need to fill with the following information to make `yum` aware of the presence of the repository as a source:

   ```
   [opengeo]
   name=opengeo
   baseurl=http://yum.opengeo.org/suite/v4/
   centos/$releasever/$basearch
   enabled=1
   gpgcheck=0
   ```

3. This tells yum that there is a repository called opengeo that is available to search at the given baseurl address. The enabled=1 flag tells yum that the repository is available for use. Save the file and exit the vi text editor. From this point forward, all the yum commands will look inside the opengeo repository for packages.

 If at some point in the future you want to prevent yum from using the opengeo repository, then simply edit the /etc/yum.repos.d/OpenGeo.repo file and change the value of the enabled flag from 1 to 0. The repository will no longer be used by yum, until you set the flag back to 1 again.

4. Now we can perform an installation of the GDAL library and all its dependencies issuing the following command:

    ```
    $ sudo yum install gdal gdal-mrsid
    ```

5. This command instructs yum to install the core GDAL package (including the Java binding) along with the MrSID format plugin so that we can use the MrSID raster files. If all goes well, you should see an installation success message. To verify that GDAL was correctly installed, issue the following command:

    ```
    $ gdalinfo --formats
    ```

6. If GDAL was correctly installed, you should see a long list of all the different formats GDAL can use.

That's it! GDAL is installed and working, ready for you to install the GeoServer GDAL plugin.

Installing on Windows Server 2008 R2 SP1

In this section, we will take a look at how to install the GDAL binary libraries on Windows Server 2008. As with Linux, Windows users also have a couple of options to install the GDAL libraries:

*   Compiling from the source code
*   Downloading precompiled binaries as an installation package

Compiling the source code on Windows can be a real pain, and the vast majority of users will be unaware of how to go about doing it, let alone actually have access to the necessary software. In the world of Windows, it is best to always install compiled binaries rather than attempt the compilation yourself.

Tamas Szekeres has been doing a great job of maintaining a continuous build of the GDAL libraries for the Windows platform. These binaries can be downloaded as MSI installers, making this installation the same as any other Windows software installation. We will use his build of Version 1.9.2 of GDAL for consistency, though more recent versions are available. First, we need to download the GDAL core installer along with the GDAL MrSID plugin installer. These two files can be downloaded at the following locations:

- **GDAL core**: `http://www.gisinternals.com/sdk/Download.aspx?file=release-1400-gdal-1-9-2-mapserver-6-2-0\gdal-19-1400-core.msi`

- **GDAL MrSID plugin**: `http://www.gisinternals.com/sdk/Download.aspx?file=release-1400-gdal-1-9-2-mapserver-6-2-0\gdal-19-1400-mrsid.msi`

First, we need to start by running `gdal-19-1400-core.msi` to install the core GDAL library components. Double-click on the downloaded file and work through the installation wizard:

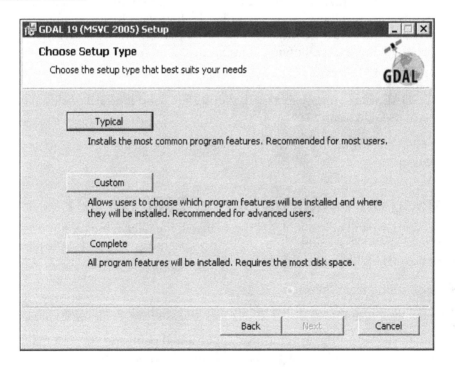

When you reach the **Choose Setup Type** page, you have three choices available. **Typical** will install the most commonly used components of GDAL and will be sufficient for the majority of users. **Custom** allows you to specify the exact components of GDAL to install; clicking on the button will open the selection page shown in the following screenshot:

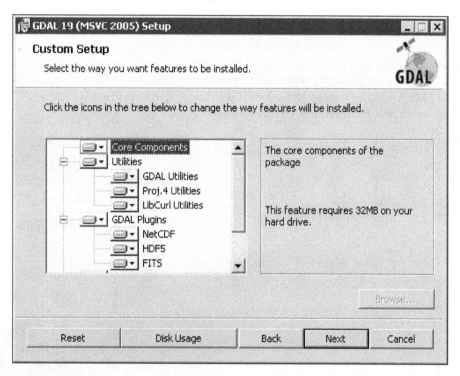

Finally, the **Complete** button will perform an installation of all GDAL components. Unless you have a specific reason not to, you should go ahead and click on the **Complete** button to install everything. On the next page that appears, click on the **Install** button to begin the installation. Follow the remaining steps to complete the installation.

After installing the core package, we can install the MrSID plugin. Double-click on the downloaded file, gdal-19-1400-mrsid.msi, to begin the installation wizard. There are no options to set for this installation, so simply click on **Next** until you reach the **Choose Setup Type** page; click on the **Complete** button to begin the installation.

Setting environment variables

Using the installers provided by Tamas Szekeres enables us to use GDAL on Windows by running the **GDAL 19 (MSVC 2005) Command Prompt** shortcut from the start menu. This opens a command prompt with all the appropriate environment variables set so that the GDAL tools can be used.

In order for GeoServer — and potentially other applications — to be aware of the installed GDAL library, we must create some environment variables to point to the binary files. To do this, we need to open the **Environment Variables** dialog from **Advanced System Settings**, which can be accessed from the **System** applet in **Control Panel**. First, we need to add the GDAL installation directory to the PATH variable, as shown in the following screenshot:

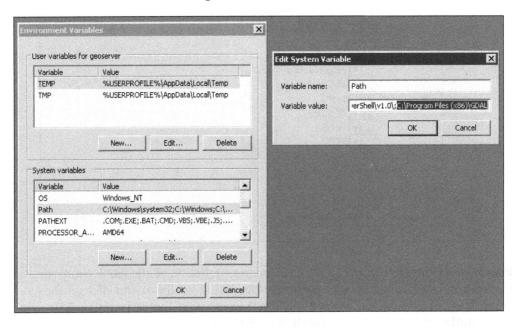

Adding the C:\Program Files (x86)\GDAL location to the PATH environment will allow other applications to use the GDAL library and tools; make sure to have ; preceding the entry. Next, we need to add the following system variables to support GDAL's functions:

Variable name	Variable value
GDAL_DATA	C:\Program Files (x86)\GDAL\gdal-data
GDAL_DRIVER_PATH	C:\Program Files (x86)\GDAL\gdalplugins
PROJ_LIB	C:\Program Files (x86)\GDAL\projlib

GDAL is now installed and configured on our Windows environment. To test that the environment variables have been set correctly, we can open a command prompt and enter the following command:

```
C:\> gdalinfo --formats
```

If the PATH environment is correct, we should receive a response to this command in the form of a long list of available formats. Within this list, we need to look for an entry for MrSID; if we find it, then GDAL_DRIVER_PATH has also been correctly set. Now we are ready to install the GeoServer GDAL plugin.

Installing the GeoServer GDAL plugin

Once we have GDAL installed and configured on our system, getting the GeoServer plugin is as easy as copying the contents of a ZIP file into our GeoServer deployment. First, we need to head over to the GeoServer download page at http://www.geoserver.org/release/stable:

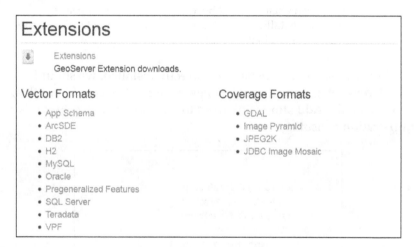

Make sure that you go to the download page that corresponds to the version of GeoServer that you installed. If you take the most recent version, then the downloads you need are on the **Stable** page. If you have a previous version, then you need to look on the **All Releases** page. If you do not download the matching version of the extension, errors will occur.

On the download page, there is a section titled **Extensions**, and within this, there's a grouping of downloads called **Coverage Formats**. We need to click on the **GDAL** link and save it somewhere on our system.

To perform the installation, we just need to extract the `.jar` files contained within the archive into the `WEB-INF/lib` folder of our GeoServer installation. For example, on a Linux installation, the command will look something like:

```
$ unzip geoserver-2.4.4-gdal-plugin.zip *.jar -d /opt/apache-
tomcat-7.0.50/webapps/geoserver/WEB-INF/lib/
```

This command will tell `unzip` to extract only files with a `.jar` extension from the location specified by the `-d` switch. The command will work the same on both Windows and Linux variants of `unzip`.

 If you run your environment from GUI, then you can just use standard drag-and-drop copy methods to move the files from the zip package to the GeoServer directory.

In order for GeoServer to be aware of the new extension, we need to restart it.

If you run a cluster of GeoServers, remember to repeat the process of installing GDAL and the GeoServer extension across all the instances in your cluster.

If GDAL and the GeoServer extension are correctly installed, we should see an expanded list of options to create a new raster data store. To see this, we need to click on the **Add stores** link from the front page of GeoServer's **web administration console**:

Raster Data Sources

- AIG - Arc/Info Binary Grid (AIG) Coverage Format
- ArcGrid - Arc Grid Coverage Format
- ArcSDE Raster - ArcSDE Raster Format
- DTED - DTED Coverage Format
- EHdr - EHdr Coverage Format
- ENVIHdr - ENVIHdr Coverage Format
- ERDASImg - Erdas Imagine Coverage Format
- GeoTIFF - Tagged Image File Format with Geographic information
- Gtopo30 - Gtopo30 Coverage Format
- ImageMosaic - Image mosaicking plugin
- ImageMosaicJDBC - Image mosaicking/pyramidal jdbc plugin
- ImagePyramid - Image pyramidal plugin
- JP2MrSID - JP2K (MrSID) Coverage Format
- MrSID - MrSID Coverage Format
- NITF - NITF Coverage Format
- RPFTOC - RPFTOC Coverage Format
- RST - IDRIS (RST) Coverage Format
- WorldImage - A raster file accompanied by a spatial data file

How to optimize raster data for better performance

As talented as the GeoServer developers are, there is only so much they can do from a software perspective to help us run high-performing web mapping servers. As users of the software, we also have a part to play to get the best performance out of it. In the first instance, this is achieved through optimizing our deployment strategy and ensuring that our production environment is configured optimally, as we saw in *Chapter 1, Installing GeoServer for Production*. Secondly, and arguably more importantly, it's the way we prepare the data that we will deliver through GeoServer.

Unfortunately, it is the second element that most people overlook when setting up their web mapping servers—irrespective of the software they use. Well-structured and organized data can make a huge difference on the response times of a mapping server. While GeoServer is very flexible in the number of formats it can handle, and the many flavors of each format it can manipulate, there will always be an overhead in processing time if we expect it to do too much for each map request. For example, it will take GeoServer longer to respond to a request if the source image is a multiband (RGBA—4 bands) TIFF image with LZW compression rather than an uncompressed 8-bit (indexed color palette) TIFF image. There is a processing overhead in decompressing the image data, and the more bands an image has, the more memory is required to manipulate it. Higher memory requirements per request will reduce the number of concurrent requests that the server can handle.

There are a number of things to consider when looking at optimizing the raster data we plan on serving. However, before considering the different options, it must be stressed that the most fundamental thing to understand is the source material that we work with and what our intended end use case is. Understanding our source data is critical to make the right decisions about how to prepare and serve it. There is no hard-and-fast rule about how to optimize the raster data ready for efficient serving, but there are some key concepts to consider that can make a difference to response times.

Understanding your source data

We configured GDAL on our system to increase the range of raster formats supported; we also have a very useful toolkit that we can use to understand and process our source data. The best way to understand our data is to use the gdalinfo command. It inspects raster files and exposes their internal structure:

```
$ gdalinfo <raster_file>
```

Here, `<raster_file>` is the location of the image that you want to inspect. For example, we can apply the `gdalinfo` command to a raster file from an Ordnance Survey (Great Britain's national mapping agency) product OS VectorMap District, which will generate the following output:

```
OSGeo4W Shell
Driver: GTiff/GeoTIFF
Files: \\10.44.20.36\osdata\OpenData\StreetView\tq\tq93nw.tif
       \\10.44.20.36\osdata\OpenData\StreetView\tq\tq93nw.TFW
Size is 5000, 5000
Coordinate System is ''
Origin = (590000.000000000000000,140000.000000000000000)
Pixel Size = (1.000000000000000,-1.000000000000000)
Metadata:
  TIFFTAG_COPYRIGHT=ORDNANCE SURVEY CROWN COPYRIGHT 2012
  TIFFTAG_DATETIME=2012:09:29 07:48:36
  TIFFTAG_IMAGEDESCRIPTION=OS Street View TQ93NW
  TIFFTAG_RESOLUTIONUNIT=2 (pixels/inch)
  TIFFTAG_XRESOLUTION=254
  TIFFTAG_YRESOLUTION=254
Image Structure Metadata:
  COMPRESSION=LZW
  INTERLEAVE=BAND
Corner Coordinates:
Upper Left  (  590000.000,  140000.000)
Lower Left  (  590000.000,  135000.000)
Upper Right (  595000.000,  140000.000)
Lower Right (  595000.000,  135000.000)
Center      (  592500.000,  137500.000)
Band 1 Block=5000x1 Type=Byte, ColorInterp=Palette
  Color Table (RGB with 256 entries)
    0: 255,246,238,255
    1: 98,65,74,255
    2: 213,230,131,255
    3: 90,82,82,255
    4: 255,148,131,255
    5: 255,90,98,255
    6: 238,246,246,255
    7: 57,24,24,255
    8: 222,98,98,255
    9: 115,74,65,255
   10: 8,16,8,255
   11: 230,238,238,255
   12: 0,8,0,255
   13: 230,213,164,255
   14: 230,238,230,255
   15: 32,32,16,255
   16: 139,180,189,255
   17: 238,230,90,255
   18: 255,255,148,255
   19: 32,32,32,255
   20: 222,246,164,255
   21: 16,8,8,255
   22: 189,180,74,255
   23: 213,246,148,255
   24: 8,0,0,255
-- More --
```

Throughout this chapter, you will see references being made to some source raster datasets. These are used merely for illustration of the commands and concepts; however, if you want to follow along using the same data, then you can go online and order the free dataset from Ordnance Survey (Great Britain), which is called OS StreetView™. In these examples, I will use data from the National Grid tile named **TQ**. The data can be ordered from http://www.ordnancesurvey.co.uk/opendata.

This output tells us that we are dealing with a TIFF world format image that is 5,000 pixels wide and 5,000 pixels high. We can also see that the image is compressed using the LZW compression (COMPRESSION=LZW), and it is a single stripped file (Block=5000x1) with an indexed color palette of 256 colors (ColorInterp=Palette). Now that we understand a little bit more about the dataset we are dealing with, we can start to consider how we might process it ready for GeoServer.

Single file versus multifile

The image that we just inspected is part of a much larger dataset from Ordnance Survey that consists of a total of 10,592 images to cover Great Britain. Later, we will see how we can use the ImageMosaic format to treat the dataset as a single coverage. However, before we do so, there are some things we must consider in advance. The number of files that constitute a complete dataset will have a bearing on the performance of GeoServer when accessing it. Many small files are less efficient than fewer larger files. This statement might seem counter-intuitive at first; after all, surely a larger image takes more effort and time to read than several smaller files. However, it is important to consider what the system has to do in order to read each image. There will be a system overhead for each read operation on the disk and the system must seek the location on the disk of the file and then open a stream so that the data can be read; multiply this by the number of images required to construct a view and there will be a lot of wasted time as a result of costly disk I/O.

In contrast, a single larger file will only have the disk I/O overhead once. From this point forward, it will be up to the memory and CPU to process the data. In our example of Ordnance Survey's StreetView product, we can see that each file is named according to where they are situated in the National Grid. If you know the British National Grid, then you will know that TQ93NE can be converted into a 12-figure grid reference of 595000 easting and 135000 northing.

 Ordnance Survey provides a guide to the British National Grid, and it can be downloaded from http://www.ordnancesurvey.co.uk/docs/support/guide-to-nationalgrid.pdf.

We know that a single image in this dataset is 5,000 pixels by 5,000 pixels, and we also know that the letters NE, SE, SW, and NW represent a quadrant of a larger grid square; in this case, TQ93:

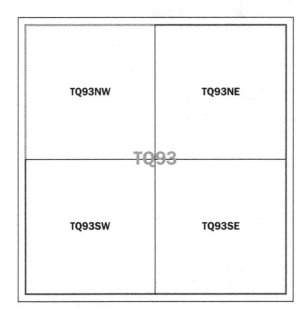

Therefore, we can merge all the files representing quadrants into a larger (10,000 pixel by 10,000 pixel) image and give it the name of the parent tile. This means that we can reduce the number of total files for the dataset by a factor of four, giving us 2,648 files in total. GDAL provides a Python script that can be used to perform the merging operation, gdal_merge.py. Although each image will be larger, there are fewer of them, so we gain some time in disk I/O operations.

> Details on the different utilities provided by GDAL can be found at http://www.gdal.org/gdal_utilities.html, with specific information on gdal_merge.py available at http://www.gdal.org/gdal_merge.html. GeoSolutions provide a tutorial on using GDAL for raster processing at http://geoserver.geo-solutions.it/edu/en/raster_data/processing.html.

This is an extreme case, and the number of files is large because of the spatial coverage of the dataset (Great Britain). However, the principle can be scaled down and still deliver benefit. For example, if you consider using the GeoTIFF format, then it is feasible to have a single image, that is, <= 2 GB, and still serve it with great performance.

GeoTIFF overviews and tiling

The GeoTIFF format is very versatile, and in the vast majority of cases, it will be a good fit for your needs. GeoTIFF is an extension of the TIFF format, but includes additional elements to enable it to store spatial information, for example, the header can store the Coordinate Reference System information rather than storing it in a separate world file. A GeoTIFF file can have what are known as **overviews**, and the data can be organized either in **strips** or **tiles**.

GeoTIFF overviews

An **overview** is a reduced scale version of the complete image held in GeoTIFF. This can be useful as it opens the prospect to create image pyramids within the GeoTIFF file. GeoTIFF has the ability to store overviews internally as well as externally (through an .ovr file, or the **Erdas Imagine** format, .aux). The ability to store overviews internally is extremely useful as it makes managing the dataset much easier by not having to handle multiple files for the dataset.

This example depicts an image with two overview levels applied, one at level 2 and another at level 4:

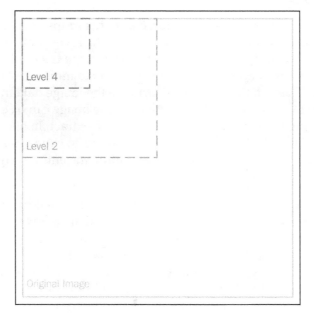

The number of the level determines the down-sampled size of the overview. So, a level of 2 will result in an overview that is half the size (width and height) of the original image.

GeoServer is capable of reading overviews if they are present in the GeoTIFF file, and this means that it can quickly fetch a suitable image to return without the need to process the complete GeoTIFF image data.

Overviews can be added to a GeoTIFF file using the GDAL tool, gdaladdo. An example command for gdaladdo will be:

```
$ gdaladdo -r nearest -b 1 tq93ne.tif 2 4 8 16
```

This command will create overviews using the nearest neighbor resampling method (-r nearest), with the first band (-b 1) being used to generate the overviews. The numbers at the end are the levels to create overviews at. It is difficult to define what options you should set to get the best performance as it very much depends upon your source data. The preceding command is a sensible start point, but I will encourage you to experiment with different settings for your own datasets and use cases.

GeoTIFF tiles

The image data within GeoTIFF can be stored as either strips or tiles. This refers to the internal structure of the bytes that constitute the image data of GeoTIFF. A stripped structure means that the byte array for the image is stored in one or more sequential strips of data, and there are index pointers to indicate where each strip resides in the file. Tiles, on the other hand, arrange the image data in blocks. Storing the image data in this way means that portions of the image can be extracted very easily by referencing the location within the image to extract. Image data arranged in strips must be worked through sequentially in order to extract the portion of the image required, which, in essence, means reading the entire image stream into memory so that a specific portion can be extracted.

With a tiled structure, only the required portion of the image needs to be read and held in memory. For very large raster files, you should always consider arranging the data in tiles, which can be done by specifying a format creation option for any GDAL tool that creates the GeoTIFF output. Simply add the -co "TILED=YES" command switch, and GDAL will write the image data in a tiled structure. The size of the tiles can also be controlled using the command switches -co BLOCKXSIZE=n and BLOCKYSIZE=n, where n is the size in pixels for the tiles.

Converting raster formats to GeoTIFF

GDAL provides us with a nifty utility to convert raster data from one format to another. The `gdal_translate` utility can be used to convert our OS StreetView TIFF world image to GeoTIFF, considering the fact that the image is in the British National Grid coordinate system. We can also control other aspects of the output, such as whether the image data should be compressed and whether there should be tiling. For example, from a command line, we can execute the following command:

```
$ gdal_translate -of GTiff -a_srs EPSG:27700 -co "COMPRESS=NONE" -co
"TILED=YES" tq93nw.tif tq93nw_gtiff.tif
```

This will create a new file, `tq93nw_gtiff.tif`, from the source file, `tq93nw.tif`. As a part of the translation, we ask for the output file to have no compression (`-co "COMPRESS=NONE"`) and for the data to be tiled using default values instead of stripped values (`-co "TILED=YES"`). If we run `gdalinfo` on the newly created file, we will see a confirmation of these changes:

```
OSGeo4W Shell

Driver: GTiff/GeoTIFF
Files: D:\Temp\tq93nw_gtiff.tif
Size is 5000, 5000
Coordinate System is:
PROJCS["OSGB 1936 / British National Grid",
    GEOGCS["OSGB 1936",
        DATUM["OSGB_1936",
            SPHEROID["Airy 1830",6377563.396,299.3249646000044,
                AUTHORITY["EPSG","7001"]],
            TOWGS84[446.448,-125.157,542.06,0.15,0.247,0.842,-20.489],
            AUTHORITY["EPSG","6277"]],
        PRIMEM["Greenwich",0],
        UNIT["degree",0.0174532925199433],
        AUTHORITY["EPSG","4277"]],
    PROJECTION["Transverse_Mercator"],
    PARAMETER["latitude_of_origin",49],
    PARAMETER["central_meridian",-2],
    PARAMETER["scale_factor",0.9996012717],
    PARAMETER["false_easting",400000],
    PARAMETER["false_northing",-100000],
    UNIT["metre",1,
        AUTHORITY["EPSG","9001"]],
    AUTHORITY["EPSG","27700"]]
Origin = (590000.000000000000000,140000.000000000000000)
Pixel Size = (1.000000000000000,-1.000000000000000)
Metadata:
  AREA_OR_POINT=Area
  TIFFTAG_COPYRIGHT=ORDNANCE SURVEY CROWN COPYRIGHT 2012
  TIFFTAG_DATETIME=2012:09:29 07:48:36
  TIFFTAG_IMAGEDESCRIPTION=OS Street View TQ93NW
  TIFFTAG_RESOLUTIONUNIT=2 (pixels/inch)
  TIFFTAG_XRESOLUTION=254
  TIFFTAG_YRESOLUTION=254
Image Structure Metadata:
  INTERLEAVE=BAND
Corner Coordinates:
Upper Left  (  590000.000,  140000.000) (  0d42'56.27"E, 51d 7'37.89"N)
Lower Left  (  590000.000,  135000.000) (  0d42'46.80"E, 51d 4'56.20"N)
Upper Right (  595000.000,  140000.000) (  0d47'13.22"E, 51d 7'31.84"N)
Lower Right (  595000.000,  135000.000) (  0d47' 3.50"E, 51d 4'50.16"N)
Center      (  592500.000,  137500.000) (  0d44'59.95"E, 51d 6'14.04"N)
Band 1 Block=256x256 Type=Byte, ColorInterp=Palette
  Color Table (RGB with 256 entries)
    0: 255,246,238,255
    1: 98,65,74,255
    2: 213,230,131,255
    3: 90,82,82,255
    4: 255,148,131,255
    5: 255,90,98,255
    6: 238,246,246,255
-- More --
```

From the output of `gdalinfo`, we can see that we now have the Coordinate Reference System information stored inside the file rather than externally in a world file. We can also see that there is no compression on the image data and that it is arranged in tiles of 256 pixels by 256 pixels (`Block=256x256`), which is the default value when nothing else is specified in the creation options.

 Have a look at `http://www.gdal.org/gdal_translate.html` for an in-depth discussion of `gdal_translate` and the different options available.

How to serve very large raster datasets

So far in this chapter, we looked at how we can increase the number of raster formats that GeoServer can serve, and considered how we can prepare our raster data for efficient serving. However, in these discussions, we only looked at relatively small numbers of raster images. We have not yet given any consideration to how we might approach the not-so-insignificant issue of serving large volumes of high resolution imagery. For example, how might we approach the challenge of serving raster data at a national scale such as large-scale aerial surveys or a national map product such as Ordnance Survey's OS StreetView?

We can stitch all the individual raster images together to create a single file containing the complete coverage. However, this will result in a considerably large file for processing (and, in fact, one that it might not be possible to store). The OS StreetView product, for example, requires approximately 10,592 files to cover Great Britain and roughly 12.1 GB of storage. Merging to a single file is not a practical solution to this particular challenge as aside from the time it will take to process the single image, the format won't support the creation of an image that's large enough.

What we need is a solution that will enable us to keep the individual files in our filesystem, but allow GeoServer to consider them as a complete spatial coverage. Select the most appropriate files from the filesystem, stitch them together, and then chop out the part of the combined image that has been requested. Luckily for us, this is actually a common problem in the world of spatial data management, and solutions exist to handle it. The answer is to create a virtual mosaic of all the images that combine to create the complete spatial coverage. Systems will use different terminologies to express the same function, and in the majority of cases, you will either come across the term **image mosaic** or **image catalog**.

Irrespective of the term used to describe the capability, they will have one thing in common — the use of an index file that describes the name and location of each of the constituent components of the mosaic or catalogue.

 Since we are looking at the ImageMosaic format in GeoServer, we will adopt the terminology used by GeoServer to describe the function. **Mosaic** is the term used to describe the complete coverage as a single entity. **Granule** is the term used to describe a single component of the mosaic. One or more **granules** combine to construct the complete **mosaic**.

It is worth noting that granules within the mosaic can be spatially contiguous, overlap, have no spatial connectivity whatsoever, or be a mixture of all the three types.

GeoServer comes with a built-in format that will allow us to create a mosaic to serve large coverages of raster data, which is called the ImageMosaic format. It supports the creation of mosaics whose granules are in a standard supported image format such as GeoTIFF or **WorldImage** (standard image formats such as **PNG**, **JPEG**, or **TIFF** with supporting world files). If you followed the steps to add support for GDAL within GeoServer, then granules can also be in any of the supported GDAL image formats.

When creating and using ImageMosaics in GeoServer, you should be aware of the following limitations and ensure that your granules adhere to them:

- Each granule in the mosaic must be in the same Coordinate Reference System
- The same ColorModel and SampleModel should be used for all granules
- The same spatial resolution and overviews should be used in all granules; if not, then any overview present will be ignored

Using the ImageMosaic format

The ImageMosaic format is a standard out-of-the-box format for GeoServer. To function correctly, it requires the following four components to be present:

- An **index file**: The features of this file are the polygons representing the spatial extents of each granule in the mosaic. Each feature must contain an attribute that provides the location of the granule's file on the host filesystem; the location can be expressed either relative to the index file or as an absolute reference. As of Version 2.4.4 of GeoServer, the ImageMosaic format only supports an index file in the Esri Shapefile format (.shp).

- A **projection file** (.prj): The name of this file is the same as that of the index (.shp) file that provides the Coordinate Reference System information for the mosaic. Although a standard component of Esri Shapefiles, it is not always generated by software that support the format. If the projection file is present, then GeoServer will utilize it to determine the Coordinate Reference System for the mosaic. If it is not present, then we will need to provide this information at the point we publish a layer based on the mosaic.

- A **properties file** (.properties): This is the configuration file that provides information about the mosaic, such as the x and y cell size, and whether the file location attribute is absolute or relative.

- Granules: These combine to construct the mosaic.

Creating ImageMosaic automatically

By far, the easiest way to create ImageMosaic is to use the format's built-in capability to automatically create the spatial index and configuration files. This approach assumes that we already prepared a directory structure with all the granules for the mosaic.

ImageMosaic is a data store format. So, to create a new one using our directory of granules, we need to use the GeoServer web administration console. Perform the following steps to create a new ImageMosaic:

1. Select the **Stores** link from the **Data** section of the left-hand side menu on the web administration console.

2. Click on the **Add New Store** link to open the **New data source** page.

3. Look for the entry, **ImageMosaic**, under the **Raster Data Sources** section, and click on the link to open the configuration page for ImageMosaic:

On this page, we need to set some properties so that the configuration and index files can be properly generated.

4. Select the workspace to create the data store from the **Workspace** drop-down list.

5. Give the data store a name in the **Data Source Name** textbox.

6. Provide a brief description for the data store in the **Description** textbox.

7. Finally, specify the location where GeoServer can find the granules for our mosaic by typing it into the **URL** textbox.

The value for the **URL** connection parameter should point to the root of the directory structure containing our granules (or if we already configured an index shapefile, we can provide its location directly). GeoServer will check for a pre-existing shapefile with the same name as the value for **Data Source Name**. If it finds one, then it is used, if it does not, then it will begin to recursively scan our directory of granules. Any file found within the directory structure that is a supported format is inspected to determine its spatial extents and ColorModel. The location of the image file along with its envelope is added as a feature in a new shapefile. Once the scan process is complete, a new set of files will be created at the root of the data store.

The ImageMosaic data store is so configured that we can go ahead and publish a new coverage layer specifying the details of how we want our users to see and access the data.

Be patient! While the automatic index file creation process is useful, it can also be time consuming. Relax and let GeoServer do its thing, especially if you are creating ImageMosaic with thousands of files.

Creating ImageMosaic manually

If we want to have fine control over the ImageMosaic creation process, for example, we want to select certain images from a directory of many others, then we will need to create the index shapefile and properties file manually.

The index shapefile has minimal requirements. In essence, all that is required is for there to be a polygon representing the spatial extents of each granule in the index, with an attribute whose value is the location on the disk of the raster image. The value can either be relative or absolute to the index. The name of the attribute is not important. However, by convention, it is normally called `location`. There are many different approaches that we can take to create the index file, but for this example, we will use the excellent Open Source GIS package, QGIS (`http://www.qgis.org`). QGIS has a **Tile Index** tool that is a wrapper around a GDAL utility. If you don't already have it, head over to the link and download the latest version. At the time of writing this book, this is version 2.4.0; install it and then launch it.

From the QGIS main menu, navigate to **Raster | Miscellaneous | Tile index** to open the tool:

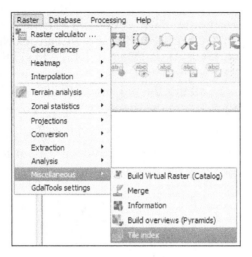

The **Tile Index** tool allows us to select a source directory to scan for compatible image formats, and optionally, recursively scan subdirectories. As we select options on the dialog, notice how the text in the large textbox changes:

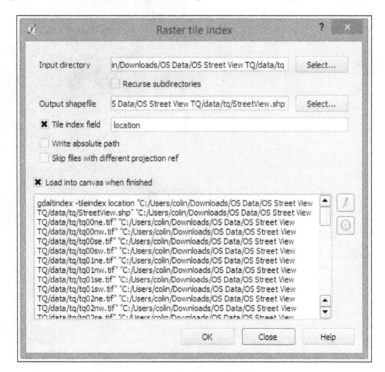

This is the GDAL command that QGIS will execute in order to create the tile index shapefile. If you are comfortable with GDAL, then it is possible to edit and fine tune the generated command string by clicking on the edit button (the one with a pencil icon). For now, we will accept the GDAL command as generated; we need to specify a name and location for the output shapefile, and we can also specify the name to give to the tile index field. The tile index field will hold the path to the image file, so we'll check the box and then enter the value, location, into the text box that becomes active. Finally, we will tick the box that loads the result into the canvas so that we can check the output is what we expect.

Click on the **OK** button and wait for the tool to complete its work. Once completed, we will be prompted for the spatial reference information for the index file, and then, if all's well, it will be loaded into the map window:

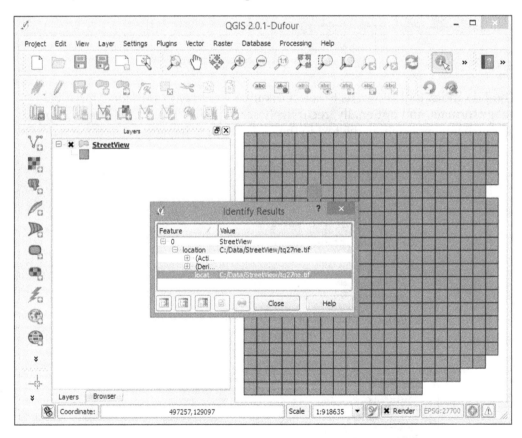

Now that we have our granules index shapefile, we need to create the accompanying properties file. The properties file is a simple text file whose name should be the same as the index shapefile, but with a `.properties` extension. The contents of the properties file is a `<key>=<value>` pair on each line to describe the configuration of the mosaic. Valid properties for this file are shown in the following table:

Key	Purpose
Levels	These are the resolutions for each of the levels of granules contained within the mosaic.
Heterogenous	This determines whether the granules in the mosaic are diverse or broadly the same. If set to true, resolutions are not checked when creating the granules index.
AbsolutePath	This determines whether the location attribute stores the reference to granules as an absolute or relative reference.
Name	This is the name of the mosaic that will be used.
Caching	This decides whether GeoServer caches the details of the mosaic. Setting this to false allows control of the mosaic content, without GeoServer losing synchronization.
ExpandToRGB	This determines whether to expand the color model from indexed to RGBA. There is a performance penalty using RGBA, so if all your granules are indexed colors, set this to false for a performance increase.
LocationAttribute	This is the name of the attribute that holds the location of the granule.
LevelsNum	This is the number of reduced resolution layers available for each granule overview in GeoTIFF.

Create a new text file and give it the name `<your mosaic>.properties`, where `<your mosaic>` is the name of the mosaic you create. For this example, we will call the `StreetView` mosaic, so we need to create a file called `StreetView.properties`. This file needs to be saved to the same location as the tile index shapefile. For this example, the content of the file should be:

```
Levels=1.0,1.0
Heterogeneous=false
AbsolutePath=false
Name=StreetView
TypeName=StreetView
Caching=false
ExpandToRGB=false
LocationAttribute=location
LevelsNum=1
```

When creating the `.properties` file manually, it is important to understand the source mosaic granules. In particular, it is important to know the levels that will be used. With the `.properties` file saved, we are ready to create the ImageMosaic data store much the same way we did automatically. This time, however, instead of specifying the parent directory of our mosaic granules, we will specify the index shapefile.

Follow the same procedure as automatically generating the mosaic to open the configuration page for an ImageMosaic data store:

Notice the key difference here from when we created ImageMosaic automatically in the value for the **URL** property. When creating ImageMosaic automatically, we simply specified the location of the parent directory containing the granules. This time, we told GeoServer whereto find the granules index shapefile directly. GeoServer will now create the ImageMosaic data store, and we are now free to create any layer we like from this data store.

How to use the ImageMosaic JDBC extension

In the previous section, we looked at using GeoServer's built-in ImageMosaic format to serve large coverages of raster data. Now, we will take a look at installing and using an optional extension that will enable us to store the granules for a mosaic in a JDBC database. There is potentially a performance penalty with storing rasters inside a database, this is particularly true if the database is not tuned and optimized. Due to the potential performance penalty, it is worth considering some of the reasons why we might decide to store rasters inside a database:

- **Portability**: When migrating servers, instead of having to move hundreds, or even thousands, of files around the network, we can use database backup, restore, and replication functions.

- **Shared Database**: Organizations might choose to store rasters in databases for cataloguing purposes. This is particularly true if they have a large library of raster files, for example, terabytes of aerial survey files. It is often easier to store and catalogue this volume of raster files in a database.

- **Faster Searching**: One of the biggest features of a database is their ability to rapidly search indexes. If the coverage contains a large number of files, then the index searching performance of a database will be of benefit.

The ImageMosaic JDBC plugin can also be used in place of the shapefile index file, where the database is used to store the granules index, but the granules themselves are still kept on the filesystem. This approach provides the dual benefit of faster granule lookup (by the database) and fast raster serving (by the filesystem).

Installing the extension

In order to serve raster data from a JDBC database, we must install the JDBC ImageMosaic extension. As with all other extensions for GeoServer, it is very important to download the version of the extension matching your installed version of GeoServer. We have been using Version 2.5.2, so we must go to the corresponding download page at `http://geoserver.org/release/stable` to get the correct version.

Navigate to **Extensions | Coverage** store section and select the **JDBC Image Mosaic** option to download a ZIP file containing the following extension:

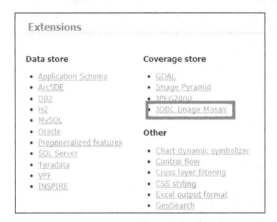

To perform the installation, we just need to extract the `.jar` files contained within the archive into the `WEB-INF/lib` folder of our GeoServer installation. For example, on a Linux installation, the command will look something like:

```
$ unzip geoserver-2.5.2-gdal-plugin.zip *.jar -d /opt/apache-
tomcat-7.0.50/webapps/geoserver/WEB-INF/lib/
```

This command will tell `unzip` to extract only files with a `.jar` extension into the location specified by the `-d` switch. This command will work in the same way on both Windows and Linux variants of `unzip`. In order for GeoServer to be aware of the new extension, we need to restart it, go ahead, and restart the service using the method most appropriate to our system.

Configuring the extension

The JDBC ImageMosaic extension has been designed to support a range of different databases, irrespective of whether they have a spatial extension. The extension reads the raster data from a column in the database where the data has been stored in its binary form, usually as a BLOB (`http://en.wikipedia.org/wiki/Binary_large_object`). To make use of the extension, we must perform these five main steps:

1. Prepare and load the raster data into our database.
2. Create a metadata table for the extension.
3. Create extension configuration files.
4. Create a data store in GeoServer linked to the configuration files.
5. Publish the contents of the data store as a layer.

Preparing and loading raster data

The method of loading raster data into the database will very much depend on the database platform that you're using. The objective is to create a single table to contain all of the granules that will make the mosaic, with each granule being a separate record in the table. You can also choose to create additional tables to hold overviews of the mosaic, which will aid in faster rendering of data when the users zoom out. The overview versions of each granule should be stored in their own separate tables; the configuration files will tell GeoServer where to find the data.

For this example, we will use PostGIS since it has a raster data type called **PGRASTER** (`http://postgis.net/docs/manual-2.0/using_raster.xml.html`), and the JDBC ImageMosaic plugin has support for the built-in data type. Another reason to choose this plugin is that it is very straightforward to set up, and being open source, it is accessible to all. To load raster data into PostGIS, there is a tool that comes as part of the package called, which is called `raster2pgsql`. Providing a detailed description of how to use `raster2pgsql` is outside the scope of this book, but there is a good description of the tool and how to use it at `http://postgis.refractions.net/docs/using_raster.xml.html`. We will use the tool to load some free Ordnance Survey raster data called OS VectorMap District. Go to the Ordnance Survey's website at `http://www.ordnancesurvey.co.uk/opendata` and order yourself some raster data. For this example, I simply ordered data for the British National Grid square TQ, but you can order anything you like, after all, it is free! Once you receive your raster data and download it, unzip the contents to a folder on your system. Open a command line and enter the following command:

```
$ raster2pgsql -c -I -C -s 27700 -l 2 -M -Y <path_to_data>/*.tif osvmd >
insert_osvmd_tiles.sql
```

Before running this command, make sure that the `raster2pgsql` command is in your environment path. This command will generate an SQL script that you can then use to load the raster data into PostGIS. The `-c` switch will create a new table (in this case, we call it `osvmd`) and `-I` will create a spatial index for the table. The `-c` switch will ensure that all constraints are set properly, and `-s 27700` will create the output tables in the British National Grid spatial reference system. The `-M` switch will trigger a vacuum analyze that will update the table statistics and help with performance, and the `-Y` switch will use the `COPY` commands rather than table inserts as they are faster. The `-l 2` switch will create overviews for the raster at two levels. Overviews will help in performance of display as the lower resolution images re-return at certain scale ranges.

Once the process is complete, we will be left with an SQL script called insert_osvmd_tiles.sql, which contains all of the raster data and the commands necessary to load them into the database. All that remains is to execute the script against our database and wait for the data to load in. You can execute the script from a command prompt by issuing the following command:

```
$ psql -d [database name] -f insert_osvmd_tiles.sql
```

Change [database name] to the name of your PostGIS database and hit *Enter*. Depending on the size of your source raster file(s), this script might take some time to execute.

Creating the metadata table

In order to function correctly, the JDBC mosaic plugin requires a metadata table to be present in the database. The name of the metadata table is irrelevant since we will tell the plugin what it is called in an XML configuration file; for this example, we will call the table MOSAIC, but in a production environment, you might want to consider a different name. The table can be created inside PostgreSQL using the following SQL:

```
CREATE TABLE mosaic (
    name varchar(254) not null,
    tiletable varchar(254) not null,
    minx FLOAT8,
    miny FLOAT8,
    maxx FLOAT8,
    maxy FLOAT8,
    resx FLOAT8,
    resy FLOAT8,
    primary key (name, tiletable)
);
```

With the table created, we now need to populate it with some values. The values need to describe the tables where the raster data can be found. The first insert statement describes the raster table containing the full resolution images:

```
INSERT INTO public.mosaic(
        name, tiletable, maxx, maxy, minx, miny, resx, resy)
   VALUES ('vmap', 'osvmd', 600000, 200000, 500000, 100000, 2.5,
-2.5);
```

The next insert statement will add an entry for the first overview level:

```
INSERT INTO public.mosaic(
          name, tiletable, maxx, maxy, minx, miny, resx, resy)
   VALUES ('vmap', 'o_2_osvmd', 600000, 200000, 500000, 100000, 5,
-5);
```

The final insert statement will add an entry for the second overview level:

```
INSERT INTO public.mosaic(
          name, tiletable, maxx, maxy, minx, miny, resx, resy)
   VALUES ('vmap', 'o_4_osvmd', 600000, 200000, 500000, 100000, 10,
-10);
```

The metadata table is now populated so that when we add the datastore to GeoServer the ImageMosaicJDBC extension will know where to find the data in our database.

Creating the extension configuration files

For the plugin to function correctly, it needs to have an XML file that describes the mapping necessary to allow it to get all the tiles for the mosaic from the database. The configuration file has three sections to it describing the database connection details, table mappings, and coverage properties.

Since the connection and mapping details will likely be the same for multiple mosaics, it is best practice to divide the configuration into three separate files, and then use XML inclusion to bring them all together into a mosaic configuration. The following steps will take us through the process of creating the three files required to create the XML mapping file:

1. First, let's create the XML fragment file to hold the database connection details for our PostGIS database where we loaded the tiles. Let's create a folder inside the GeoServer data directory to hold our coverage:

   ```
   $ mkdir <geoserver_data_dir>/coverages/osvmd
   ```

2. Remember to change <geoserver_data_dir> to the location of your GeoServer data directory. Within this folder, create a new text file called pgraster.connect.xml.inc, and then enter the following XML fragment:

   ```
   <connect>
     <dstype value="DBCP" />
     <username value="[username]" />
     <password value="[password]" />
     <jdbcUrl value="jdbc:postgresql://[server]:[port]/[database] />
     <driverClassName value="org.postgresql.Driver" />
     <maxActive value="10" />
     <maxIdle value="0" />
   </connect>
   ```

3. Replace the values inside square brackets with those relevant to your environment. The main purpose of this fragment is to provide the connection details to the database; in this case, PostgreSQL/PostGIS.

4. Next, we need to create the table mappings fragment. Create another text file called `pgraster.mapping.xml.inc` and enter the following XML fragment:

```xml
<spatialExtension name="pgraster" />
<mapping>
  <masterTable name="MOSAIC">
    <coverageNameAttribute name="name" />
    <maxXAttribute name="maxx" />
    <maxYAttribute name="maxy" />
    <minXAttribute name="minx" />
    <minYAttribute name="miny" />
    <resXAttribute name="resx" />
    <resYAttribute name="resy" />
    <tileTableNameAttribute name="tiletable" />
  </masterTable>
  <tileTable>
    <blobAttributeName name="rast" />
  </tileTable>
</mapping>
```

The first element of this fragment is `<spatialExtension>`, whose `name` attribute should be a value indicating the type of spatial database connection the plugin should use. In this case, we specify the `pgraster` value that tells the plugin to use the native PostGIS PGRASTER spatial data type. The rest of the fragment tells the plugin about the metadata table. This is an important element of the configuration since it will allow us to specify our own metadata table if we decide to deviate from convention. For example, if we want to call our coverage name column in the metadata table, `coverage_name`, then we will simply need to make sure that the correct value is present for the `name` attribute of the `<coverageNameAttribute>` element. The other thing to note about this XML fragment is the `name` attribute of the `<blobAttributeName>` element. In this case, the value is `rast`; the important thing to note is that this value should be the name for the column that contains the raster data.

5. The final file to create is an XML file that will import the separate components to create a complete configuration. This file will be the one that we point GeoServer at when creating the data store. The name of the file can be anything you like, but it is a good practice to use the following naming convention:

```
[coverage_name]_[spatial_type].xml
```

Here, [coverage_name] is the name of the coverage you want to serve through GeoServer, and [spatial_type] is the JDBC spatial database type being used. In our case, we create a coverage called VectorMap, and we use the PGRASTER spatial type, so our file will be called vectormap.pgraster.xml. Create the file and then edit it in a text editor so that it looks like the following:

```
<?xml version="1.0" encoding="UTF-8" standalone="no"?>
<!DOCTYPE ImageMosaicJDBCConfig [
      <!ENTITY mapping PUBLIC "mapping"  "mapping.pgraster.xml.
inc">
      <!ENTITY connect PUBLIC "connect"  "connect.pgraster.xml.
inc">
]>

<config version="1.0">
    <coverageName name="vmap"/>
    <coordsys name="EPSG:27700"/>
    <!-- interpolation 1 = nearest neighbour, 2 = bipolar, 3 =
bicubic -->
    <scaleop  interpolation="1"/>
  <axisOrder ignore="false"/>
    &mapping;
    &connect;
</config>
```

What you should notice is that the last file imports the previous two fragments that we created. The reason for doing this is to allow us to quickly create new coverage configurations without having to repetitively write the connection and mapping elements. This is particularly useful if we have all our coverages in the same database. The two !ENTITY elements in the header link to the files to import and are relative to this file. The relevant sections from these files are then imported by the &mapping and &connect entries.

Make sure that all the three files are in the same directory as they will be required to build the configuration that GeoServer will use to create the data store.

Creating the GeoServer data store

With the data loaded, the metadata table created, and the configuration files written, we are now ready to create the data store in GeoServer. Perform the following steps to create the data store:

1. Start by selecting the **Stores** option from the left-hand side menu on the GeoServer web administration console:

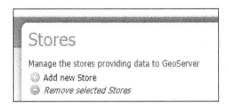

2. On the **Stores** page, click on the **Add new store** link to open the **New data source** page.

3. From the **Raster Data Sources** section, find the **ImageMosaicJDBC** entry and select it:

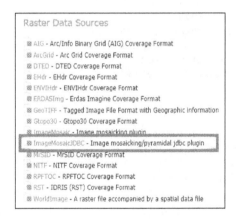

4. This will open the data store configuration page, where we can specify the details for the coverage that we want to serve:

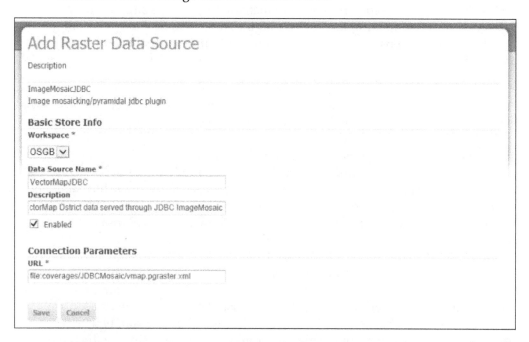

You will notice that there is not much difference between this and any other data store configuration. As usual, we specify a name and description for the data store to be referred to and make sure it is enabled. The main thing we need to do is specify the location of our XML configuration file as this is what the plugin will use to know how to connect to the database and read the image mosaic granules. The value for this field should be:

```
file:coverages/JDBCMosaic/vmap.pgraster.xml
```

The location of the file that we specify is relative to the GeoServer data directory, so if our data directory is `C:\Data` on Windows, then the preceding location will be interpreted by GeoServer as `C:\Data\coverages\JDBCMosaic\vmap.pgraster.xml`. Once the data store configuration details are entered, click on the **Save** button.

GeoServer will now connect to our PostGIS database and read the metadata table, looking for entries related to the coverage we specified in the configuration file. You can now select the coverage and publish it as a layer in the same way that any other layer is published in GeoServer.

Summary

In this chapter, we looked at how we can increase the formats supported by GeoServer by implementing the GDAL plugin. To do this, we have to install the GDAL binaries and ensure that our environment is appropriately configured so that GeoServer is aware of it.

We looked at how important it is to consider the raster data that we want to serve through GeoServer, and learned how we can use gdalinfo to inspect our raster files to learn more about their structure. Having understood the structure of our raster images, we looked at strategies to manipulate them so that they are optimized; this included considering whether they should be merged to create larger single files. Other strategies to optimize our raster data included adding overviews and ensuring that the image data is organized internally as tiles. We saw how gdaladdo can be used to manage overviews and learned about the format creation options to control tiled-image data structures. We looked at how the ImageMosaic format can be used to enable us to deliver large spatial coverages of raster data consisting of multiple files. We considered how ImageMosaic can be created manually as well as automatically, and we looked at how tools can be used to prepare the granule index files. Finally, we took this concept of ImageMosaic and looked at how the granules can be stored to, and read from, a spatial database. To illustrate this, we looked at loading Ordnance Survey VectorMap District into a PostGIS database in the PGRASTER format, and then publishing it through GeoServer using the ImageMosaic JDBC extension.

The key lesson we learned is how important it is to understand the raster dataset you are trying to deliver and the importance of taking the time and effort to preprocess your raster data to decrease the processing burden on GeoServer. Ultimately, this means that your implementation of GeoServer will be able to server more concurrent requests efficiently.

In the next chapter, we will take a look at methods for the efficient serving of vector datasets from spatial databases.

3
Working with Vector Data in Spatial Databases

In the previous chapter, we looked at how we can optimize our raster datasets in to be able to serve them more efficiently. In this chapter, we will take a look at how we can work with vector datasets in a production environment, with our focus being on serving the data through spatial database platforms. Although GeoServer is very good at serving data from flat file formats such as Esri shapefiles, you can't beat the performance benefits from utilizing a spatial database platform in a production environment with large datasets. Out of the box, GeoServer will support connecting to a PostGIS database; however, GeoServer's pluggable architecture can be used to support other platforms. At the time of writing this book, there are official extensions for the following database platforms:

- Esri ArcSDE (database extensions for use with the Esri technology)
- DB2
- MySQL
- Oracle
- Microsoft SQL Server and SQL Azure
- Teradata

Additional database platforms, such as SpatiaLite, can be supported through the use of community extensions. Providing support for an additional dataset is as simple as installing the appropriate extension into the GeoServer installation directory. Sometimes, there will be the need to install and configure additional database platform support files such as JDBC drivers. Once the appropriate database extensions and support files are installed, the database can be used within GeoServer as if it were any other source format.

By the end of this chapter, we will have a much better understanding of the use of spatial database platforms in GeoServer, and in particular, we will understand the following concepts better:

- The benefits of database connection pooling and the settings to use
- Choosing a JNDI connection over a standard JDBC
- Understanding the parameters that are common to all the database formats
- Connecting to and serving data from a PostGIS database
- Connecting to and serving data from an Oracle database
- Connecting to and serving data from Microsoft SQL Server or a SQL Azure database
- Utilizing SQL Views to create layers from multiple database tables

Database connection pooling

Before we get into the details of setting up specific database platforms, it is worth having a conversation about database connection pooling, what it is, and why we should care about it.

Understanding database connection pools

If database connection pooling was not utilized, every time GeoServer receives a request for the data stored in a spatial database, the following sequence of events occurs:

- A connection to the database is made
- SQL commands are executed to select data
- The results from the query are read and processed
- The database connection is closed

A lot of things happen to fetch some data to be rendered (WMS) or processed and streamed (WFS). Consider this happening for a lot of requests, and you can imagine things getting very busy with connections being opened and closed all the time. A lot of the connections from GeoServer to spatial databases are short-lived; in most cases, they might only need to gather a few hundred features. This means that the opening and closing of the connection for these short-lived requests are a significant overhead and will impact the performance.

A database connection pool is designed to overcome this issue. Each time a connection to the database is created, and then closed, instead of the connection being destroyed, it is added to the pool, providing an open connection to the database. The next time a connection to the database is requested, Java will first look to the pool to see if any existing connections are idle. If there is an idle connection, it is used, thus removing the overhead of creating a new database connection. If an idle connection is not available, Java will look to see if the maximum number of connections for the pool has been reached; if not, then it will create a new database connection that will then be added to the pool once it is finished with.

If the maximum number of connections has been reached for the pool, the request will be queued until an existing connection becomes available. There are occasions when a database connection can become stale, that is to say, JVM believes that the connection still exists, but in fact, the database itself has closed the connection. This will result in an error condition when JVM attempts to use the stale connection to service a request. Often, software can implement strategies to prevent this condition from occurring, and so a combination of database-managed connections and Java-managed database connection pools will result in a stable connection infrastructure that can self-manage.

A database connection pool is a set of persistent database connections that allows GeoServer to access database content without the overhead of having to open and close connections. Given that the vast majority of database activity from GeoServer is short-lived, it is not typical for GeoServer to have a long-running transaction. A database connection pool is essential to ensure responsiveness and performance of our GeoServer instance.

Configuring a database connection pool

When creating a data store that uses a spatial database backend, GeoServer provides a number of configuration options to control connection pooling for the data source. The following table describes the database connection pool options that can be set:

Option	Description
Max connections	This determines the total number of database connections the pool should hold. Once this number of connections is reached, no more connections will be created.
Min connections	This determines the minimum number of connections to the database that the pool should hold, irrespective of its current database activity.
Validate connections	This determines whether database connections should be validated before they are used.

Option	Description
Fetch size	This determines the number of records to read from the database in each network exchange.
Connection timeout	This determines the time, in seconds, to wait before the connection pool should abort its attempt at getting a new connection to the database.

Right now, we know what the options are; the next question is what we should set for them. Unfortunately, the answer to this is, *it depends*. You need to have an understanding of the data you serve, and the likely volume of requests that you will get for this data. For example, very complex detailed polygons with a high-request concurrency will benefit from a large database connection pool. This is because the volume of data to be transferred in each network exchange is likely to be high, which in turn suggests that each connection to the database will be longer than, say, a simpler sparse point dataset. Therefore, to handle the high-request concurrency, we need a larger database connection pool. Setting the `max connections` option to a suitable value will be the key to ensuring that the right level of concurrency can be attained.

The `max connections` option defaults to 10, but this can be set higher to allow greater database connection concurrency, which translates to a better concurrency on GeoServer. When the maximum number of connections is reached, any further database connection requests are halted until a connection in the pool becomes available. You need to strike a balance between setting the number too high so that you consume too many resources, and too low so that you end up causing a bottleneck waiting for database connections.

The `min connections` option determines how many connections the pool will hold, irrespective of any database activity. If there are no active connections to the database servicing data requests, the connection pool will always ensure that the minimum number of connections is open. When this minimum number is exceeded, the pool will create new database connections until `max connections` is reached.

The `validate connections` flag determines whether the connections in the pool should be validated before they are used. As discussed previously, it is possible for database connections in the pool to become invalid because the database server closes the connection due to an inactive period timeout being reached. If a stale or broken connection is used, then this can often lead to a client error; setting this flag will check the connection before it is utilized.

The benefit is that no invalid connection will be used, but the trade-off is that it will come at a slight performance penalty, since validating the connection will take time. However, the overall benefits of the connection pool will outweigh the slight performance penalty. If you have requirements for availability, then it is usually best to have this flag on.

The fetch size option determines how many records should be retrieved from the database in each network exchange. This is a form of paging; if a request requires 2,000 records to be fulfilled, and the fetch size is set to 500, then there will need to be 4 round-trips to the database to retrieve all the required records. This is where the network latency will start to play its part; if, for example, you set the value too low, say 25, then the overall time to fetch all the required data will be much longer than if you set the value to 1,000. Although the database will take longer to retrieve 1,000 records than it will take to retrieve 25, the network latency overhead from many network exchanges will far outweigh slightly longer, but fewer, network exchanges. The default value is 1,000, which for the vast majority of cases will be adequate. Bear in mind that the larger the fetch size you set, the greater memory requirements you are placing on GeoServer.

 Too many very large fetches can result in an out of memory condition. Again, understanding the data that you are serving and the likely mix of traffic is the key to tuning this option.

The connection timeout option defaults to 20 seconds and determines how long the connection pool should wait for a database connection. Setting this value too high will result in a lot of delays that ultimately results in failed responses. It is better to fail faster since a lot of database connection failures can often be flagged up in monitoring. Conversely, setting the value too low will result in the database server not being given enough time to respond, and will lead to a lot of incorrect database connection error messages. Understanding your database platform and network environment is the key to setting this property to an appropriate value. If you find that you need to set the property higher than the default, then you should probably think about optimizing your database and/or your network environment.

JNDI connection or JDBC

When creating spatial database connections in GeoServer, you might notice that you are frequently provided with two options for the data store as highlighted in the following screenshot:

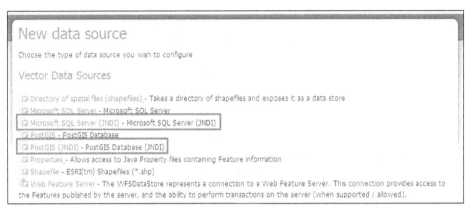

Vector data sources

In the preceding example, we can see that for Microsoft SQL Server and PostGIS, there is a standard data source option as well as one with **(JNDI)** after the name. If you noticed this, then you might have thought to yourself, "What's the difference?", and if you are aware of the difference, you might be wondering why you would want to use it over the standard JDBC version.

JNDI appended to the name of the data source stands for **Java Naming and Directory Interface,** which is a Java technology that enables software to look up objects and data using a common name. It is a fairly broad technology that can be used for a multitude of things such as connecting to an LDAP server or allowing a servlet to look up configuration information from a container. It is this ability to look up configuration information from a servlet container that GeoServer utilizes in the JNDI flavors of a data source.

Database connections are expensive in terms of resource utilization, and as we discussed, they are often pooled. However, if you have several components running in your servlet container, and each requires access to database connections, then each component will be responsible for setting up its own database connection pool. With more components creating their own connection pools resources on your server, it will become constrained very quickly. Furthermore, you will be responsible for ensuring the configuration of a connection pool in one application will not cause problems to others by requesting too many connections.

To overcome this challenge, it is possible to create a global database connection pool at the container level, and then reference this connection pool by its name in each of the applications that need access to database connections. Having a single connection pool at the container level means that resource utilization can be optimized and management will be simpler. It also becomes possible to change the configuration of the database connections. For example, a change to the database server location will instantly be reflected across all the applications utilizing the global pool. This is achieved without having to make any changes to the individual applications. An implementing application only needs to be aware of the name and no other specific details.

Configuring JNDI at the servlet container

Now that we understand the distinction between a standard JDBC connection and a JNDI connection pool, let's take a look at how to configure a JNDI connection pool in Tomcat.

Setting up a JNDI connection pool in Tomcat involves three stages:

1. Installing a JDBC driver for the database in Tomcat.
2. Configuring Tomcat connection pool properties.
3. Making GeoServer aware of the presence of the JNDI connection pool.

For Tomcat to be able to create a connection pool to your database platform, it must first have a copy of the relevant JDBC drivers installed to its shared `libs` directory, — `<tomcat_home>/lib`, where `<tomcat_home>` is the installation directory for your instance of Tomcat. The database platform you create a connection pool for will determine the most appropriate JDBC driver to use. The following table lists the most common platforms and their associated JDBC driver download locations:

Database platform	JDBC driver download
PostgreSQL (PostGIS)	GeoServer currently uses Version 8.3 of the PostgreSQL driver; therefore, it is recommended to use the same in our JNDI pool. Copy the `postgresql-8.4-701.jdbc3.jar` file from `<tomcat_home>/webapps/geoserver/WEB-INF/lib` to ensure compatibility.
Microsoft SQL Server	Check out `http://www.microsoft.com/en-us/download/details.aspx?id=19847`.
Oracle 11*g* R2	Check out `http://www.oracle.com/technetwork/database/enterprise-edition/jdbc-112010-090769.html`.
MySQL	Check out `http://dev.mysql.com/downloads/connector/j/`.

Download the appropriate JDBC driver for your database platform and copy the relevant `.jar` files into the `<tomcat_home>/lib` directory. How you choose which drivers to download will depend on what your database platform is. The following table lists how to find the version for the most common database platforms:

Database platform	Procedure
PostgreSQL	Run the query `SELECT version()` in psql
Microsoft SQL Server	Follow the procedure outlined at `http://support2.microsoft.com/kb/321185`
Oracle	Run the `SELECT * FROM V$VERSION` query

With the driver installed in the Tomcat-shared `lib` folder, we now need to configure the JNDI resource name and connection pool properties. This is done by adding an entry to the `<tomcat_home>/conf/context.xml` file. For example, a PostgreSQL entry in the file will be:

```
<context>
  <Resource name="jdbc/postgres" auth="container" type="javax.
sql.DataSource" driverClassName="org.postgresql.Driver" url="jd
bc:postgresql://<server>:<port>/<dbname>" username="<username>"
password="<password>" maxActive="20" maxIdle="5" maxWait="-1" />
</context>
```

Replace the `<server>`, `<port>`, `<dbname>`, `<username>`, and `<password>` values with the ones appropriate to your environment. This particular fragment will create a connection pool with the following characteristics:

- A maximum of 20 concurrent connections to the database
- A minimum of five connections open in the pool
- The pool will wait indefinitely for a connection to free up and will, therefore, not throw a connection exception as a result of timeout waiting

There are many other parameters that can be specified to control the connection pool; the full documentation of them is available from the DBCP pages at `http://commons.apache.org/proper/commons-dbcp/configuration.html`.

Of all the potential parameters, the following are worth considering for inclusion:

Parameter	Description
poolPreparedStatements	This is a Boolean flag indicating whether prepared statements should be pooled. This is an important setting from a performance perspective. It is disabled by default.
maxOpenPreparedStatements	This is the maximum number of prepared statements that can be kept open in the connection pool. Be careful with this setting as allowing too many can cause stability problems. It is unlimited by default.
validationQuery	This is a statement to execute to that a connection is active before it is used. This is not necessary if you can guarantee stability of connections in your database environment.

If we want to use any additional parameters, then we just need to include them in the `<context><resource>` element of the `<tomcat_home>/conf/context.xml` file.

Out of these parameters, the `poolPreparedStatements` parameter is the most interesting. A **prepared statement**, sometimes referred to as a **parameterized statement**, is a feature that allows databases to run repeated statements more efficiently. Each time a database executes a statement, it goes through a cycle of parsing, compiling, and optimizing before executing. This cycle adds overhead to each SQL statement executed. In systems that repeatedly run the same queries, with only some parameters being different on each run, this inefficiency will become very apparent in performance. By preparing the statement through parameter substitution, the database platform can parse, compile, and optimize the statement once and hold it in memory. Each time a query comes to match the statement, the ready-compiled statement can be executed straightaway. This will provide tremendous performance increases in systems that repeatedly execute similar statements, and GeoServer can execute many statements in this way.

Now that the Tomcat container has been configured, we need to make GeoServer aware of the JNDI resource name so that we can use it when creating data store connections. An entry needs to be added to GeoServer's `web.xml` file in `<tomcat_home>/webapps/geoserver/WEB_INF/web.xml`.

At the end of this file, we need to add an entry so that GeoServer is aware of the resource that was created at the container level:

```
<web-app>
    <!-- Existing file content -->
    <resource-ref>
        <description>PostgreSQL Data Source</description>
        <res-ref-name>jdbc/postgres</res-ref-name>
        <res-type>javax.sql.DataSource</res-type>
        <res-auth>Container</res-auth>
    </resource-ref>
```

This statement in the `web.xml` file will make GeoServer aware of the naming resource and utilize it in data connections. To ensure that the configuration changes are emitted to the Tomcat container, you should restart your services.

Once the services restart, we can connect to our Tomcat database connection pool by selecting the **PostGIS (JNDI)** option when creating a new data source. To use the example JNDI resource name we created previously, we need to enter it into the `jndiReferenceName` textbox:

So, for the example resource name we created for PostgreSQL, the value will be `java:comp/env/jdbc/postgres`. The `java:comp/env` element of the value is the part of the JNDI namespace where the configured entries and resources are placed. The `jdbc/postgres` portion is the name that we give to our connection pool in the name attribute of the `<Resource>` element in Tomcat's `context.xml` file. So, if we call our connection pool `jdbc/postgis`, the `jndiReferenceName` name will be `java:comp/env/jdbc/postgis`. With the data source configured, layers can be published just like when using the standard JDBC version of the database connection. The difference is that our database connection pool is now being managed at the servlet container level, rather than at the GeoServer application level.

General database connection parameters

Irrespective of the database platform you use to serve your vector data, there is a set of parameters that is common to all. In this section, we will take a look at:

- How primary keys can be managed
- Database startup session scripts
- Database shutdown session scripts

The primary key metadata table

While not necessary, it is usually best practice to have your database tables configured with a primary key. A primary key should be a unique value for each record in the table, and most often, it's not a simple integer incremented by some value, often 1, for each newly inserted record. GeoServer usually derives its feature ID values from the table's primary key column, and it will make assumptions about how to generate new IDs when inserting features, for example, as a result of a **WFS-Transaction (WFS-T)** insert transaction. These will usually be based on common conventions for a database platform, for example, looking for an auto-incrementing column in PostGIS. If GeoServer can't find a source for its new value, it will generate a random value and use it instead. If no primary key is set for a layer, then GeoServer treats it as a read-only layer, and therefore, does not make it available to WFS-T.

This automatic discovery behavior can be switched off by specifying a primary key metadata table. This table, when present, is used by GeoServer to make decisions about how to determine the correct value to use for a feature ID, in other words, a primary key. For example, setting the pk_policy value to sequence tells GeoServer to use the next available value from the sequence identified in the pk_sequence column.

The table can be named anything you like; just make sure you specify the correct name of the table when adding it to a data source in the **primary key metadata table** textbox.

 GeoServer defaults to looking for a table named gt_pk_metadata_ table in our database, if we do not set a value for the **primary key metadata table** textbox. If we use this name for our metadata table, then we do not need to specify a value for the textbox.

Although the table can be named anything, the structure must adhere to the following columns:

Column	Type	Description
table_schema	VARCHAR	This determines the name of the database schema the table belongs to.
table_name	VARCHAR	This determines the name of the table.
pk_column	VARCHAR	This determines the name of the column to be used to create feature IDs.
pk_column_idx	INTEGER	This determines the index of the column in a multicolumn key.
pk_policy	VARCHAR	This determines the policy to use when creating new IDs. It can be either assigned, sequence, or autogenerated.
pk_sequence	VARCHAR	This determines the name of the database sequence to get the next value from when pk_policy is set to sequence.

You will need to create this table according to the SQL conventions for the database platform that you run. The GeoServer documentation contains an example of creating the primary key metadata table in a PostGIS database at http://docs.geoserver.org/stable/en/user/data/database/primarykey.html.

The database session startup SQL

GeoServer has the ability to execute a SQL script each time it grabs a connection from the database connection pool. You can use the script to perform a wide range of tasks, but the most common use for the script will probably be to perform some form of database-level authorization of user access. This will enable a much finer-grained control over data security than is possible at the GeoServer security subsystem level.

The startup script can be parameterized by expanding the environment variables, and environment variables can even be passed along with the OGC request parameters. In this case, the env parameter is appended to the OGC service request and contains a key:value pair for each parameter to be passed:

```
&env=name1:value1;name2:value2
```

The database session close-up SQL

A database session close-up script is similar in nature to a startup script in that it is executed on each request; the difference is that the script is executed when the session is closed. The close-up script should be used to clean up anything opened, created, or started in the startup script. For example, if some database-access-level security is applied on a session at startup, it should be removed at close-up to ensure that no security issues occur.

The geometry metadata table

Depending on the database platform you are connecting to, GeoServer will adopt a different strategy for the autodiscovery of geometry types and spatial reference information. In some cases, it will use data inspection to examine the first record of the table, and read the geometry to determine its type and spatial reference, for example, with Microsoft SQL Server. In other cases, it will use the built-in database metadata tables or views to get the information, as with Oracle databases.

For situations where GeoServer's default strategy to discover the geometry type and spatial reference information is unreliable or error-prone, a **geometry metadata table** can be used to manually specify the details for each table. The following table lists the columns that should be present in the geometry metadata table:

Column name	Type	Description
F_TABLE_SCHEMA	VARCHAR(30)	This determines the name of the schema that the table belongs to
F_TABLE_NAME	VARCHAR(30)	This determines the name of the table
F_GEOMETRY_COLUMN	VARCHAR(30)	This determines the name of the column that holds the geometry of the features
COORD_DIMENSION	INTEGER	This determines the dimension of the coordinates, which is either 2 or 3
SRID	INTEGER	This determines the spatial reference identifier
TYPE	VARCHAR(30)	This determines the type of the geometry held in the table, which can be POINT, LINE, POLYGON, COLLECTION, MULTIPOINT, MULTILINE, MULTIPOLYGON, or GEOMETRY

You can create this table in your database using a SQL script appropriate to the platform that you use; for example, for Microsoft SQL Server, it will be:

```
CREATE TABLE GEOMETRY_COLUMNS(
    F_TABLE_SCHEMA VARCHAR(30) NOT NULL,
    F_TABLE_NAME VARCHAR(30) NOT NULL,
    F_GEOMETRY_COLUMN VARCHAR(30) NOT NULL,
    COORD_DIMENSION INTEGER,
    SRID INTEGER NOT NULL,
    TYPE VARCHAR(30) NOT NULL,
    UNIQUE(F_TABLE_SCHEMA, F_TABLE_NAME, F_GEOMETRY_COLUMN),
    CHECK(TYPE IN ('POINT','LINE', 'POLYGON', 'COLLECTION',
'MULTIPOINT', 'MULTILINE', 'MULTIPOLYGON', 'GEOMETRY') ));
```

Once you create this table in your database, you need to populate it with all the tables that you will publish as layers in GeoServer. In the preceding example, we set the name of the table to GEOMETRY_COLUMNS. However, the table you create can be given any name. Make sure to use the name you give the table when entering the value into the **Geometry metadata table** textbox when creating the data store.

Serving data from PostGIS

PostGIS (http://www.postgis.net) is, without question, the most popular open source spatial database platform available today. PostGIS is not actually a database in itself; it is in fact an open source library that spatially enables the open source PostgreSQL database. However, the name is so frequently used when referring to a PostgreSQL database with the extension installed, that it is the term we will adopt when discussing it in this book. In the open source geospatial world, GeoServer and PostGIS are perhaps the most common combination of spatial database and web mapping server. It is the database that GeoServer supports out of the box, without the need for any further configuration.

Publishing a PostGIS table as a layer

To publish a PostGIS table as a layer in GeoServer, we must first create a data store that connects to a PostGIS database. From the main page of the web administration console, choose the **Add stores** option to open the **New data source** page:

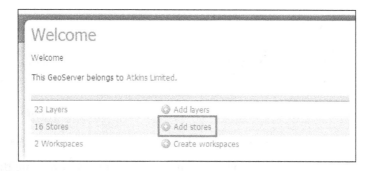

The **New data source** page lists all available formats that GeoServer can use as a data source. PostGIS is available as standard on all installations. To publish a table from PostGIS, select either the **PostGIS** or **PostGIS (JNDI)** option:

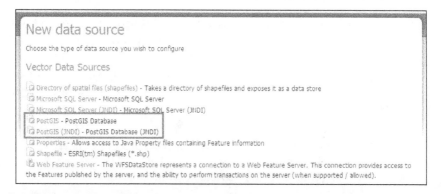

On the **New Vector Data Source** page, select the **Workspace** option from the drop-down list that you want this data source to belong to, and then give it a meaningful name and description.

Next, we need to specify the connection parameters so that GeoServer knows how to communicate with our database. The following table describes the main connection parameters:

Parameter	Description
host	This determines the host IP address or URL for your database server.
port	This determines the port your PostGIS server is listening for connections on. Normally, this is port 5432, but you should consider implementing a different public port such as 5432, which is often probed by malicious software looking for exploits.

Parameter	Description
database	This determines the name of the database on your server to connect to.
schema	This determines the name of the database schema containing your data. Typical PostGIS installations will have this in Public, but you should consider partitioning your database using schemas.
user	This determines the name of the user to connect to the database as.
passwd	This determines the password for the specified user.

Once we have the basic connection parameters set, we need to examine the database connection pooling parameters (max connections, min connections, fetch size, connection timeout, and validate connections). For most cases, the default values will be good enough, but do bear in mind the discussion we had at the start of this chapter on optimizing the settings.

Consider creating a primary key metadata table and entering its name in the textbox, especially if you plan on publishing your data so that it is updatable through WFS-T insert operations. Having a reliable and stable primary key column is fundamental to WFS-T working effortlessly. If you only plan on publishing your data through WMS, then primary keys are less of an issue, and GeoServer's default strategy will be sufficient for your needs.

 Although not essential, it is always a good practice to have primary keys on your database tables. This will be important if you want your table to be available through WFS-T.

It is worth considering what the **Loose BBOX** checkbox will do for you if you enable it. This is a potential performance-enhancing setting, but it does come with a caveat. It can increase performance because rather than considering the full geometry of a feature when doing a spatial selection, it uses the minimum bounding rectangle of the geometry. Consider the following example:

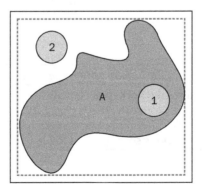

Let's say we want to do a point-in-polygon selection query using feature **(A)** as the selection polygon. If **Loose BBOX** is enabled, then the spatial query will use the minimum bounding rectangle of feature **(A)**, which is shown as the dashed line. This will result in point features **(1)** and **(2)** being returned, even though point **(2)** is clearly outside of feature **(A)**. However, the time to return the result will be significantly faster than if we use the full geometry of feature **(A)** to return the accurate result of only point **(1)**. So, the increased performance will come at the cost of some degree of accuracy. If you plan on only serving up your data as a WMS service, or if you think that users will not try and perform complex filtering with WFS, then it is worth turning on the **Loose BBOX** option as the drawback of reduced accuracy is far outweighed by the performance gains. If, however, you require accuracy in your system, then keep the option switched off.

Another performance-enhancing parameter to consider turning on is `preparedStatements` and its associated `Max open prepared statements`. Prepared statements, sometimes called parameterized SQL, is a database feature that allows it to run repeated statements more efficiently. Each time a statement is executed on a database, it must first be parsed, compiled, and then optimized – this takes time. Multiply this time by potentially thousands of the same type of statement, and you will see that a significant amount of time can be wasted due to overhead. A prepared statement overcomes this by taking the parsed, compiled, and optimized statement, and storing it for future use. When another statement arrives at the database with the same signature as the prepared statement, but with only variable values differing like a column in a `WHERE` clause, then the database can omit the parse, compile, and optimize steps and go straight to execution, thus saving time that will manifest in your environment as better performance. The `Max open prepared statements` value is an integer indicating how many prepared statements should be kept open in the connection pool. Each prepared statement will have a resource requirement associated with it, so setting this value too high can lead to instability as resources can potentially run out. It is, however, worth setting `preparedStatements` on as it will provide better performance.

Once all the settings have been set, hit the big green **Save** button and wait for GeoServer to set itself up. If everything works, GeoServer will present you with a page containing a table listing all the tables that you can publish as a layer. Layer publishing follows the same pattern as any other type of data store.

Serving data from Oracle

Out of the box, GeoServer does not support Oracle databases as a data source. However, there is an extension available that enables support for it as a data source. We just need to add the extension into our GeoServer instance and configure a connection to our database.

Installing the Oracle extension

To add support for Oracle databases, we need to download the extension. We must ensure we choose the download matching the version of GeoServer that we installed. We have been using the stable version (which at the time of writing is 2.5.2), so this is the version of the extension that we need to download. In your favorite browser, go to http://geoserver.org/release/stable and choose the **Oracle** option under the **Extensions | Data** store section, as shown in the following screenshot:

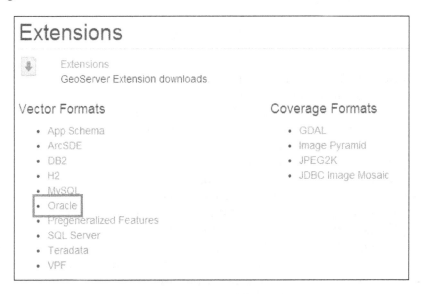

Download the file to a location on your system and issue the following command from a command line; this command will work whether you are running a Linux or Windows environment:

```
$ unzip geoserver-2.5.2-oracle-plugin.zip *.jar -d <tomcat_home>/webapps/
geoserver/WEB-INF/lib/
```

Change <tomcat_home> to the location where you have Tomcat installed. This command will extract the Java files from the ZIP archive and copy them straight into our GeoServer directory. Repeat this process for all instances of Tomcat that you are running.

The GeoServer extension comes with the Oracle 10*g* JDBC driver that should work with Oracle 11*g* as well as previous versions. However, there have been some reported issues when using the driver to connect to 11*g* and 12*c* databases. If you experience problems creating connections to an 11*g* or 12*c* database, then you should first update the JDBC driver by downloading the latest version from Oracle's website (`http://www.oracle.com/technetwork/database/enterprise-edition/jdbc-112010-090769.html`). Download the `ojdbc6.jar` file and copy it into `<tomcat_home>/webapps/geoserver/WEB-INF/lib`. Delete the `ojdbc4.jar` file in the same directory to prevent any driver clashes.

Validating the installation

Now that we installed the GeoServer extension, we need to confirm that everything has worked. If you haven't done so already, restart your GeoServer instances and log in to the web administration console. From the left-hand-side menu, navigate to **Data | Stores,** and then click on the **Add new store** link on the **Stores** page. The **New data source** page will be displayed and should be similar to the following one:

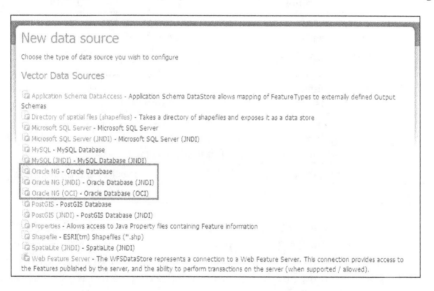

If you can see the three options for Oracle NG highlighted in the preceding screenshot, then the extension has been installed and configured correctly. You will notice an entry called **Oracle NG (OCI)** in the list of options. This type of data store will use the OCI driver rather than the JDBC driver, and will only work if your server has an Oracle client, such as Oracle Instant Client, installed on it. However, in most cases, the standard JDBC or JNDI drivers will be sufficient.

Publishing an Oracle table as a layer

Now that we configured the GeoServer extension and verified that it is working correctly, we can publish our data tables as layers in GeoServer. First, we need to create a data store, which is the connection to our Oracle database containing the tables we want to publish as layers. From the main page of the web administration console, choose the **Add stores** option to open the **New data source** page.

From the list of available **Vector Data Sources,** choose the **Oracle NG** option. Select the workspace from the drop-down list that you want this data source to belong to, and then give it a meaningful name and description.

Next, we need to specify the connection parameters so that GeoServer will know how to communicate with our database. The following table describes the main connection parameters:

Parameter	Description
host	This determines the host IP address or URL for your database server.
port	This determines the port your Oracle server is listening for connections on. Normally, this is port 1521, but you should consider implementing a different public port as 1521 is often probed by malicious software.
database	This determines the name of the database on your server to connect to. This is actually interpreted by Oracle as a SID name, but if you need to connect as a Service, then prefix the name with a /.
schema	This determines the name of the database schema containing your data. It is highly recommended that you set this value as it will drastically increase the performance of data discovery.
user	This determines the name of the user to connect to the database as.
passwd	This determines the password for the specified user.

Once we have the basic connection parameters set, we need to examine the database connection pooling parameters (max connections, min connections, fetch size, connection timeout, and validate connections). For most cases, the default values will be good enough, but do bear in mind the discussion we had at the start of this chapter on optimizing the settings.

The final parameter to consider is the textbox named **Geometry metadata table**. This is an optional parameter and can be safely left empty; however, it is worth pausing for a moment to consider what benefit it can have. For Oracle data sources, GeoServer utilizes the built-in metadata views from the MDSYS schema, in particular, USER_SDO* and ALL_SDO*. These views are usually populated when you use software to load spatial data into Oracle.

However, if you add spatial information yourself for scripts or some other means, then you will need to ensure the views are updated to reflect the data you have added. Although use of the metadata views is generally robust, there might be situations where GeoServer is unable to read them; for example, if the connection pool uses **impersonation** to connect to the database. In these circumstances, the manual geometry metadata table, discussed earlier in this chapter, can be used. Just specify the name of the table you create in the database in the **Geometry metadata table** textbox. It is worth considering creating this table and populating it with information. GeoServer will first use the table if it is present, and then use the metadata views if it cannot find an entry in the table. Therefore, you can be assured of always having your geometry type and spatial reference information properly identified. If the metadata views don't discover the information, you can add an entry to the geometry metadata table instead.

Once you have set all the parameters for the data source, go ahead and click on the **Save** button. If there are any problems with your configuration, a red box will appear, giving you details of the error. If all is well, then GeoServer will connect to your database and discover what tables are available to it for publishing as a layer. The **New Layer** page is then opened and the tables available for publishing are listed.

Serving data from Microsoft SQL Server and SQL Azure

GeoServer does not come with support for Microsoft SQL Server or SQL Azure out of the box. To enable support for Microsoft SQL Server databases as a source format, we need to install the GeoServer extension and supporting Microsoft JDBC drivers.

Installing the Microsoft SQL Server extension

To get support for Microsoft SQL Server as a data store, we need to install two components. First, we must install the GeoServer extension to enable the format, and then we need to install some supporting Microsoft files. Due to licensing restrictions, the GeoServer extension does not come with the necessary Microsoft JDBC driver files, and so, these will need to be installed separately.

We need to download the GeoServer extension for SQL Server, ensuring we choose the download matching the version of GeoServer that we installed. We have been using the current stable version (which at the time of writing is 2.5.2), so this is the version of the extension we need to download.

In your favorite browser, go to `http://geoserver.org/release/stable` and choose the SQL Server option under the **Extensions | Vector Formats** section, as shown in the following screenshot:

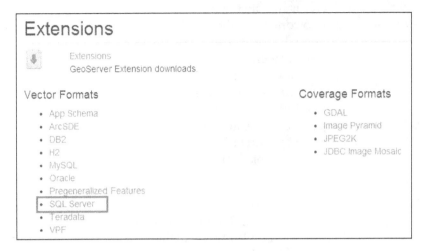

Download the file to a location on your system and issue the following command from a command line; this command will work whether you are running a Linux or Windows environment:

```
$ unzip geoserver-2.5.2-sqlserver-plugin.zip *.jar -d <tomcat_home>/
webapps/geoserver/WEB-INF/lib/
```

Change `<tomcat_home>` to the location where you have Tomcat installed. This command will extract the Java files from the ZIP archive and copy them straight into our GeoServer directory. Repeat this process for all instances of Tomcat that you are running. Next, we need to download the Microsoft JDBC driver files.

Installing Microsoft JDBC drivers on Linux

Irrespective of the distribution of Linux you are running, the installation process for the JDBC driver is the same. To download the file, go to `http://www.microsoft.com/en-us/download/details.aspx?id=19847` and click on the big red **Download** button. A pop-up window will appear, allowing you to choose the file to download, which is either a `*.exe` file or a `*.tar.gz` file. We can't run a `.exe` file on Linux, so we need to choose the `.tar.gz` file instead. At the time of writing, the current name of the file is `sqljdbc_3.0.1301.202_en.tar.gz`.

Check the box for the file, as shown in the preceding screenshot, and then click on the big blue **Next** button:

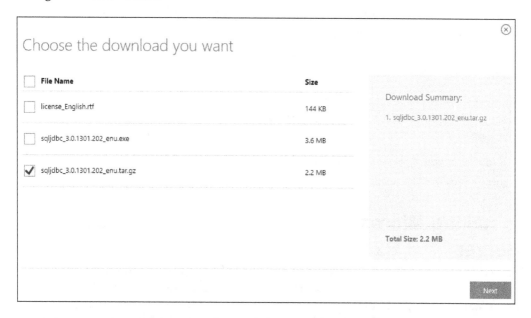

Save the downloaded file somewhere on your system so that you can access, for example, your home directory. If you followed the advice in *Chapter 1, Installing GeoServer for Production*, and installed a base server installation of Linux, you will not be able to go through the Microsoft web page to perform the download, in which case you can download the necessary file directly by issuing the following command on the command line:

```
$ cd ~
$ wget http://download.microsoft.com/download/E/A/9/EA9CAD06-1716-4CFE-
8339-0BBB9C5E588E/sqljdbc_3.0.1301.202_enu.tar.gz
```

These commands will change into your home directory; then, download the tarball file containing the JDBC driver file that we want. Now, we just need to copy the necessary file into GeoServer:

```
$ tar -xvzf sqljdbc_3.0.1301.202_enu.tar.gz
$ sudo cp sqljdbc_3.0/enu/sqljdbc4.jar <tomcat_home>/webapps/geoserver/
WEB-INF/lib/
```

These commands will unpack the tarball, and then copy the `sqljdbc4.jar` file into the `lib` directory of GeoServer. Replace `<tomcat_home>` with the location of your Tomcat instance. Remember to perform the copy command for each instance of GeoServer that you are running. Once you copy the file to all instances of GeoServer, you can clean up your system by removing the directory:

```
$ rm -rf sqljdbc_3.0/
```

To have GeoServer recognize the presence of the format, you must restart all the instances of GeoServer. If you followed the instructions in *Chapter 1, Installing GeoServer for Production*, then we will issue the following commands:

```
$ sudo service tomcat-1 restart
$ sudo service tomcat-2 restart
```

Installing Microsoft JDBC drivers on Windows Server 2008 R2

The process to install the JDBC drivers on Windows is similar to Linux, except that we also need to copy some additional files into the `System32` directory. To download the file, go to `http://www.microsoft.com/en-us/download/details.aspx?id=19847` and click on the big red **Download** button. Choose the option for the `.exe` file, and then click on the big blue **Next** button. When prompted with the file download, save it to a location on your system.

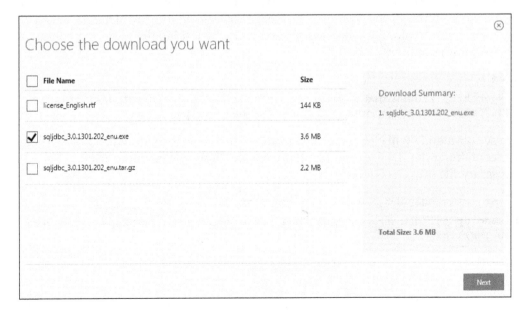

Open the file explorer and navigate to the location you saved the file to. Double-click on the downloaded file, `sqljdbc_3.0.1301.202_enu.exe`, to open it:

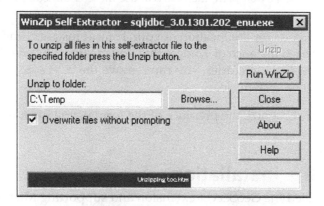

In the **WinZip Self-Extractor** dialog, specify a location for the **Unzip to folder:** textbox, which is where the contents will be extracted to. To keep things simple, specify `C:\Temp` for the location, and then click on the **Unzip** button. If all goes well, you will get a message box telling you that it successfully extracted 1,232 files. These files will now be in the `C:\Temp\sqljdbc_3.0` directory.

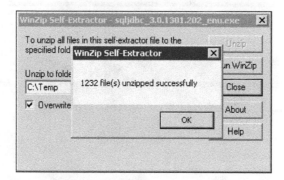

There are three files that need to be copied from this directory; use the following table to see which files should be copied where:

Source file	Destination directory
`C:\Temp\sqljdbc_3.0\enu\sqljdbc4.jar`	`<tomcat_home>/webapps/` `geoserver/WEB-INF/lib`
`C:\Temp\sqljdbc_3.0\enu\xa\x86\` `sqljdbc_xa.dll`	`C:\Windows\System32`
`C:\Temp\sqljdbc_3.0\enu\auth\x86\` `sqljdbc_auth.dll`	`C:\Windows\System32`

The preceding examples assume we are running a 32-bit JVM. If we use a 64-bit JVM, then we will use the x64 directory instead.

Change `<tomcat_home>` for the location of your Tomcat instance, and remember to copy this file to each instance of Tomcat that you created. Once you copy these files into their respective directories, you can remove the `C:\Temp\sqljdbc_3.0` directory to keep your system clean.

To have GeoServer recognize the presence of the format, you must restart all the instances of GeoServer.

Validating the installation

Now that we installed the GeoServer extension and supporting Microsoft JDBC driver, we need to confirm that everything worked. If you haven't done so already, restart your GeoServer instances and log in to the web administration console. From the left-hand-side menu, navigate to **Data | Stores**, and then click on the **Add new store** link on the **Stores** page. The **New data source** page will be displayed and should be similar to the one shown in the following screenshot:

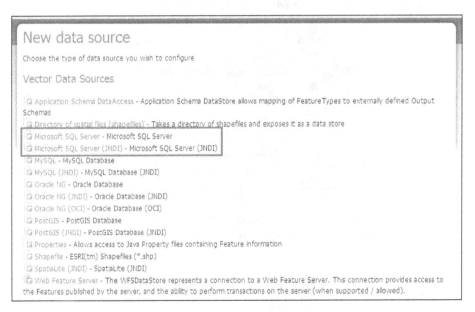

If you can see the two options for Microsoft SQL Server highlighted, then the extension and driver have been installed and configured correctly.

Publishing a Microsoft SQL Server table as a layer

Now that we configured the GeoServer extension and verified that it is working correctly, we can publish our data tables as layers in GeoServer. First, we need to create a data store that is the connection to our Microsoft SQL Server database containing the tables that we want to publish as layers. From the main page of the web administration console, choose the **Add stores** option to open the **New data source** page.

From the list of available **Vector Data Sources,** choose the **Microsoft SQL Server** option. From the drop-down list, select the workspace that you want this data source to belong to, and then give it a meaningful name and description.

Next, we need to specify the connection parameters so that GeoServer will know how to communicate with our database. The following table describes the main connection parameters:

Parameter	Description
host	This determines the host IP address or URL for your database server.
port	This determines the port that your database server is listening for connections on. Microsoft SQL Server usually defaults to port 1432 or 1433, but you might need to check your configuration or consult your database administrator.
database	This determines the name of the database on your server to connect to. If you leave this blank, then the default database associated with the user you connect with will be used.
schema	This determines the name of the database schema containing your data. If you leave this blank, then the connection will use the default schema assigned to the user you connect as.
user	This determines the name of the user to connect to the database as. If you connect to a SQL Azure database, then you will need to append @azure_server_name to the end of the username, where azure_server_name is the name of the Azure server hosting your database.
Password	This determines the password for the user you are connecting to the database as.

Once we have the basic connection parameters set, we need to examine the database connection pooling parameters (max connections, min connections, fetch size, connection timeout, and validate connections). For most cases, the default values will be good enough, but do bear in mind the discussion we had at the start of this chapter on optimizing the settings.

If your Microsoft SQL Server installation supports **Integrated Security**, and you are running GeoServer under a Windows domain account that has access rights granted to the database, you can check the box on the page to enable this. If, on the other hand, you are not, or are not sure, then leave this box unchecked.

The final parameter to consider is the textbox named **Geometry metadata table**. This is an optional parameter and can be safely left empty. However, it is worth pausing for a moment to discuss what this is and the benefit it can have. As we discussed previously in the *General database connection settings* section, when GeoServer connects to a database, it uses strategies to discover metadata about the table being published, which consists of important information, such as the geometry type and spatial reference information. For Microsoft SQL Server, it does this by inspecting the table's first row of data. The data inspection can be error-prone, perhaps because the geometry contained in the first row is not valid and causes an error state to arise. To make it possible for GeoServer to reliably understand what data is available to publish, the geometry metadata table can be created and specified. It is highly recommended to create the geometry metadata table for Microsoft SQL Server.

Once you have set all the parameters for the data source, go ahead and click on the **Save** button. If there are any problems with your configuration, a red box will appear giving you details of the error. If all is well, then GeoServer will connect to your database and discover what tables are available to it to publish as a layer. The **New Layer** page is then opened, and the tables available to publish are listed:

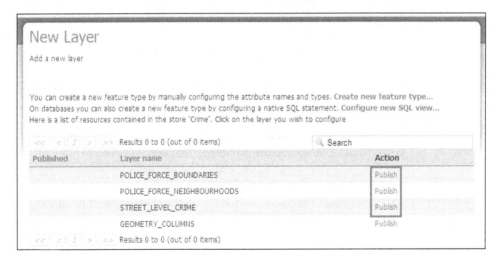

Next to each table that you can publish as a layer, there is a **Publish** link; click on this for the layer that you want to publish. At this point, the process to publish the layer is the same as for any other data source type.

Creating SQL View layers

So far in this chapter, we have looked at publishing layers based on traditional database tables; so now, we will look at GeoServer's ability to create **SQL View** layers. A SQL View layer is a kind of dynamic layer within GeoServer that allows for a custom SQL script to be executed on each request for data. A SQL View layer can be used to perform complex database queries to derive content for a layer, for example, selecting all the points of a certain type within a polygon and adding a count value to that polygon. The generated polygon layer can then be rendered with a color ramp to show the range of values.

GeoServer SQL Views versus database views

You might be looking at this and thinking to yourself, "Why will I use a GeoServer SQL View over a database view?" There are a couple of reasons why GeoServer SQL Views might be preferable to database views:

- You do not require access to the underlying database to create SQL View. However, you will require SQL-level access to the database to create a database view.

- Changing a database view requires SQL-level access to the database, whereas changing SQL View only requires access to the GeoServer web administration console.

- GeoServer SQL View can be dynamically altered at runtime, based on a set of request parameters.

SQL View is read-only, and therefore, cannot be updated through a WFS-T transaction without some additional configuration, whereas some database platforms do allow views to be updated as if they were a regular database table. If WFS-T is important to your use case and you want to use views, then SQL Views will not be appropriate, and you should instead look to the database level to manage views.

That being said, it is the last reason in the list that is the real benefit to SQL Views in GeoServer. SQL View can be passed as parameters that are part of a WMS or WFS request to control its output; the default values can be set to handle situations where the parameter might be missing from the request, and regular expressions (http://en.wikipedia.org/wiki/Regular_expression) can be used to validate the parameter values. The use of regular-expression validation on parameters is very useful as it will allow you to safeguard against potential SQL Injection attacks that a parameterized SQL View can open you up to.

Creating a SQL View layer

So SQL Views, and in particular parameterized ones, are a very useful feature. So, how do we go about creating them in GeoServer? The process is actually quite straightforward. With a database data store already defined, for example, Microsoft SQL Server, we simply create a SQL View layer the same way we will create any other.

For the following examples, we downloaded a dataset of street-level crime reporting for August, 2014 from the UK Police Data Portal at `http://data.police.uk/data`. I selected the data for all Police Forces and imported the CSV files into my Microsoft SQL Server database using `ogr2ogr` (`http://www.gdal.org/ogr2ogr.html`) and spatially indexing it.

The following steps will take our downloaded dataset, in this case, `2014-08-avon-and-somerset-street.csv`, and show how we can load it into Microsoft SQL Server:

1. Before we can load the CSV file, we need to create a VRT (`http://www.gdal.org/drv_vrt.html`) that will tell `ogr2ogr` how to interpret the CSV file as a point dataset. Use a text editor to create a file called `2014-08-avon-and-somerset-street.vrt`, and save it to the same location as the `.csv` file. The content of the file should look like the following:

```
<OGRVRTDataSource>
    <OGRVRTLayer name="AvonSomersetStreetCrime">
        <SrcLayer>2014-08-avon-and-somerset-street</SrcLayer>
        <SrcDataSource>2014-08-avon-and-somerset-street.csv</SrcDataSource>
        <GeometryType>wkbPoint</GeometryType>
        <LayerSRS>WGS84</LayerSRS>
        <GeometryField encoding="PointFromColumns" x="Longitude" y="Latitude"/>
    </OGRVRTLayer>
</OGRVRTDataSource>
```

2. Next, we need to run a test to ensure that OGR will interpret the CSV file through the VRT definition correctly. Enter the `ogrinfo -ro -al 2014-08-avon-and-somerset-street.vrt` command that should generate an output similar to the following:

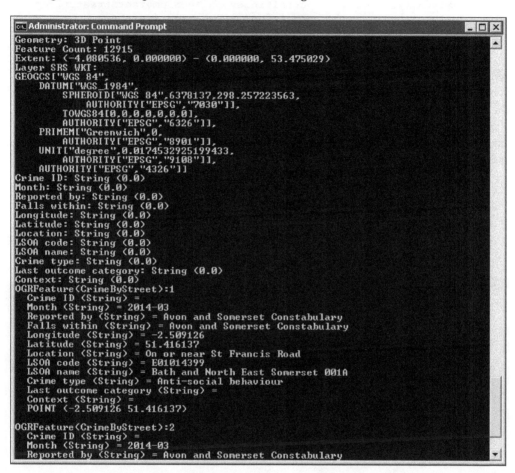

3. Having confirmed that OGR can read the data through VRT, we can now issue the command to load it into SQL Server, changing the values inside the curly braces to match your database connection:

```
ogr2ogr -f MSSQLSpatial "MSSQL:Server={server_
name},{port};Database={database_name};Uid={user_name};Pwd={passwo
rd};Encrypt=yes;Connection Timeout=30;" 2014-08-avon-and-somerset-
street.vrt
```

4. Next, we need to create a spatial index on the newly created table with the following command. Again, replace the values in curly braces to match your database connection:

```
ogrinfo -sql "create spatial index on AvonSomersetStreetCrime"
"MSSQL:Server={server_name},{port};Database={database_
name};Uid={user_name};Pwd={password};Encrypt=yes;Connection
Timeout=30;"
```

With the crime data loaded into our database, we will first create a SQL View layer that will filter the crime data to show only records with CRIME_TYPE of Drugs, then alter the view so that we further filter based on a LAST_OUTCOME_CATEGORY value of Under investigation, and finally change SQL View so that CRIME_TYPE is parameterized, thus allowing us to dynamically change the view for different types of crimes on request.

Creating a SQL View layer follows much the same pattern as any other layer. In the web administration console, you click on the **Layers** option from the left-hand side menu to open the page showing a list of published layers. From this page, clicking on the **Add a new resource** link opens the **New Layer** page where we select our data store to add a layer from:

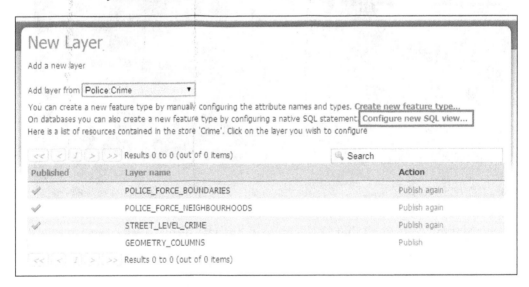

Notice how when we select a data source that has a database backend, we get some additional options, one of which is the **Configure new SQL view...** link. Clicking on this link will take us to a page where we can define our SQL View properties:

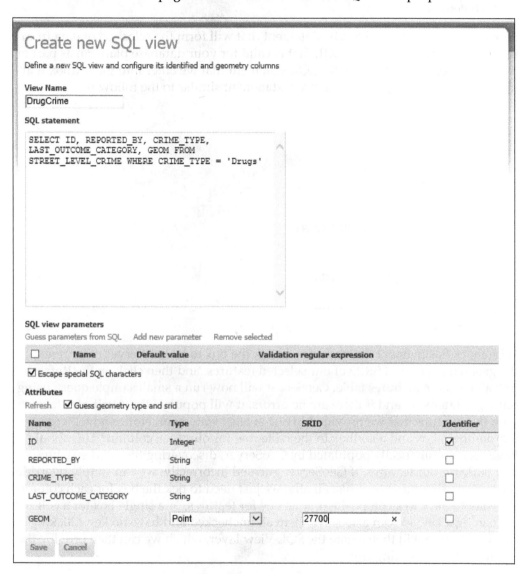

The first thing we must do is provide a name for our SQL View layer. This will be the name of the layer in GeoServer, the same as any other type of layer you might create. In this case, we shall call the layer `DrugsCrime` to make it descriptive of what the layer content is.

Next, we need to define the SQL statement that will form the selection of data from the database. This can be any SQL that is valid for your database platform as part of a `FROM` clause. So, in this case, the SQL statement that we enter into the textbox will be translated into a SQL Server `SELECT` statement similar to the following:

```
SELECT
    *
FROM (
    SELECT
        ID,
        REPORTED_BY,
        CRIME_TYPE,
        LAST_OUTCOME_CATEGORY,
        GEOM
    FROM
        STREET_LEVEL_CRIME
    WHERE
        CRIME_TYPE = 'Drugs'
) AS vtable;
```

With the SQL statement defined, we can tick the box to let GeoServer determine the geometry type and SRID of our selected features, and then click on the **Refresh** link above the **Attributes** table. GeoServer will now run a small sample query using our SQL statement, and if there are no errors, it will populate the **Attributes** table with the columns that we provided in our `SELECT` statement. Notice how there is a drop-down box and a textbox in the table row for our `GEOM` column? This should have been automatically populated by GeoServer, discovering the geometry type and SRID for our features. If GeoServer guessed incorrectly, we can simply override the values using these controls. Finally, we just need to tick the box for each column we want to have in a composite unique key for features, or a single box for a column containing a key; we can also leave them all unchecked and have no key. Clicking on the **Save** button will then create the SQL View layer, which we can then provide the usual publishing settings for.

Here is a map view showing all the CRIME_TYPE records, without any filtering applied to the layer; in effect, this SQL View will be the SELECT * query without a WHERE clause. In this case, it is the normal layer read straight from SQL Server and rendered:

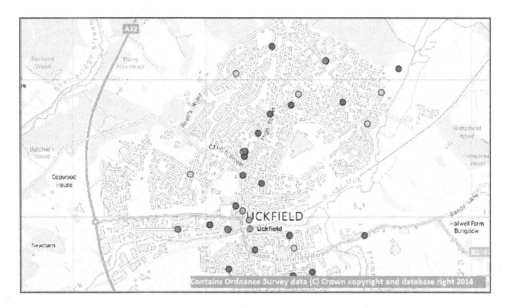

Here is the same map, but with our SQL View layer showing only records with a CRIME_TYPE value of Drugs:

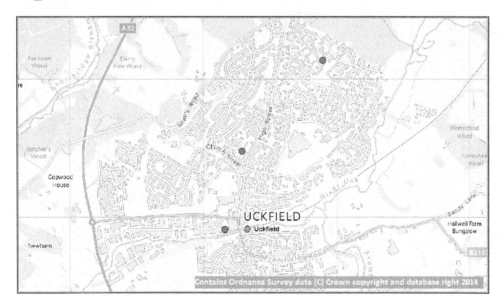

Now, we will adapt SQL View so that we further filter the data it returns by adding an additional WHERE condition to select crimes of the Drugs type, with a last outcome type of Under investigation. To do this, we need to edit the DrugCrime layer that we created previously by selecting it from the list of published layers in the web administration console. On the **Edit Layer** page, we can scroll down to the **Feature Type Details** section, and then click on the **Edit sql view** link below the table:

Feature Type Details			
Property	Type	Nillable	Min/Max Occurences
ID	Integer	false	1/1
REPORTED_BY	String	true	0/1
CRIME_TYPE	String	true	0/1
LAST_OUTCOME_CATEGORY	String	true	0/1
GEOM	Point	true	0/1

Edit sql view

The only change we need to make is to alter the SQL statement that is being used to drive our SQL View. Click in the box and change the statement to the following:

```
SELECT
    ID,
    REPORTED_BY,
    CRIME_TYPE,
    LAST_OUTCOME_CATEGORY,
    GEOM
FROM
    STREET_LEVEL_CRIME
WHERE
    CRIME_TYPE = 'Drugs'
    AND
    LAST_OUTCOME_CATEGORY = 'Under investigation'
```

Now, we can save the SQL View definition and accept the same publishing parameters, or change them if we wish. Our map changes to reflect the different views on the data; notice how the bottom feature is no longer visible; there are only two drug crimes (represented by purple dots) in this area, when there were three previously:

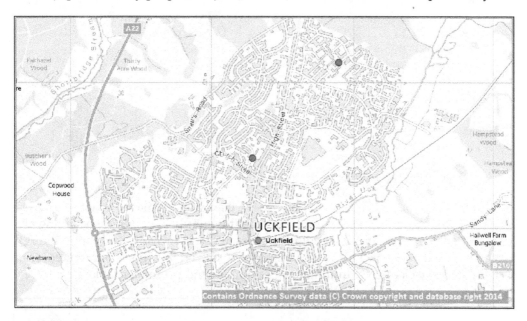

This is great! So far, we have been able to change the content of a layer by filtering data out of a much larger table by simply editing a view definition within GeoServer. We did not go anywhere near the database backend, which means that our administrative or trusted users can define and edit SQL Views without any risk of data loss in our database. What will be really good though is to allow our end users to dynamically change the data they see on a per-request basis. This is where the real power of GeoServer's SQL Views comes into effect. Now, we will make some minor changes to our SQL View definition to make it dynamic. As before, edit the DrugCrime layer and click on the **Edit sql view** link.

There are two changes that we need to make to turn this SQL View layer into a dynamic one. First, we need to change the SQL statement to specify where we want to include our parameters:

```
SELECT
    ID,
    REPORTED_BY,
    CRIME_TYPE,
    LAST_OUTCOME_CATEGORY,
    GEOM
FROM
    STREET_LEVEL_CRIME
WHERE
    CRIME_TYPE = '%crime_type%'
    AND
    LAST_OUTCOME_CATEGORY = 'Under investigation'
```

Notice that we removed `Drugs` from our `where` clause and replaced it with `%crime_type%`. Adding parameters to the SQL statement is simply a matter of specifying a value and adding a leading and trailing `%` character. When GeoServer parses the SQL statement, it will recognize these as parameters. Click on the **Guess parameters from SQL** link to have GeoServer automatically populate the parameter table:

Our `crime_type` parameter has been recognized and added to the table. We can specify a default value for the parameter, so if a request comes in without the parameter attached, we can return some default data; in this case, our original `Drugs` filter. The **Validation regular expression** box allows us to enter a regular expression to use to validate the parameter before it is used. This is a useful protection against SQL injection attacks (`http://en.wikipedia.org/wiki/SQL_injection`), but it also allows us to ensure properly structured input, such as e-mail addresses, is received. In this case, we added the `^[\w\s]+$` value, which means that we will accept any alphanumeric or white-space characters as input.

To control the SQL Views response, we just need to add an additional query parameter to the OGC service request. The parameter is `viewparams`, and it is in the form of `key:value` pairs; multiple pairs are separated using a semicolon. For example, in our case, we will add the following to a WMS request to show only crimes of the `Burglary` type, which are currently `Under investigation`:

```
&viewparams=crime_type:Burglary
```

The ability to add `viewparams` to an OGC service request is a vendor parameter of GeoServer and not part of the formal OGC specification for web services.

Adding this to the end of an OGC WMS GetMap request for the area previously mentioned will yield the following result:

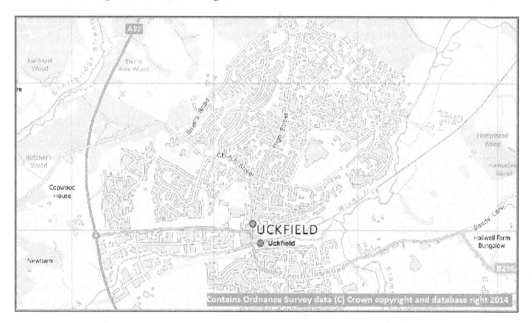

Summary

Now, we are really starting to make progress! Over the last three chapters, we discussed how to install GeoServer in a production environment, preparing raster data for high-performance serving; now, we looked at how we can serve vector data from an enterprise database platform.

We now have a much better understanding of what a database connection pool is and how we can optimize it for our environment. We also discussed how a servlet-container-level connection pool can be created using JNDI. We now have a better understanding of what common parameters we can set on database-backed stores such as the primary key metadata and geometry columns metadata tables.

We looked at how to create database connections, as data stores for the most common enterprise-database environments are likely to come across in production environments. We now understand how to set up GeoServer so that it can connect to Microsoft SQL Server and Oracle databases through the extension infrastructure.

Finally, we looked at how we can use the SQL View layer type to create layers that are dynamically populated from our database by using it to filter contents of a much larger table based on a per-request parameter.

We now have a production-ready instance of GeoServer with a bunch of raster and vector data connections. Now, it is time to start digging into the more advanced capabilities of GeoServer and really start to explore its capabilities.

4

Using GeoServer to Serve Complex Features

In the previous chapter, we looked at setting up vector data stores from spatial databases and then publishing tables as layers. This type of data is known as simple features, and is the type of data that will most commonly be served through GeoServer. However, it is possible that you will need to deliver a more complex dataset that is relational in nature and built from multiple data sources.

With a little bit of effort, it is possible to set up GeoServer so that you can deliver complex feature datasets to your users. In this chapter, we will discuss how this can be achieved using GeoServer's app-schema extension. By the end of this chapter, you will have a better understanding of:

- What a complex feature is and how it differs from a simple feature
- What an application schema is and how it can be used
- How to install and configure the app-schema extension
- How to configure the app-schema extension to serve a complex feature

The difference between simple and complex features

In the previous chapter, we looked at how to efficiently store and serve vector data. One of the things we did not discuss is how GeoServer considers the vector data that you store in your database and, therefore, how it is served in a vector format through WFS.

Simple features – GeoServer's default

GeoServer considers all vector data, irrespective of the storage format, to be simple features. There are three simple feature profiles defined by the Open Geospatial Consortium, and GeoServer delivers features similar to the simplest profile, SF-0.

 For more details on the OGC simple features specification, take a look at the information on OGC's website at http://www.opengeospatial.org/standards/sfs.

A simple feature, delivered through WFS, is the one where there is a straight one-to-one mapping between the underlying data storage format and the output XML file. For example, data stored in a database table is delivered by WFS in an XML output where each feature attribute is a straight one-to-one mapping with a column in the database table. The XML will contain one feature for every row returned by the database in response to the WFS request. Consider the following database record selected from the Police data we loaded in the previous chapter:

ID	Force	Neighborhood
8715	Sussex	EE1NH11

A WFS request for this particular feature will yield the following XML output:

```
<wfs:FeatureCollection numberOfFeatures="1" timeStamp="..."
xsi:schemaLocation="...">
  <gml:featureMember>
    <Police:ForceNeighbourhoods gml:id="ForceNeighbourhoods.8715">
      <Police:FORCE>Sussex</Police:FORCE>
      <Police:NEIGHBOURHOOD>EE1NH11</Police:NEIGHBOURHOOD>
      <Police:GEOM>
        <gml:Polygon srsDimension="2" srsName="urn:x-
ogc:def:crs:EPSG:27700">
          <gml:exterior>
            <gml:LinearRing srsDimension="2">
              <gml:posList>560137.1812000136 98379.21078293558
560329.9312763263 98406.08010795392 560740.4317393883
98792.07872016821 560769.1816489289 98684.70860240335
561500.8014195256 98219.95597274863 561121.9309060494 97770.0772481022
560430.4309366472 98005.5797026777 560367.0511290649 98234.5799618616
560137.1812000136 98379.21078293558
              </gml:posList>
            </gml:LinearRing>
          </gml:exterior>
        </gml:Polygon>
      </Police:GEOM>
```

```
      </Police:ForceNeighbourhoods>
    </gml:featureMember>
  </wfs:FeatureCollection>
```

The highlighted sections of the output demonstrate the one-to-one mapping of the database table column to the XML output element. The actual mapping is shown in the following table:

Database table column name	XML element
ID	gml:id
FORCE	<Police:FORCE />
NEIGHBOURHOOD	<Police:NEIGHBOURHOOD />

The content of the XML output from the WFS request can be directly mapped back to the underlying database table columns that GeoServer is querying. The XML output in this case is often referred to as a **flat representation**.

Complex features

In contrast to simple features, a complex feature does not result in a *flat* output representation from a WFS request. The XML representation of a complex feature can have properties that can themselves contain additional nested properties, either complex or simple. A complex feature can also make reference to another feature within one of its own elements; this makes the XML output a collection of related objects that can be identified. In this case, the XML output is often referred to as being a **relational representation.**

The best way to consider what a complex feature is will be to look at a real-world example. Let's suppose that we have a routable road network that we would like to share with other users. The base model for our road network will consist of road links and road nodes, where each road link has an identified start and end node, and there are no duplications of road nodes.

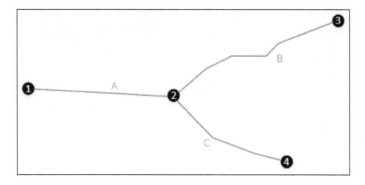

In this simplified example, we have four road node features and three road link features. Within our database model, we will have these two different feature types stored as separate tables with, perhaps, a foreign key relationship between the road nodes and road links. This will allow us to identify that the start road node of the road link **A** is **1**, and its end road node is **2**. The following diagram shows what this relational table structure might look like:

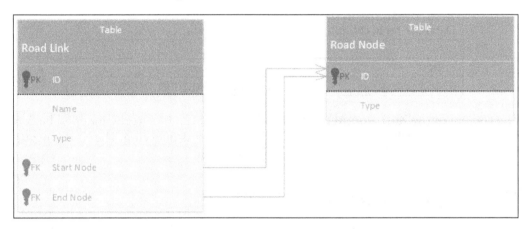

When sharing this data with other users, we will need to provide not only the road links that comprise the road network but also the road nodes. This is where a *relational* representation in the XML output comes into play. We can elect to output the start and end road node for each road link as a nested property of the road link, or we can supply the road nodes as separate features within the XML output and then reference these separate features through their identifier. Being able to make these types of associations and provide all the features that belong to the association in the output is one of the main strengths of a complex feature output. This is also commonly known as **Feature Chaining** and allows the delivery of a complex feature that is constructed from smaller, potentially simpler features. It is a very useful pattern as it allows for the construction of a complex feature using constituent features that are useful within their own right. For example, a single road node feature can also be used to denote a roundabout on the network as well as indicate the start or end node of a road link to provide the network with direction.

Using GeoServer application schemas

Understanding the difference between complex and simple features is the beginning; knowing what to do about it is the next step. Given that GeoServer will only serve simple features by default, there needs to be a mechanism to enable us to deliver complex features when the need arises. Such a need might be to deliver vector data to our users through some community-derived schema. For example, the European Union INSPIRE Directive (`http://inspire.jrc.ec.europa.eu`) mandates the use of GML in delivering harmonized data models for the delivery of key datasets across EU member states in an effort to drive interoperability and standards. If you are responsible for INSPIRE compliance or would like to deliver your data in an INSPIRE-compliant way, then the ability to deliver complex features from GeoServer will be important.

Perhaps you want to be able to deliver multiple data tables from a database as a single package of related features for use in an application. Once again, making GeoServer deliver complex features will enable this.

Fortunately for us, this is something that others have required, and in the true spirit of open source collaboration, a GeoServer extension has been created to meet it. The application schema extension, or the app-schema, adds a data store format to GeoServer. This enables it to take data from any supported format and combine it into a complex feature collection for output as a WFS response. The GeoServer documentation at `http://docs.geoserver.org/stable/en/user/data/app-schema/index.html` contains a very detailed description of the app-schema extension and how to use it, and it is well worth reading for a detailed background.

Installing and configuring the extension

As with other extensions for GeoServer, to use the app-schema extension, it must first be installed on all of your instances of GeoServer. The extension itself can be downloaded from the GeoServer project pages, but make sure that you download the version of the extension that matches the version of GeoServer you are using. Until now, we have been using the current stable version (which, at the time of writing this book, is 2.5.2), so we can download the corresponding extension from `http://geoserver.org/download`.

The app-schema extension provides GeoServer with a new type of data store, so it can be found by navigating to **Extensions | Vector Formats** on the download page.

Download the file to a location on your system, and then issue the following command from a command line. This command will work whether you are running a Linux or Windows environment:

```
$ unzip geoserver-2.5.2-app-schema-plugin.zip *.jar -d <tomcat_home>/
webapps/geoserver/WEB-INF/lib/
```

Change `<tomcat_home>` to the location where you have Tomcat installed. This command will extract the Java files from the ZIP archive and copy them straight into your GeoServer directory. Repeat this process for all the instances of Tomcat that you have running. Before restarting GeoServer to enable the extension, we must make a small change to the WFS service configuration.

Configuring the WFS service

When using GeoServer to serve complex features, it is best practice to change two WFS service settings. These changes can be made using the WFS configuration page, which can be accessed by navigating to **Services | WFS** on the left-hand side panel of the web administration console, or by editing the `wfs.xml` configuration file. As we still have GeoServer running, it is simpler to use the web administration console rather than editing the XML file. Click on the **WFS** link from the **Services** section on the left-hand side menu of the web administration console. Scroll to the bottom of the page and locate the **Conformance** and **Encode response with** sections, as shown in the following screenshot:

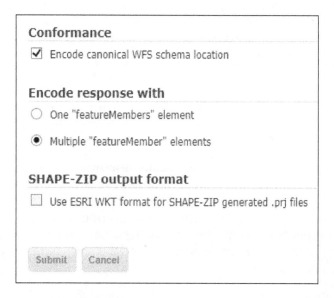

It is important to set the **Conformance** setting if we want our GeoServer to play nicely with other systems and clients. By default, GeoServer will use its own internal WFS schema file when encoding WFS responses by creating a `schemaLocation` attribute that references its internal schema file. The following is an example of the GML output generated by default:

```
<wfs:FeatureCollection xmlns="http://www.opengis.net/wfs"
xmlns:wfs="http://www.opengis.net/wfs" xmlns:police="http://www.
police.uk" xmlns:gml="http://www.opengis.net/gml" xmlns:xsi="http://
www.w3.org/2001/XMLSchema-instance" xsi:schemaLocation="http://www.
police.uk http://<server>:<port>/geoserver/police/wfs?service=WFS&v
ersion=1.0.0&request=DescribeFeatureType&typeName=police%3Aboundary
http://www.opengis.net/wfs http://<server>:<port>/geoserver/schemas/
wfs/1.0.0/WFS-basic.xsd">
```

The `xsi:schemaLocation` attribute has links directly back to the GeoServer instance that serves the dataset, linking to `WFS-basic.xsd`. This means that clients will have to connect to and download the GeoServer schema file, without knowing whether it is consistent with the WFS schema published at `http://schemas.opengis.net`. Ticking the box next to **Encode canonical WFS schema location** will change the default behavior of GeoServer. It will encode the WFS response with `schemaLocation` for WFS by pointing to `http://schemas.opengis.net`, as seen in the following extract:

```
<wfs:FeatureCollection xmlns="http://www.opengis.net/wfs"
xmlns:wfs="http://www.opengis.net/wfs" xmlns:police="http://www.
police.uk" xmlns:gml="http://www.opengis.net/gml" xmlns:xsi="http://
www.w3.org/2001/XMLSchema-instance" xsi:schemaLocation="http://www.
police.uk http://<server>:<port>/geoserver/police/wfs?service=WFS&v
ersion=1.0.0&request=DescribeFeatureType&typeName=police%3Aboundary
http://www.opengis.net/wfs http://schemas.opengis.net/wfs/1.0.0/WFS-
basic.xsd">
```

With the setting changes, the `xsi:schemaLocation` attribute now contains a link to the official WFS schema document. Connecting clients will now know that the official schema for WFS is being used for the dataset.

The second change to make is to set the **Encode response with** setting to **Multiple "featureMember" elements**. This option controls how GeoServer will encode features in a WFS 1.1 response. By default, it encodes all the features inside a single `gml:featureMembers` element. When dealing with application schemas, this can lead to invalid output being generated in certain circumstances. Changing this setting will make GeoServer encode each individual feature in the response inside a `gml:featureMember` element.

We used the web administration console to make these changes; however, if you would prefer to do this by manually editing the XML file (perhaps because your GeoServer instance has been shut down), then you can do it by opening the `<geoserver_data_dir>/wfs.xml` file (where `<geoserver_data_dir>` is the location of your GeoServer data directory) inside a text editor and then adding the following elements before the closing tag at the end of the file.

```
<canonicalSchemaLocation>true</canonicalSchemaLocation>
<encodeFeatureMember>true</encodeFeatureMember>
```

With the WFS settings configured, we can now restart all of our GeoServer instances to activate the app-schema extension and the changes to the WFS configuration. To check whether the app-schema extension is working, attempt to create a new data store.

Application Schema DataAccess should be a choice under **Vector Data Sources**, as shown in the following screenshot:

New data source

Choose the type of data source you wish to configure

Vector Data Sources

Application Schema DataAccess - Application Schema DataStore allows mapping of FeatureTypes to externally defined Output Schemas
Directory of spatial files (shapefiles) - Takes a directory of shapefiles and exposes it as a data store
Microsoft SQL Server - Microsoft SQL Server
Microsoft SQL Server (JNDI) - Microsoft SQL Server (JNDI)

Application schema mapping file

An application schema is defined much like any other data store in GeoServer, the difference being that the data store points to an XML file called the app-schema **mapping file**. The mapping file has an associated schema document called `AppSchemaDataAccess.xsd`; this document is not required by GeoServer for the extension to function but is provided for use in XML editors that utilize an `.xsd` file for context-sensitive help and schema validation.

The mapping file contains six sections that describe how the extension should read source data and translate it into a target application schema. The following table describes each section and its purpose:

Section	Required	Purpose
namespaces	Yes	This section provides the definition of all the namespaces that will be used in the mapping file.
includedTypes	No	This section enables additional elements to be included in the mapping file without themselves being mapped. In other words, the items are not accessed individually, and they are included for reusability.
sourceDataStores	Yes	This section gives details of where the data for the features will come from. There must be at least one source data store defined in a mapping file, but more than one can also be used.
catalog	No	This section gives the reference to an OASIS XML catalog configuration file that allows GeoServer to process entity references.

Section	Required	Purpose
`targetTypes`	Yes	This section provides a list of all the application schemas (`.xsd` files) required to create the mapping. In most cases, only one will be required, but sometimes, more than one will need to be specified.
`typeMappings`	Yes	This is where the actual work is done. This section is used to describe the mappings needed to transform simple features from source data stores into complex features for output.

The GeoServer documentation goes into a lot of detail about how the mapping file is constructed and how to use it. We will take a look at the key parts of the file, but it will be worth spending some time reading the GeoServer documentation for a fuller explanation (`http://docs.geoserver.org/stable/en/user/data/app-schema/index.html`).

The `namespaces` section is where you can define the namespaces that will be used in the mapping file. The following fragment is an example of what the namespace element can look like, in this case, for using a single namespace:

```
<namespaces>
  <Namespace>
    <prefix>xlink</prefix>
    <uri>http://www.w3.org/1999/xlink</uri>
  </Namespace>
</namespaces>
```

For each namespace, you need to reference in your mapping file; there must be a corresponding `<Namespace>` element in the `namespaces` section. Each `<Namespace>` element consists of two child elements that describe the namespace prefix (for example, `xlink`) and the URI (for example, `http://www.w3.org/1999/xlink`).

The `sourceDatastores` section allows you to specify the sources of data for the app-schema extension to use. All references to values within the `<OCQL>` elements will be translated into data elements from the source, for example, tables or views in the case of a database store. Any valid GeoServer data store can be used, and more than one source data store can be specified, but each one must have a unique name. Definitions of the properties for the data store are provided using a list of parameters. The following is the definition for a PostGIS data store connection. A complete example is provided in the downloadable code that accompanies this book:

```
<sourceDataStores>
    <DataStore>
```

```
        <id>pg_datastore</id>
        <parameters>
        database connection parameters
        </parameters>
    </DataStore>
</sourceDataStores>
```

The `<parameters>` element contains the child `<parameter>` elements, each consisting of the `<name>` and `<value>` elements. Each `<parameter>` element equates to standard data store settings that you would expect to find when defining a data store for PostGIS through the GeoServer web administration console. To define multiple sources of data, simply add additional `<DataStore>` elements, ensuring each one has a unique value for the `<id>` element.

The `targetTypes` section provides details of all the application schema (`.xsd`) files that will be needed to correctly create the feature type from the mapping file. In the majority of cases, you will only need to specify the location of one schema file that holds the definition of the complex feature being created from the mapping file. However, in some cases, it might be necessary for you to specify multiple `xsd` files for the mapping file to function correctly. For example, the following is an example of `targetTypes` for the **INSPIRE Road Transport Network** application schema:

```
<targetTypes>
        <FeatureType>
                <schemaUri>http://inspire.jrc.ec.europa.eu/schemas/tn-
ro/3.0/RoadTransportNetwork.xsd</schemaUri>
                <schemaUri>http://inspire.jrc.ec.europa.eu/schemas/tn/3.0/
CommonTransportElements.xsd</schemaUri>
                <schemaUri>http://inspire.jrc.ec.europa.eu/schemas/
net/3.2/Network.xsd</schemaUri>
                <schemaUri>http://inspire.jrc.ec.europa.eu/schemas/gn/3.0/
GeographicalNames.xsd</schemaUri>
                <schemaUri>http://inspire.jrc.ec.europa.eu/schemas/
base/3.2/BaseTypes.xsd</schemaUri>
        </FeatureType>
    </targetTypes>
```

There is a single `<FeatureType>` element that contains multiple `<schemaUri>` elements, the contents of each being the web address for that particular `xsd` file. When GeoServer first parses the mapping file, it will attempt to go out to the web to fetch the specified schema files, and it will then store them in the data directory in a folder called `app-schema-cache`. Subsequent parsing of the mapping file will not trigger an external web call; instead, GeoServer will go to the cache of files.

It is important to note that GeoServer will never go back to the Web to refresh the cache once it is created. If you need to have the cache refreshed, then you must delete the app-schema-cache folder contents so that the fetch method is triggered on the next reading of the mapping file.

If your instance of GeoServer sits behind a firewall and is unable to make outbound web calls, then you will need to find an alternative method of supplying the schema files. The GeoServer documentation at http://docs.geoserver.org/stable/en/ user/data/app-schema/app-schema-resolution.html provides some strategies for how this can be achieved.

The typeMappings section is where the actual substance of the mapping file is. All the previous elements are more concerned with the setup and configuration of the mapping file rather than the business of generating content. Within the typeMappings section, there should be one or more <FeatureTypeMapping> elements, which is the main instruction to create a new feature. Each <FeatureTypeMapping> element identifies the source data to feed the type through the <sourceDataStore> element, the value of which should match one of your <DataStore> elements in the sourceDataStores section. For example, if we want to use the PostGIS definition from our previous example, we will specify pg_datastore as the value for the element. The <targetAttribute> element allows you to specify the target output feature type, and the <attributeMappings> section allows you to specify how attributes should be created.

Publishing data with an application schema

Now, we have an understanding of what an application schema is, and we have our instance of GeoServer ready to serve data based on one. It is time to get our hands dirty with a simple example. For this example, we are going to continue with the idea (presented earlier) of delivering a road network dataset using the **INSPIRE Annex I Road Transport Network** schema. Specific details on what this schema is can be found in the INSPIRE data-specification document, D2.8.1.7, available at http://inspire.jrc.ec.europa.eu/documents/Data_Specifications/ INSPIRE_DataSpecification_TN_v3.1.pdf.

We will use the following steps to create a simple implementation of the Road Transport Network schema using some free **OpenStreetMap** data:

1. We will first prepare our source dataset in a PostGIS database.

2. Then, we will configure the data store to hold our application schema dataset.

3. After that, we will create the application schema mapping file.

4. Finally, we will bring it all together to publish the data through WFS.

Source data preparation

For this simple example, we are going to use some free OpenStreetMap data. There are a number of ways in which you can obtain the OpenStreetMap data, either by manually specifying an area of interest from the OpenStreetMap website (http://www.openstreetmap.org) or by downloading pre-prepared extracts of the data.

To download a custom area of data from the OpenStreetMap website, go to http://www.openstreetmap.org and use the map controls to center the map on the area you are interested in. Then, click on the **Export** button to open the data export window.

As you pan and zoom the map, the data extents will change and update. When you are happy that the map window is displaying the area of data you are interested in, click on the blue **Export** button. After a few moments, you will get a download response from the server; save the file somewhere on your system. The downloaded file will be an OSM .pbf binary file.

A simpler way to get hold of the OpenStreetMap data is to download a predefined data extent. Probably the best online resource is offered by Geofabrik at http://download.geofabrik.de. The page provides a table that allows you to drill down to a specific area and then download it.

Click on the region name to see the overview page for that region, or select one of the file extenstion links for quick access.

Sub-Region	Quick Links		
	.osm.pbf	**.shp.zip**	**.osm.bz2**
Africa	[.osm.pbf]	✖	[.osm.bz2]
Antarctica	[.osm.pbf]	[.shp.zip]	[.osm.bz2]
Asia	[.osm.pbf]	✖	[.osm.bz2]
Australia and Oceania	[.osm.pbf]	✖	[.osm.bz2]
Central America	[.osm.pbf]	✖	[.osm.bz2]
Europe	[.osm.pbf]	✖	[.osm.bz2]
North America	[.osm.pbf]	✖	[.osm.bz2]
South America	[.osm.pbf]	✖	[.osm.bz2]

Clicking on the name of a subregion will drill down into further pages of locations. In most cases, it is possible to drill down into the county level. For my example, I am going to use the predefined area for West Sussex in the United Kingdom. We are going to use the osm2po toolset to process and load the downloaded data, and this tool works best with the .osm.pbf format of OpenStreetMap data.

We are using the osm2po software to translate and clean up the OpenStreetMap dataset; however, it is useful to know that in addition to being a translated software, it is also a very capable routing engine.

Download the latest version of osm2po from http://osm2po.de, and then unzip the contents to a location on your system. At the time of writing this book, the current version of osm2po is 4.8.8. With the contents extracted, open a command prompt in the directory you extracted to and issue the following command:

```
$ E:\Utilities\osm2po>java -Xmx512m -jar osm2po-core-4.8.8-signed.jar
prefix=ws tileSize=x postp.1.class = de.cm.osm2po.plugins.PgVertexWriter
http://download.geofabrik.de/europe/great-britain/england/west-sussex-l

atest.osm.pbf
```

As you can see, osm2po is a Java application, so you need to make sure that Java is configured on your system and is on the path. The `-Xmx512m` switch tells the JVM how much memory to reserve; adjust this according to your system specification and the size of the area that you will process. The `prefix=ws` argument will create the processed data in a folder that matches the value that you specify; in this case, the data will be placed in a folder called `ws`. The `postp.1.class` switch tells osm2po to output the nodes as well as the links. The last item should be either the location of a downloaded OpenStreetMap dataset or the URL where the data can be downloaded. In this case, we went for the latter and specified the download location. There are a number of different commands, so check out the help and documentation at `http://osm2po.de/` to learn more. If everything goes well, then we will see the following as the last line in the console:

```
Services started. Waiting for requests at http://localhost:8888/
Osm2poService
```

If you open a web browser and navigate to that location, you will be presented with the osm2po routing service test bed. Play around a little with it; it's a very capable routing engine and might prove useful in some of your applications.

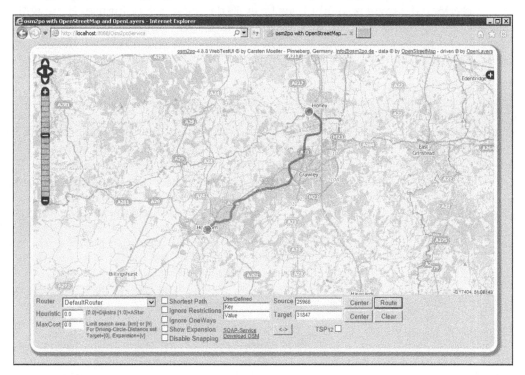

Now, you might be asking yourself why are we going through all this trouble to get hold of some OpenStreetMap data that we can then spit out from GeoServer in an INSPIRE schema. Well, apart from the fact that it is great fun to play with all these tools and it is interesting to see how powerful an open source and open data toolset can be for routing, it creates a SQL script for us that we can use to load the data into our PostGIS database. More important, though, is that the OpenStreetMap data would have been cleaned and topologically structured, giving us a nice clean dataset to work with. If you take a look inside the folder created when the data was processed, in our case ws, then you will see two SQL scripts that we can run to load the data into our PostGIS database. From a command line in the directory of the scripts, run the following commands:

```
$ psql -U [username] -d [dbname] -q -f "E:\Utilities\osm2po\ws\
ws_2po_4pgr.sql"
```

```
$ psql -U [username] -d [dbname] -q -f "E:\Utilities\osm2po\ws\ws_2po_v.
sql"
```

Remember to change the paths to the SQL files in your system and also specify your database name and username to connect with. Once the scripts have executed, the OpenStreetMap data will be held in our PostGIS database, ready for use. There will be a table that contains the road link features and another table that contains the start and end nodes for each road link. The two tables are linked through the use of unique identifiers on the road nodes.

The application schema mapping file

With the data prepared, we are now ready to create a mapping file to take the data stored in our PostGIS database and publish it in an INSPIRE-compliant schema. Before we can create the mapping file, we need to set up a workspace within GeoServer to hold it. There is an important requirement here; the name of the workspace and its namespace should match the target schema for which we are generating the mapping file. In our case, this is going to be the same as the INSPIRE Road Transport Network namespace of *tn-ro*.

Create a new workspace and enter the details shown in the following screenshot:

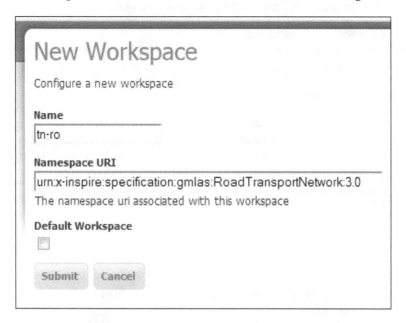

Note that the value for **Namespace URI** is the reference to the INSPIRE schema for Road Transport Network, Version 3.0. This will create a new folder called `tn-ro` in our GeoServer directory inside the `workspaces` folder. Remember how the mapping file is going to be the definition for the data store? Well, this means that we should create a folder inside the workspace folder to hold the data store that we will define. The name does not particularly matter, but try and make it something relevant. As this is a Road Network dataset, we will create a folder called `RoadNetwork`, which will be our data store. Go ahead and create the folder; you should have `<geoserver_data_dir>/workspaces/tn-ro/RoadNetwork` if you followed the naming convention that we used. We are going to create a mapping file inside the `RoadNetwork` folder, and we will call it `TN-RO_RoadLink.xml` to contain the details of the schema mapping we want to perform. I will simply take you through the key sections and highlight the areas of most interest rather than including the full script here. The complete XML file can be downloaded from this book's website.

The XML file must be valid, so the usual opening elements are required. The root of the document is the **as:AppSchemaDataAccess** element:

```
<?xml version="1.0" encoding="UTF-8"?>
<as:AppSchemaDataAccess xmlns:as="http://www.geotools.org/app-schema"
    xmlns:xsi="http://www.w3.org/2001/XMLSchema-instance"
xsi:schemaLocation="http://www.geotools.org/app-schema
AppSchemaDataAccess.xsd">
```

Notice the xsi:schemaLocation attribute on this element. Strictly speaking, this is not necessary as GeoServer is aware of the schema for this XML. However, it is useful to include this attribute, especially if you want to edit this file in an XML editor that can use schema documents for highlighting, validation, and code completion.

The next section of the file contains the namespace definitions for all the namespaces that we will be using:

```
<namespaces>
    <Namespace>
        <prefix>gml</prefix>
        <uri>http://www.opengis.net/gml</uri>
    </Namespace>
    <Namespace>
        <prefix>tn-ro</prefix>
        <uri>urn:x-inspire:specification:gmlas:RoadTransportNetwo
rk:3.0</uri>
    </Namespace>
    <Namespace>
        <prefix>tn</prefix>
        <uri>urn:x-inspire:specification:gmlas:CommonTransportElem
ents:3.0</uri>
    </Namespace>
    <Namespace>
        <prefix>net</prefix>
        <uri>urn:x-inspire:specification:gmlas:Network:3.2</uri>
    </Namespace>
    <Namespace>
        <prefix>gn</prefix>
        <uri>urn:x-inspire:specification:gmlas:GeographicalNam
es:3.0</uri>
    </Namespace>
    <Namespace>
        <prefix>base</prefix>
        <uri>urn:x-inspire:specification:gmlas:BaseTypes:3.2</uri>
    </Namespace>
```

```
<Namespace>
     <prefix>gmd</prefix>
     <uri>http://www.isotc211.org/2005/gmd</uri>
</Namespace>
<Namespace>
     <prefix>xlink</prefix>
     <uri>http://www.w3.org/1999/xlink</uri>
</Namespace>
<Namespace>
     <prefix>xsi</prefix>
     <uri>http://www.w3.org/2001/XMLSchema-instance</uri>
</Namespace>
</namespaces>
```

Each `<Namespace>` element consists of the prefix that will be used and then the URI that the prefix resolves to. These are the ones required for the INSPIRE transportation schema; add any additional ones that you want to use.

Next, we come to the `<sourceDataStores>` section:

```
<sourceDataStores>
    <DataStore>
        <id>pg_datastore</id>
        <parameters>
            <!-- Add connection parameters in here -->
        </parameters>
    </DataStore>
</sourceDataStores>
```

Recall how we talked about a complex schema being supplied data from multiple sources? This section is where you define these data connections. Each data source element must have a unique name in the context of the XML file; in this case, we have called the source pg_datastore, as it is a PostGIS data source we are describing. The name of the data source does not matter, but it is a good practice to make the name descriptive of the source itself, to make it easier to follow in the XML code.

The next section of the XML file is where we specify the locations of all the XSDs that will be required to service our complex feature. There must be at least one reference in this section, and most of the time, one will be sufficient. However, there will be complex cases where more than one reference is necessary:

```
<targetTypes>
    <FeatureType>
        <schemaUri>http://inspire.jrc.ec.europa.eu/schemas/tn-
ro/3.0/RoadTransportNetwork.xsd</schemaUri>
        <schemaUri>http://inspire.jrc.ec.europa.eu/schemas/tn/3.0/
CommonTransportElements.xsd</schemaUri>
```

```
          <schemaUri>http://inspire.jrc.ec.europa.eu/schemas/
net/3.2/Network.xsd</schemaUri>
          <schemaUri>http://inspire.jrc.ec.europa.eu/schemas/gn/3.0/
GeographicalNames.xsd</schemaUri>
          <schemaUri>http://inspire.jrc.ec.europa.eu/schemas/
base/3.2/BaseTypes.xsd</schemaUri>
        </FeatureType>
      </targetTypes>
```

If your target feature type requires multiple schemas for it to be validated, then you would simply create a `<schemaUri>` element for each one. GeoServer will download these schemas and place them into a local cache to make it quicker to work with them when processing data.

The final section is where all the magic happens. This is where you describe the different type mappings that your application schema publishes. Each type is expressed through a `<FeatureTypeMapping>` element and has the instructions of how a simple feature is mapped into a complex feature:

```
<typeMappings>
  <FeatureTypeMapping>
      <sourceDataStore>pg_datastore</sourceDataStore>
      <sourceType>ws_2po_4pgr</sourceType>
      <targetElement>tn-ro:RoadLink</targetElement>
```

The start of a `<FeatureTypeMapping>` element contains a child element that points to one of the data sources defined at the start of the XML file. In this case, it is the PostGIS (`pg_datastore`) data source that we defined. The `<sourceType>` element is the name of the PostGIS table that GeoServer should use to read the data from. The `<targetElement>` element is the name of the output's complex feature that the `app-schema` extension should create, and the attribute mappings for which are described in the following `<AttributeMappings>` element:

```
<AttributeMapping>
    <targetAttribute>tn-ro:RoadLink</targetAttribute>
    <idExpression><OCQL>osm_id</OCQL></idExpression>
</AttributeMapping>
```

This particular `<AttributeMapping>` element is a special case, as it instructs GeoServer to create a `gml:id` attribute on our output complex feature element. The `<OCQL>` element tells GeoServer which column in our database table contains the value to use for the `gml:id` attribute's value:

```
<AttributeMapping>
<targetAttribute>net:inspireId/base:Identifier/base:localId</
targetAttribute>
```

```
        <sourceExpression>
            <OCQL>osm_id</OCQL>
        </sourceExpression>
    </AttributeMapping>
    <AttributeMapping>
    <targetAttribute>net:inspireId/base:Identifier/base:namespace</
    targetAttribute>
        <sourceExpression>
            <OCQL>'tn-ro.rn.temp'</OCQL>
        </sourceExpression>
    </AttributeMapping>
```

These two `<AttributeMapping>` elements are interesting for two reasons. First, they both demonstrate the reason for the `app-schema` extension by allowing us to express a complex attribute mapping from a simple table column. In this case, the complex attributes are ultimately `base:localId` and `base:namespace`, but the reason they are complex is because they are nested. In the output feature, the `base:localId` will be written as follows:

```
<net:inspireId>
    <base:Identifier>
        <base:localId>
            <!-- the value would be here -->
        </base:localId>
    </base:Identifier>
</net:inspireId>
```

The second reason that these elements are of interest is because they also demonstrate how a constant can be supplied as the value for the `<sourceExpression>` element. Look at the second example of the two. Notice how the source expression is written such that the value inside the `<OCQL>` element is the constant value `tn-ro.rn.temp`. Any value contained inside single quotes will be printed verbatim by the `app-schema` extension when it writes the output.

This is a relatively simple script, and there is a lot more that can be done with the mapping file. I highly recommend that you spend some time reading the GeoServer documentation for mapping files at `http://docs.geoserver.org/stable/en/user/data/app-schema/mapping-file.html` to get more details. For now, we will just look at some of the key implementation points.

The meat of the mapping file is the content within the `<attributeMappings>` element, as these are the instructions to the app-schema extension for how to generate the output complex feature. The first interesting point to look at is the first attribute mapping that provides the feature with its unique identifier:

```
<AttributeMapping>
    <targetAttribute>tn-ro:RoadLink</targetAttribute>
```

```
<idExpression>
    <OCQL>osm_id</OCQL>
</idExpression>
</AttributeMapping>
```

The key part here is the use of an `<idExpression>` element. This is a **Common Query Language** (CQL) expression that the extension will use to create a `gml:id` attribute on the feature itself. The value inside the `<OCQL>` element should be the name of the table column that holds the value to use it as the `id`. In this case, we are using the `osm_id` column.

> CQL is an OGC query language created for use with the Catalogue Web Services specification. Unlike other filter languages, it is designed to be written in plain text rather than XML; this makes it far more accessible to most users.

Most attributes are mapped using the `<sourceExpression>` element that holds a CQL expression, either the name of a table column or a string literal, to set for the attribute. The power of complex features is the ability to create nested, multivalued attributes in the output, instead of straight one-to-one database column to attribute mappings. A good example of this is highlighted in the following mapping file content:

```
<AttributeMapping>
    <targetAttribute>
        net:inspireId/base:Identifier/base:localId
    </targetAttribute>
    <sourceExpression>
        <OCQL>osm_id</OCQL>
    </sourceExpression>
</AttributeMapping>
<AttributeMapping>
    <targetAttribute>
        net:inspireId/base:Identifier/base:namespace
    </targetAttribute>
    <sourceExpression>
        <OCQL>'tn-ro.rn.temp'</OCQL>
    </sourceExpression>
</AttributeMapping>
```

This example will create a complex attribute with nested elements on the output feature. Notice how a standard XPath query (http://www.w3schools.com/xpath/) is used to define the `<targetAttribute>` value. This will be used to generate the correct nesting of the opening and closing elements; the second attribute mapping contains a string literal and will manifest as a second nested element at the same level as the first one. For example, this mapping will yield the following on our output feature:

```
<net:inspireId>
    <base:Identifier>
        <base:localId>
            225
        </base:localId>
        <base:namespace>
            tn-ro.rn.temp
        </base:namespace>
    </base:Identifier>
</net:inspireId>
```

This is only a simple example, but it should give you a good idea of what can be possible within a mapping file.

Data store and feature type configuration

With the mapping file created, all we need to do now is set it up as a data store and then configure a feature type from it. Open up the GeoServer web administration console and click on the **Stores** link from the left-hand side menu. Click on the **Add new store** button, and then select the **Application Schema DataAccess** option in the vector data sources section.

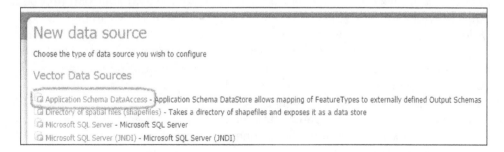

This will open the standard data store creation page that you should be familiar with by now. Enter some details for the name and description of the data store.

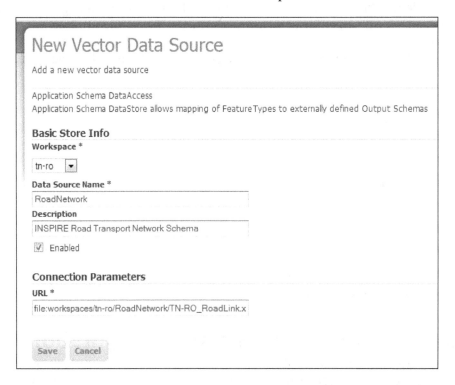

Notice how the URL connection parameter is a location of our mapping file, relative to the route of the GeoServer data directory. In this case, it is `<geoserver_data_dir>/workspaces/tn-ro/RoadNetwork/TN-RO_RoadLink.xml`. Once the details have been filled, click on the **Save** button to get a list of the available feature types to publish. Wait a minute! A list of feature types to publish? How can that be? We only defined one feature type in our mapping file. This is easily explained if you remember that we created a data store definition, and data stores contain feature types to publish. In the case of a database, these are tables, and in the case of a directory of shapefiles, these will be the individual shapefiles. In the case of an application schema, these are the available `<FeatureTypeMapping>` elements in the mapping file. The mapping file can contain more than one `<FeatureTypeMapping>` element, and the extension will read each one and present it as an option in the list of feature types to publish. So, if your application schema defines multiple types of complex features, then you can define them all in one mapping file and then publish them out separately.

Once you choose the feature type to publish and click on the **Publish** link, then the standard GeoServer functionality applies. To test whether everything worked as expected, go to the **Layer Preview** page and then select a WFS output type such as GML 3.2. If all is well, GeoServer will return a WFS XML response that contains 50 features.

> The application schema extension is built with the purpose of providing a data source to publish as a WFS service; however, it is also possible to make GeoServer render the complex feature as a WMS response. For more details, take a look at the GeoServer documentation at `http://docs.geoserver.org/stable/en/user/data/app-schema/wms-support.html`.

Summary

After finishing this chapter, we now have a good understanding of the difference between a simple feature and a complex feature. Knowing the difference and, more importantly, knowing that GeoServer defaults to delivering simple features will enable us to make informed decisions about how we deliver our data through WFS.

Complex features will allow us to really maximize the way in which we utilize GeoServer as a vector feature delivery platform. The use of standard simple feature delivery combined with the ability to deliver simple features as members of a complex feature will really open the door to a world of content delivery. This flexibility means that we can optimize storage by not having to repeat copies of data to participate in different output strategies. We saw how complex features can be used to provide output from our WFS service that conforms to a community-generated schema, such as EU INSPIRE Directive schemas. Using application schemas means that we are able to provide output for multiple schemas from a single source dataset or datasets.

In the next chapter, we are going to look at how we can extend the capabilities of other servers using GeoServer as a proxy.

5
Using GeoServer as a Proxy

What's that you say? GeoServer can be used as a proxy? What does this actually mean, and why will you want to consider doing something with it? Well, this chapter aims to enlighten you on the subject and to provide you with the understanding of cascaded WMS and WFS services, which are at the heart of being able to turn GeoServer into a proxying web mapping server.

There are a number of good reasons why one will choose to implement GeoServer in a proxying role—from providing external servers with additional or expanded capabilities to implementing it as the basis for security. Setting GeoServer up as a proxy will open the doors to a number of new and inventive scenarios in which you can use the software.

By the end of this chapter, you will have a much better understanding of:

- A cascaded service
- How to make use of cascaded services in the enterprise
- How to cascade an external WMS service
- How to cascade an external WFS service
- How to extend the capabilities of another server

Defining cascaded services

A cascaded service is one where an external server provides the WMS and/or WFS service that your local instance of GeoServer connects to and then passes through to your end clients. The service *cascades* through your implementation of GeoServer, and then moves on to the end users.

End users of a cascaded service do not know that they are actually in receipt of cascaded data unless something within the data or metadata indicates that they are. To all intents and purposes, they will consider it to be data that is controlled and hosted by you.

Using cascaded services

Now that we know what a cascaded service is, the big question on our mind is how we might go about using this in the enterprise environment. Well, the short answer is that it can be used in many ways. The more specific answer, on the other hand, is that there are three core scenarios where GeoServer can be used as a proxy using cascaded services:

- Extending the capabilities of another WMS server
- WMS enabling a WFS-only server
- As a reverse proxy

Extending the capabilities of another WMS server

The capabilities of a WMS server are very much dependent on the way they have been configured to run. For example, a configuration might have been configured to only support one spatial reference system, EPSG:27700, for British National Grid. Let's suppose that you have a web application that will benefit from using the data provided by this server, but your application has been configured to work only with Web Spherical Mercator (EPSG:3857). How can you get hold of this WMS data in your application? GeoServer's cascaded WMS service can be used in the following ways:

- Create a cascaded WMS data store to connect to the external WMS server
- GeoServer requests maps from the external WMS using the native SRS of EPSG:27700
- GeoServer performs an internal reprojection of the requested map image to EPSG:3857
- The reprojected map image is returned to the requested web-mapping application

The capabilities of the external WMS server have been extended by increasing the number of SRSes it can publish data in.

WMS enabling a WFS-only server

Enterprise systems are often a combination of different components, each with their own special data formats and interfaces. As the world of IT advances, this is thankfully becoming a thing of the past, with a much wider adoption of data standards and open APIs providing access to this data. However, there will always be exceptions where the software/hardware is simply too old or niche to consider replacing, at least for the time being. In this scenario, how does one go about utilizing the data that is trapped inside the legacy system? Well, a reasonably low-cost solution will be to adopt the principles of **Service Oriented Architecture (SOA)** and develop or deploy a WFS server that can talk to the legacy system and publish its data through the WFS protocol.

The following diagram shows how this approach can be implemented. The legacy data store has a single-purpose WFS server connected to it. The purpose of this server is to read the data in the legacy data store, and then make it available to connecting clients through WFS. GeoServer is then used to connect to the WFS service in order to be able to publish the legacy data out through WMS, or even WFS.

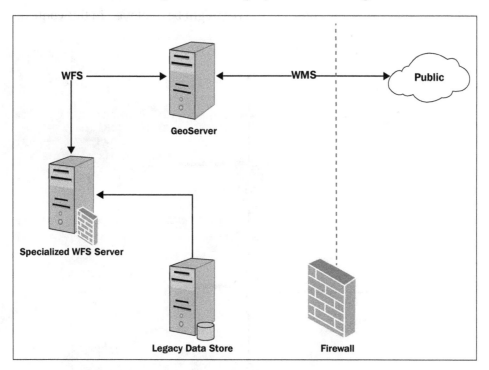

This is great! We now have a means of pushing the data out of the legacy system into a more accessible form so that applications can now work without caring about the underlying system from which the data came. However, this is only a part of the story since it is quite likely that after unlocking the data, you will need to be able to publish it as a web map. This is where GeoServer's ability to cascade a WFS service and then publish the output through WMS comes into play. GeoServer can be configured to act as a WMS publisher for the data supplied by the specialized WFS server, providing a means of delivering the legacy data through modern web standards.

Using GeoServer as a reverse proxy

This scenario is a slightly more complex implementation of cascaded services, but arguably the most powerful within an enterprise context. GeoServer can be deployed within a **demilitarized zone (DMZ)** of the corporate network in order to mask the true presence of the internal GeoServer's responsibility for map production and data serving.

The following diagram shows how GeoServer might be deployed in this context:

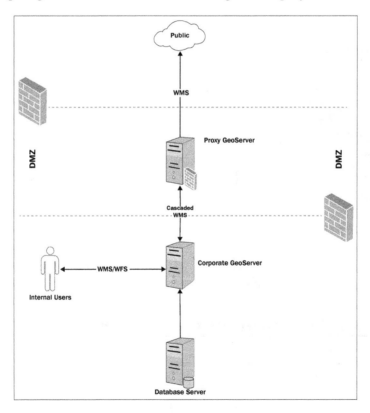

A typical information flow in this configuration will be:

1. DMZ is a zone between the outside world (protected by a public-facing firewall) and the internal network (protected by another firewall). External WMS requests are made to GeoServer that is installed and running inside DMZ.

2. GeoServer inside DMZ then forwards the WMS requests on to the internal GeoServer to process.

3. The internal GeoServer processes the WMS request and generates a response map, sending it back to GeoServer in DMZ.

4. GeoServer in DMZ receives the WMS map and then passes it on to the originator of the external WMS request.

There are a number of uses to run GeoServer inside DMZ. For example, it can be used to publish a subset of your corporate data to the general public that has undergone modification and filtering to remove sensitive or commercial information. In this scenario, GeoServer inside DMZ can be configured to use cascaded WMS services to publish data layers. These data layers can come from another GeoServer, or a cluster of GeoServers, inside the corporate network. Not only does this approach allow the separation of internal business data and publicly accessible data, but it also provides a level of security, as there is no indication or hint as to what your internal network configuration might look externally. In effect, this reduces the surface area available for attack and usually provides a better security for the underlying data sources.

DMZ is a useful concept in network security and one that is worth investing some time and effort in understanding. It provides a useful way of exposing web services to a larger, untrusted network (the Internet), while reducing the threat to your internal network. More information on DMZ can be found at `http://en.wikipedia.org/wiki/DMZ_(computing)`.

Creating a cascaded WMS connection

Now that we understand what service cascading is and some reasons why it might be useful to us, it is time to actually have a go at creating a cascaded service. For this example, we will set up a cascaded service to serve OpenStreetMap buildings to our clients.

Creating the data store

A cascaded WMS service is not really any different from other data sources that we might use with GeoServer. It still follows the same principle of having a data store connection and then publishing layers from the data store source. In this case, however, the data store is a connection to the external WMS server, and the layers we can publish are those advertised by WMS. Therefore, we must connect to the external WMS service in a way that will allow GeoServer to discover what layers can be published. To do this, we will utilize the external WMS server's published *Capabilities* document that will tell our GeoServer what layers are available. The link to the external WMS server's *Capabilities* document will be the connection details for the data store.

To create a connection to the external WMS server's *Capabilities* document, select the **Stores** link under the **Data** section of the left-hand-side menu on GeoServer's web administration console. On the **Stores** page, click on the **Add new store** link to open the **New data source** page:

At the bottom of the page, there is a section called **Other Data Sources,** and within this section, you should have an item simply called **WMS – Cascade a remote Web Map Service.** Click on the name to open the **New WMS Connection** page. It is here where we will enter the connection details to the external WMS server and create the new data store:

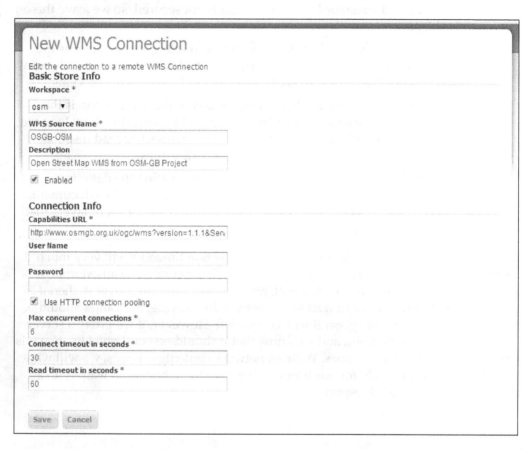

As usual, we have to provide some basic store information, such as the workspace that we want the connection to belong to and a name and description to identify it by. The main information that we must provide is the URL for the *Capabilities* document. For this example, we need to provide the URL to the OSM-GB project's WMS server, but in reality, this URL will point to the external WMS server that you cascade in your particular scenario.

To cascade the service, execute the following steps:

1. Enter the `http://www.osmgb.org.uk/ogc/wms?Version=1.1.1&Service=W MS&Request=GetCapabilities` path in the **Capabilities URL** textbox.

2. If we connect to a protected WMS server, we should also enter values for the **User Name** and **Password** fields. OSM-GB is not secured, so we leave these fields blank.

3. We can specify some rudimentary connection pooling details, such as the maximum number of concurrent connections and whether we actually want connection pooling. Tick the box for the **Use HTTP** connection pooling.

4. The last piece of information to provide, or accept the defaults for, is the request timeout. These are values that we can set to determine how long we want our GeoServer instance to sit and wait for **connect** or **read** responses before it abandons the request. Leave the default values.

5. Click on the **Save** button to begin the process of creating the data store. GeoServer will then attempt to request and read the *Capabilities* document. If everything works correctly, we will be presented with a list of layers that GeoServer can publish.

It is worth noting that the values to enter for connection timeouts will very much depend on our deployment scenario. For example, if we connect to an external third-party WMS server over the Internet, and we have no control over it, then it is reasonable to expect to have to wait for responses. In this case, the values should be set longer to accommodate general web congestion. However, if we proxy a server within our own environment, and we know that it should respond quickly, then it is preferable to reduce these values. Without network contention issues, we will want the response to fail quickly for our users, rather than them having to wait up to a minute to receive a failed response.

Publishing a cascaded WMS layer

Once GeoServer successfully reads the *Capabilities* document from the external WMS server, it will present us with a list of all the layers that can be published:

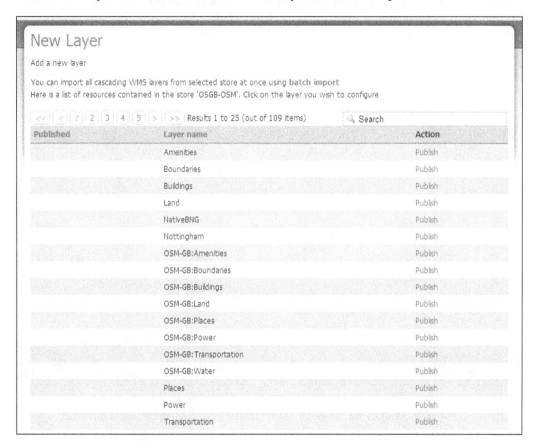

New Layer

Add a new layer

You can import all cascading WMS layers from selected store at once using batch import
Here is a list of resources contained in the store 'OSGB-OSM'. Click on the layer you wish to configure

<< | < | *1* | 2 | 3 | 4 | 5 | > | >> | Results 1 to 25 (out of 109 items)   Search

Published	Layer name	Action
	Amenities	Publish
	Boundaries	Publish
	Buildings	Publish
	Land	Publish
	NativeBNG	Publish
	Nottingham	Publish
	OSM-GB:Amenities	Publish
	OSM-GB:Boundaries	Publish
	OSM-GB:Buildings	Publish
	OSM-GB:Land	Publish
	OSM-GB:Places	Publish
	OSM-GB:Power	Publish
	OSM-GB:Transportation	Publish
	OSM-GB:Water	Publish
	Places	Publish
	Power	Publish
	Transportation	Publish

To publish a layer, we simply click on the **Publish** link next to the name of the layer. However, as we can see from this example, there are 109 layers that we can publish, so it will get very laborious to do this individually. Fortunately for us, the developers considered this scenario and provided us with a handy **batch import** tool. Clicking on the **batch import** link at the top-right of the page will provide the same list of layers, but this time with checkboxes next to each one:

Import cascading WMS layer

Import multiple cascading layers at once

<< | < | *1* | 2 | 3 | 4 | 5 | > | >> | Results 1 to 25 (out of 109 items)   🔍 Search

	Name	Action	Status
☐	Amenities	Publish	🌐 New
☐	Boundaries	Publish	🌐 New
☐	NativeBNG	Publish	🌐 New
☐	Nottingham	Publish	🌐 New
☑	OSM-GB:Amenities	Publish	🌐 New
☑	OSM-GB:Boundaries	Publish	🌐 New
☑	OSM-GB:Buildings	Publish	🌐 New
☑	OSM-GB:Land	Publish	🌐 New
☑	OSM-GB:Places	Publish	🌐 New
☑	OSM-GB:Power	Publish	🌐 New
☑	OSM-GB:Transportation	Publish	🌐 New
☑	OSM-GB:Water	Publish	🌐 New
☐	Places	Publish	🌐 New

At the bottom of the page, we have the **Import all** and **Import selected** buttons. We can publish all the layers by simply clicking on the **Import all** button, or publish some of the layers by clicking in the checkbox next to each layer we want to publish and then clicking on **Import selected**.

Once we publish one or more layers, we will be taken back to GeoServer's **Layers** list page:

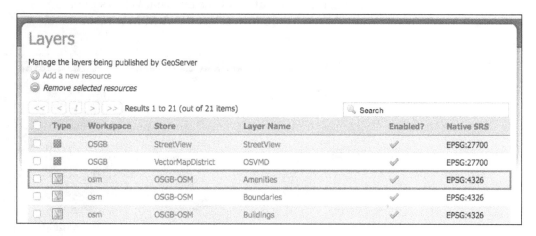

Notice how the **Type** icon for **OSGB-OSM** differs from the others? This indicates that the layer is provided by an external WMS server. It is also worth noting that the native Spatial Reference System of the external WMS server is adopted for the layer. However, one of the reasons why you might want to proxy a WMS service is to increase its capabilities, for example, the number of spatial reference systems the data can be requested in. The OSM-GB service that we consume publishes the data layers using either EPSG:4326 (WGS84 latitude and longitude) or EPSG:27700 (British National Grid), with EPSG:4326 being the default. However, because we are now publishing the data through our own GeoServer, our clients will be able to request maps in the spatial reference systems that we enabled for our GeoServer.

 We can control the spatial reference systems that our GeoServer advertises as being available by changing the global settings for WMS and WFS services.

Again, since an external WMS service is like any other data store connection (in most cases), it is possible to go back to it and publish additional layers, or republish layers; for example, if the operators of the external WMS server add additional layers to their service. To do this, select the **Add new resource** option from the **Layers** page:

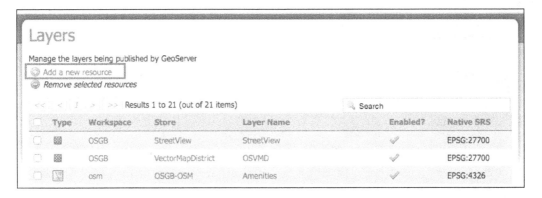

This will open the **New Layer** page where we will be provided with a list of layers that can be published or republished:

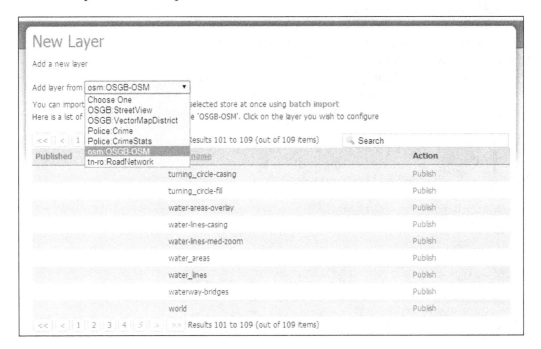

From the drop-down list, select the data store connection that you created previously. The *Capabilities* document will be read, and all the available layers to publish will be listed. Any layer currently published will have an action called **Publish again**, and any layer not previously published will have an action called **Publish**.

 Apart from being able to republish a layer from the **New Layer** page, it is also possible to select a layer in the normal layer's list, and then change one or more of its properties.

Connecting to an external WMS service handles the ability to consume external raster data. Next, we will look at how to do the same for vector data by cascading a WFS service.

Connecting to a cascaded WFS

Much like a cascade WMS service, a cascaded WFS requires some configuration to occur before it can be used. In this example, we will proxy a WFS service provided by the OSM-GB project (`http://www.osmgb.org.uk`) that delivers the **Ordnance Survey VectorMap District** data.

Creating the data store

As with a cascaded WMS service, a cascaded WFS service must first be configured as a data store before its layers can be published. Again, we must create a connection to the external WFS server's *Capabilities* document in order for our GeoServer instance to *discover* what data can be published as layers.

To create a connection to the external WFS server's *Capabilities* document, select the **Stores** link from the **Data** section of the left hand side menu on GeoServer's web administration console.

On the **Stores** page that loads, click on the **Add new store** link to open the
New data source page:

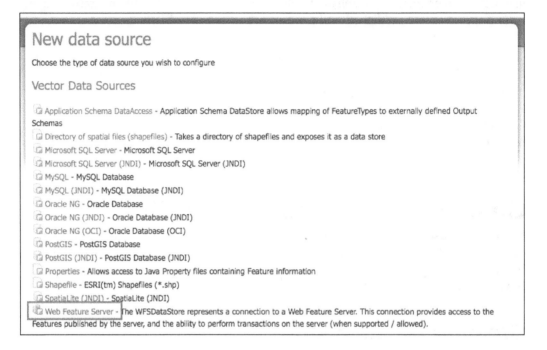

At the bottom of the **Vector Data Sources** section, there is an entry called **Web Feature Server**; click on this link to open the **Edit Vector Data Source** page. From this page, we can specify all of the connection parameters that we need in order to successfully connect to the external WFS server:

Edit Vector Data Source

Edit an existing vector data source

Web Feature Server
The WFSDataStore represents a connection to a Web Feature Server. This connection provides access to the Features published by the server, and the ability to perform transactions on the server (when supported / allowed).

Basic Store Info

Workspace *

osm

Data Source Name *

OSMGB-VectorMapDistrict

Description

OS VectorMap District WFS provided by OSM-GB projec

☑ Enabled

Connection Parameters

WFS GetCapabilities URL *

http://www.osmgb.org.uk/ogc/wfs-vmd?SERVICE=WFS&

☐ Favor HTTP POST method over GET

HTTP Authentication user name

HTTP Authentication user password

Character encoding for XML messages

UTF-8

Connection and read timeout (ms)

30000

Feature buffer size

10

☑ Use gzip encoding if server supports it

As with all data stores, we need to provide the basic information of name and description so that the store can be identified. We also need to ensure that the **Enabled** box is checked so that we can use the store once it is created. Being a vector data source, there are quite a few more configuration options for us to specify; the following table describes what each option is:

Parameter	Description
WFS GetCapabilities URL	This is where we specify the location of the external WFS server's *Capabilities* document. For our example, this is http://www. osmgb.org.uk/ogc/wfs-vmd?request= GetCapabilities&version=1.0.0.
Favor HTTP POST method over GET	When checked, GeoServer will attempt to connect using POST, before falling back to GET if POST fails.
HTTP Authentication user name	If the external WFS server requires authentication, enter the username here.
HTTP Authentication user password	If the external WFS server requires authentication, enter the password to connect with here.
Character encoding for XML messages	This is the character encoding to use for all XML messages.
Connection and read timeout (ms)	This is the time in milliseconds GeoServer should wait for the connect and read operations to complete.
Feature buffer size	This specifies the size of buffer to use and is expressed as the number of features to hold in the buffer. A larger buffer size will result in greater memory requirements.
Use gzip encoding if server supports it	Check this box if you want GeoServer to fetch data encoded as .gzip (compressed) if the external WFS server supports it. Using compressed data will reduce transfer volumes, but will place a small processing overhead on the server.

Parameter	Description
Lenient parsing	When checked, this will tell GeoServer to be more relaxed about rendering features that don't match a schema. Any errors in the rendering process are logged.
Maximum number of Features to retrieve	This specifies the maximum number of features that you will allow GeoServer to fetch from the external WFS server.
Filter compliance level	This determines how GeoServer will encode filters: • 0 is equal to low compliance and full range of filters available • 1 is equal to medium compliance, and ID and BBOX filters only • 2 is equal to strict compliance, and ID filters cannot be combined
WFS protocol strategy	This option allows you to specify whether GeoServer should implement a known workaround for specific WFS server implementations.
usedefaultsrs	Check this box if you want GeoServer to always query the external WFS server using its default SRS as advertised in *Capabilities*, and then reproject to query SRS locally on the results.
WFSDataStoreFactory:AXIS_ORDER	This sets the order for axes in coordinate pair values.
WFSDataStoreFactory:AXIS_ORDER_FILTER	This sets the order for axes in coordinate pair values in filters.
WFSDataStoreFactory:OUTPUTFORMAT	This specifies the format you want the external WFS server to output features in, providing it is supported.

Once all the parameters have been set for the store, click on the **Save** button. GeoServer will attempt to connect to the external WFS server and read its capabilities document. If everything works as expected, the **New Layer** page will open:

New Layer

Add a new layer

You can create a new feature type by manually configuring the attribute names and types. Create new feature type...
Here is a list of resources contained in the store 'OSMGB-VectorMapDistrict'. Click on the layer you wish to configure

| << | < | 1 | > | >> | Results 1 to 20 (out of 20 items) | | Search |

Published	Layer name	Action
	OS-VMD_administrativeboundary	Publish
	OS-VMD_airport	Publish
	OS-VMD_building	Publish
	OS-VMD_electricitytransmissionline	Publish
	OS-VMD_glasshouse	Publish
	OS-VMD_heritagesite	Publish
	OS-VMD_motorwayjunction	Publish
	OS-VMD_namedplace	Publish
	OS-VMD_publicamenity	Publish
	OS-VMD_railwaystation	Publish
	OS-VMD_railwaytrack	Publish
	OS-VMD_railwaytunnel	Publish
	OS-VMD_road	Publish
	OS-VMD_roadtunnel	Publish
	OS-VMD_spotheight	Publish
	OS-VMD_surfacewater_area	Publish
	OS-VMD_surfacewater_line	Publish
	OS-VMD_tidalboundary	Publish
	OS-VMD_tidalwater	Publish

The **New Layer** page provides you with a list of all the feature types that the external WFS server advertises. Click on the **Publish** link next to the name of the layer you want to publish. Data from a cascaded WFS service is treated by GeoServer like any other vector data source, and therefore, the publishing process is the same.

The difference is that a number of fields in the publishing page will be prepopulated with values read from the *Capabilities* document. If all goes according to plan, then you will be taken back to the list of available layers, where you will see the layer you just published; in this case, it is the OS-VMD_roads layer:

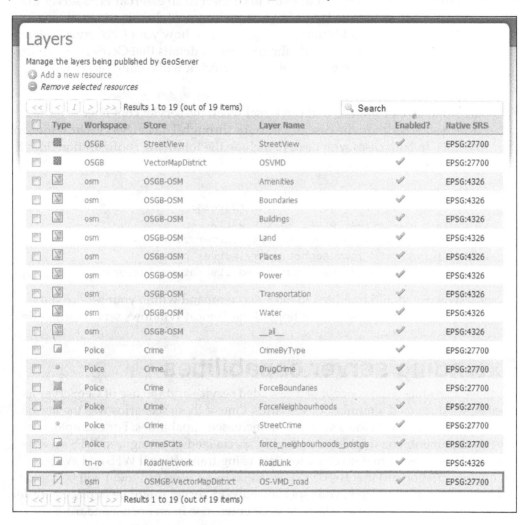

Connecting through a proxy

Not to be mistaken with what we have been talking about, using GeoServer as the proxy, your enterprise environment has its own proxy server to connect to the web. In this situation, you might find it difficult to connect to an external WFS server to successfully cascade its data as layers in your environment. In this situation, you will need to perform some additional configuration on how your GeoServer instance starts. This configuration will provide the connection details that GeoServer requires in order to connect to the proxy server through which it will communicate with external services.

There are some Java properties that can be set when the servlet container is started, either from a shell script in the case of Linux, or through Tomcat Service in Windows environments. In both cases, you need to include the following configuration lines to the Java `start` command:

```
-Dhttp.proxySet=true
-Dhttp.proxyHost=<your proxy server address>
-Dhttp.proxyPort=<your proxy server port>
-Dhttps.proxyHost=<your secure proxy server address>
-Dhttps.proxyPort=<your secure proxy server port>
-Dhttp.nonProxyHosts="<pipe delimited list of exclusions>"
```

These `-D` switches should be added to the `java` command within your service start script in Linux or through the Java settings of the Tomcat Windows service properties.

Extending server capabilities

When we introduced the concept of a cascaded service and the use of GeoServer as a proxy, we discussed a number of scenarios. One of these scenarios was the use of cascaded services to provide a server with increased capabilities. For example, within your environment, you might have a highly specialized or configured WFS server whose sole purpose is to deliver vector data using transactional WFS and WFS-T. An implementation of TinyOWS (`http://mapserver.org/tinyows`) will be a good example of this. For example, your specialized WFS server might be in place in order to make a legacy data store available to your enterprise in an open standard.

While there is nothing wrong with having a specialized WFS server within your environment (in many cases it actually makes a lot of sense, particularly if you consider it in the context of SOA), it can be limiting. What if you want to publish the legacy data as a map or make it available to other sites and services as a rendered map, especially if they are not able to support the WFS standard? This is one scenario where using GeoServer's ability to cascade services can provide additional capabilities that is not available from the source server.

In this case, GeoServer provides the capability to deliver the contents of the specialized WFS server as rendered map tiles using WMS, or any other output format supported by GeoServer such as TMS, WMS-C, or WMTS. The best thing is that this is really straightforward to set up, and in fact, it is automatic, provided you have the WMS service enabled in your GeoServer instance. This is because when you create a connection to an external WFS server, in this case, the specialized server for legacy data, the layer you *publish* behaves like any other layer published within GeoServer. This is to say that it immediately becomes available through both the WFS and WMS services. This means that you can control how the data is displayed in the rendered tiles by specifying the style that is applied, or even provide a list of styles that can be used.

When publishing a layer, there is a tab called **Publishing**, amongst others, which allows you to specify properties for the way the layer is published; for example, through WMS:

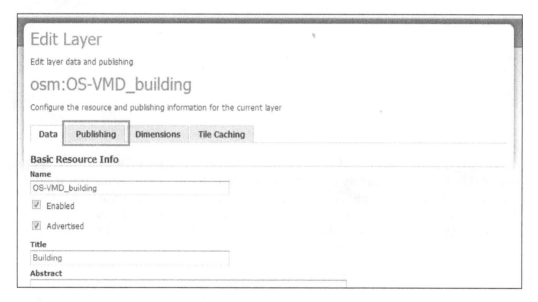

Within this tab, there are a whole host of configuration options, but perhaps the most useful is the one that enables you to set the style or styles that can be applied to this layer:

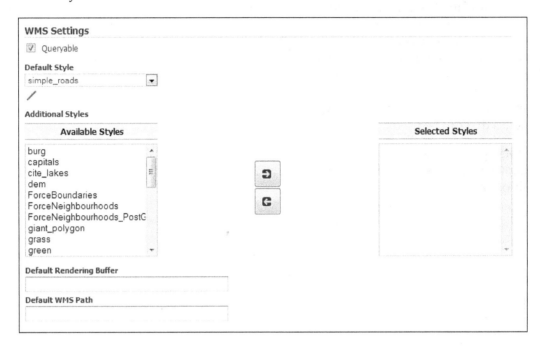

This setting allows you to set the default style that will be used to render the layer to map tiles in the absence of any other guidance about the style that should be used. In other words, this style will be applied when no specific style is requested through WMS. In addition to setting the default style, it is also possible to choose a number of other styles that can be requested. A user can request the style used to render the data through the STYLES parameter of a WMS request.

Summary

In this chapter, we took a look at what cascaded services are, some scenarios in which cascaded services might be used, and finally, we had a go at cascading some external WMS and WFS services through our own instance of GeoServer. The key point to take away from this chapter is that cascaded services will open the door to more creative deployment scenarios within the enterprise environment.

Irrespective of how you choose to implement cascaded WMS and WFS services, you are now much better placed to understand the concept, and therefore, make smarter decisions about your deployment scenarios.

In the last few chapters, we looked at the different ways in which we can consume and publish data using GeoServer. In the next chapter, we will take a look at the different ways in which we control how GeoServer outputs the data.

6
Controlling the Output of GeoServer

Until now, we have been focused on getting GeoServer installed and setting up data sources. Now, it is time for us to get to grips with controlling how GeoServer outputs this data. There are a number of different aspects of GeoServer's output that we can control and manipulate, whether it is simple map styling, dynamic data styling, or feature information manipulation, GeoServer gives us the control that we need to make it fit our needs.

In this chapter, we are going to take an in-depth look at the different ways in which we can control the output of GeoServer; in particular, we will focus on the following topics:

- Advanced use of **Styled Layer Descriptor** files to dynamically generate heat maps
- Using **Cascaded Style Sheets (CSS)** as an alternative styling language to SLDs
- Performing per-request styling of map features
- Performing per-request filtering of map data
- Using Freemarker templates to transform responses to WMS GetFeatureInfo requests

By the end of the chapter, you will have enough information to go and experiment with the different ways in which you can control the output from your own GeoServer instances.

Styling data with Styled Layer Descriptor

The standard method to style data in GeoServer is by using **Styled Layer Descriptor files**, more commonly referred to as **SLD** files. SLD is a mark-up language based on XML and offers a lot of flexibility and power when it comes to styling geospatial data. However, with this power and flexibility comes complexity. Tackling SLD files in a standard text or XML editor is not for the faint of heart and is prone to errors. Invariably, this leads to a *trial and error* approach to style the data, as you continually go back and forth, tweaking your SLD file to get the styling just right. Therefore, it is best to use a visual tool to design your styles and have this tool generate an SLD file for you.

Going into the specifics of creating an SLD file is outside the scope of this book. There are, however, several places that contain very good information about SLD files. The best source of information (this should be your first stop) is the GeoServer documentation on styling data with SLD at http://docs.geoserver.org/2.4.x/en/user/styling/index.html.

> Check out the GeoServer SLD cookbook at http://docs.geoserver.org/2.4.x/en/user/styling/sld-cookbook/index.html for some worked-through examples of SLD styles.

The second useful source of information is chapter 6 of *GeoServer Beginner's Guide, Stefano Lacovella and Brian Youngblood, Packt Publishing*. Finally, it is well worth reading the SLD specification documents from the OGC at http://www.opengeospatial.org/standards/sld. It is a complex document to work through but is undoubtedly the most authoritative reference for the standard.

Creating SLDs visually

As we discussed earlier, the SLD style language is extremely flexible and provides a lot of power to style data. However, this also means that it is complex and difficult to get into for beginners. The best way to learn about SLD is to use a visual tool to create your style and then automatically generate an SLD. This generated SLD file can then be imported to GeoServer. This becomes a great tool to learn all about SLD, as you can directly relate your actions for styling a layer to the output generated in the SLD.

There are a number of ways in which you can visually create SLD files. The simplest way is probably using QGIS (http://www.qgis.org) to work with your data, setting the styles for the layers that you will publish through GeoServer. At the time of writing this book, the current version of QGIS is 2.4.0. If you already have the dataset loaded in GeoServer, then you can use QGIS to connect to your WFS end-point and download the data. You can use the QGIS styling dialog to create the style that you want visually, alter and manipulate it, and get previews of the results inside the map. When you are satisfied with the results, you can ask QGIS to export the style for you as an SLD:

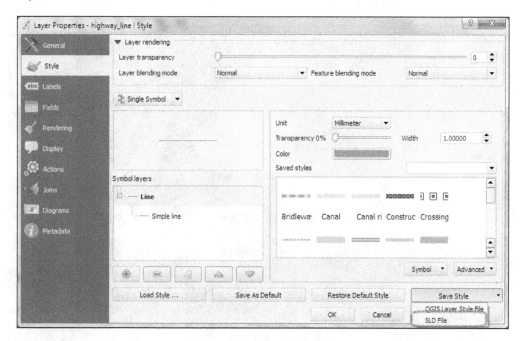

Right-click on your layer in QGIS and select the **Properties** menu option. In the **Style** tab, click on the **Save Style** dropdown and choose the **SLD File** option. This will allow you to save the generated SLD file locally, where you can then view and edit it further, or upload it to GeoServer.

 For tighter integration with GeoServer from QGIS, take a look at Boundless Geo's OpenGeo Explorer plugin. It allows you to connect directly to GeoServer from within QGIS and manage a number of aspects of the catalog, including the SLD styles. For more details on how to install and use the plugin, take a look at http://qgis.boundlessgeo.com/static/docs/index.html.

Taking SLD further – render transformations

The power of SLD and the enhancements provided by GeoServer through vendor-specific extensions to the SLD 1.0.0 standard suggest that some interesting things can be accomplished. In this example, we are going to take a look at how we can utilize render transformations to create a dynamic **heatmap** of the UK Street Level Crime data that we loaded in *Chapter 3, Working with Vector Data in Spatial Databases*. The data is interesting, but it is a mass of points styled according to a type property, and visually, it is difficult to derive any meaning. This can be seen in the following screenshot:

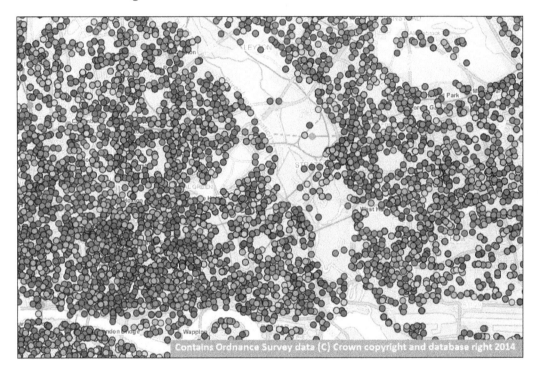

We are going to take this mass of points, filter them to a specific type of crime, and then display the results as a weighted heatmap, which will give us a quick visual impression of the level of a particular type of crime in any given area. What we aim to achieve can be seen in the following screenshot:

The ability to generate heatmaps is enabled through GeoServer's vector-to-raster rendering transformations. To take advantage of rendering transformations, we must first have the **Web Processing Service** (**WPS**) extension installed; its installation process is covered in *Chapter 9, GeoServer as a Spatial Analysis Platform*, of this book. With the WPS extension installed, it becomes possible to call functions from within the SLD, as we will see. For this example, we are going to work with the SQL Views of the UK Street Level Crime data that we created in *Chapter 3, Working with Vector Data in Spatial Databases*, to filter it based on the type of crime.

The SLD that we are going to create will be in a generic heatmap style that can actually be used on any point-based dataset where you would like to generate a weighted surface. The complete SLD is available on the Packt Publishing website and is called `Heatmap_SLD_Style.sld`; download the file and take a look at it.

 A complete discussion of how to structure calls to functions from an SLD is outside the scope of this book. Once again, the GeoServer community has created an excellent documentation that I encourage you to read. The documentation pertinent to render transformations is available at `http://docs.geoserver.org/stable/en/user/styling/sld-extensions/rendering-transform.html`.

The first part of the file that we will look at is actually the most important; it is the instruction that tells GeoServer that this SLD will use a rendering transformation function:

```
<FeatureTypeStyle>
    <Transformation>
        <ogc:Function name="gs:Heatmap">
            <!-- Function Parameters Here -->
        </ogc:Function>
    </Transformation>
    <!-- Rules Go Here -->
</FeatureTypeStyle>
```

This is the basic structure of the SLD style. After the usual SLD header information, there is the `<FeatureTypeStyle>` element, the first child element of which is `<Transformation>`. This `<Transformation>` element lets GeoServer know that we are going to use a render transformation, so it is important that this is the first element that follows the `<FeatureTypeStyle>` parent. GeoServer utilizes the `<ogc:Function>` elements for both the definitions of the render transformation that will be used, as well as for specifying the parameters that the function expects to receive. In this case, we are telling GeoServer to use the heatmap rendering transformation through the `<ogc:Function name="gs:Heatmap">` element. The `gs:Heatmap` function name is actually the name of the WPS function that GeoServer will use. The child elements of this parent are the parameters that the given function requires, for example:

```
<ogc:Function name="parameter">
    <ogc:Literal>data</ogc:Literal>
</ogc:Function>
```

Parameters are also described using the `<ogc:Function>` element, with the name attribute being `parameter`. The first child element to this function is the `<ogc:Literal>` element, whose content is the name of the parameter. The following child elements provide the value for the parameter. Some parameters can have no value, some can have a single value, and others can have multiple values. Parameter values can be specified in a number of different ways, from literal values through to predefined SLD environment variables and SLD environment variables extracted from the WMS request, also known as variable substitution.

> Variable substitution is a useful capability of GeoServer and can be used in other areas as well as within SLD files. The GeoServer documentation has a good description of variable substitution at `http://docs.geoserver.org/stable/en/user/styling/sld-extensions/substitution.html`.

The previous example was a parameter with no associated value. In this case, it is a key value that tells the render transformation to use data from the GeoServer rendering pipeline.

The following is an example of a parameter whose value is retrieved from the WMS request that invokes the map rendering:

```
<ogc:Function name="parameter">
    <ogc:Literal>outputBBOX</ogc:Literal>
    <ogc:Function name="env">
        <ogc:Literal>wms_bbox</ogc:Literal>
    </ogc:Function>
</ogc:Function>
```

This `<ogc:Function>` element tells the heatmap function about the extents of the data to generate the weighted surface across. The name of the parameter is `outputBBOX`, indicated by the `<ogc:Literal>outputBBOX</ogc:Literal>` element. The value for this parameter is another `<ogc:Function>` element with the name `env`, which indicates that its value is derived from the WMS request. In this case, it is reading the `wms_bbox` environment variable to get the extents of the map being requested.

Once all of the functions parameters have been specified, the remainder of the SLD can contain the `<sld:Rule>` elements to describe how you want the output to be rendered. If the function is the one that receives a vector dataset as its input and then outputs raster, it must contain the name of the geometry attribute from the source vector data.

Including the geometry attribute is required, despite the output not being vector, in order for the SLD to pass validation. Without it, the SLD will fail validation and not work correctly.

If you get validation errors when validating the SLD, make sure that you have a `<Geometry>` element in the SLD. For the heatmap example, we are going to create a simple color ramp from red (high) to yellow (low). High-intensity areas will be red, drifting out to yellow as the density becomes less intense:

```
<RasterSymbolizer>
    <Geometry>
        <ogc:PropertyName>geom</ogc:PropertyName>
    </Geometry>
    <Opacity>0.6</Opacity>
    <ColorMap>
      <ColorMapEntry color="#FFFFFF" quantity="0" label="nodata"
opacity="0" />
      <ColorMapEntry color="#FFFF00" quantity="0.1" label="0.1" />
      <ColorMapEntry color="#FF8000" quantity="0.5" label="0.5" />
      <ColorMapEntry color="#FF0000" quantity="1.0" label="1.0" />
    </ColorMap>
</RasterSymbolizer>
```

The output of the heatmap rendering transformation is a raster, so we need to use a `<RasterSymbolizer>` element to describe how we want the raster to be styled. The raster is a surface, with each cell having a value from 0 to 1 so that we use this to construct a color map for the range. In this case, we are creating a color map for each 0.1 value change; this will give us a very fine transition from yellow to red on the output, but if we wanted to, we could cut out some of the intermediate values and let GeoServer interpolate them itself. For example:

```
<RasterSymbolizer>
    <Geometry>
        <ogc:PropertyName>geom</ogc:PropertyName>
    </Geometry>
    <Opacity>0.6</Opacity>
    <ColorMap>
      <ColorMapEntry color="#FFFFFF" quantity="0" label="nodata"
opacity="0" />
      <ColorMapEntry color="#FAFF00" quantity="0.1" label="0.1" />
      <ColorMapEntry color="#FAE200" quantity="0.2" label="0.2" />
      <ColorMapEntry color="#FBC600" quantity="0.3" label="0.3" />
      <ColorMapEntry color="#FBAA00" quantity="0.4" label="0.4" />
      <ColorMapEntry color="#FC8D00" quantity="0.5" label="0.5" />
      <ColorMapEntry color="#FC7100" quantity="0.6" label="0.6" />
      <ColorMapEntry color="#FD5500" quantity="0.7" label="0.7" />
      <ColorMapEntry color="#FD3800" quantity="0.8" label="0.8" />
```

```
            <ColorMapEntry color="#FE1C00" quantity="0.9" label="0.9" />
            <ColorMapEntry color="#FF0000" quantity="1.0" label="1.0" />
        </ColorMap>
    </RasterSymbolizer>
```

The two are equivalent in terms of output, so go with the former to keep your SLD from becoming too bloated.

> Did you notice that in both cases, we had a `<ColorMapEntry>` element to match to the value of 0? This is a special rule that we use to set the `nodata` values to white and then make them transparent; otherwise, the `nodata` cells will obscure any underlying base mapping that we use for context. It is also worth noting that we included an `<opacity>` element with a value of 0.6 (60 percent). Again, this is so that our heatmap surface will overlay nicely with any base mapping layers that we have.

Once you have saved the style to your GeoServer, go to the **Layers** page and set the style to the parameterized SQL View of the UK Street Level Crime data. Later in this chapter, we will look at how we can use prerequest filtering of data to show only the points that we are interested in. The result of this heatmap SLD will be a nice surface that shows the density of crime within a given area:

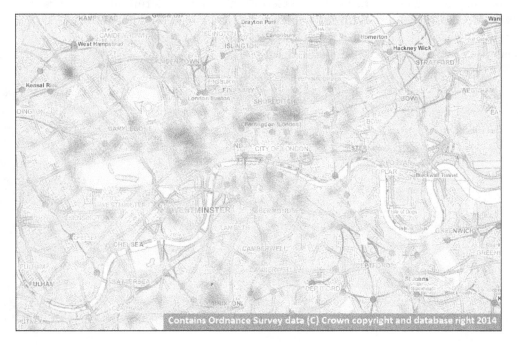

Styling data using Cascaded Style Sheets

Although SLDs are the default method to apply styles to the data served by GeoServer, it is not the only way. There is an extension available that adds the ability to provide styling information using **Cascaded Style Sheets (CSS)**. There are a couple of reasons why you might choose to use CSS styles over traditional SLDs:

- If you have built any kind of web page, then you are likely already familiar with the syntax of CSS
- The CSS syntax is much leaner than SLD, making styles more readable
- You don't need to understand XML, making CSS styles less prone to syntax errors

Getting started with CSS styles is as easy as installing the extension and restarting GeoServer.

Installing the extension

Like with all other GeoServer extensions, installation of the CSS extension is as straightforward as copying some JAR files to the `<geoserver_home>/WEB-INF/lib` folder and restarting GeoServer. First, we must download the version of the extension that matches the version of GeoServer that we are running. In our case, we are working with the current stable version, which, at the time of writing this book, is Version 2.5.2. Therefore, we need to download the extension from `http://geoserver.org/release/stable`:

Select the **CSS Styling** link from the **Miscellaneous** section on the download page and save it on your system. Open a command-line tool and execute the following command:

```
$ unzip geoserver-2.5.2-css-plugin.zip *.jar <tomcat_home>/webapps/
geoserver/WEB-INF/lib
```

This command will extract the contents of the extension's ZIP file into the `lib` directory of GeoServer. Make sure that you change `<tomcat_home>` to the location where you have installed Tomcat, and if you have more than one instance, then remember to run the command for all. Once the extension is installed, restart all of your GeoServer instances. If the **CSS Styling** extension is installed correctly, then you will see an entry for **CSS Styles** in the left-hand side menu of GeoServer's web administration console:

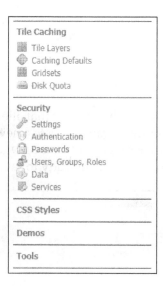

Clicking on the link will open the **CSS Styles** page and allow us to create and edit CSS styles for layers. The page has two main sections to it:

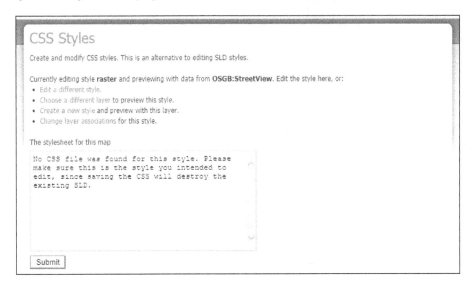

The top section of the page provides the controls that allow us to edit existing styles. Choose the layer to preview the style against, create a new style, and change the associations of layers to styles. There is a textbox area where we can create or edit the CSS style and a **Submit** button when we are ready to save the CSS style to GeoServer.

The bottom section of the page provides a tabbed view of preview panels to help us when we try to craft our masterpiece. The **Generated SLD** tab provides a preview of what the SLD equivalent of our CSS style is. This is useful if we are familiar with SLD constructs, as we can see how our CSS rules are interpreted as SLD. This is a useful feature when debugging why our CSS rules are not giving us the output we expect.

 It's useful to be able to access the generated SLD to load it into other tools such as QGIS. QGIS can be used to check the SLD for errors, edit it further visually, or simply apply it to a dataset in QGIS.

Clicking on the **Submit** button will update the generated SLD. The **Map** tab acts in the same way as the **Generated SLD** tab; the difference is that we get a visual preview of the CSS rules applied to actual map data. The **Data** tab acts as a quick reference to the layer currently being used to apply the CSS rules. The following is an example using the UK Street Level Crime data that we loaded in *Chapter 3, Working with Vector Data in Spatial Databases*.

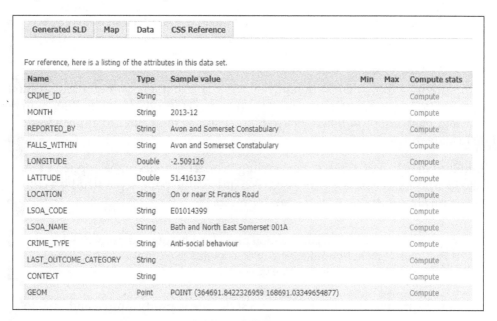

The table that is generated allows us to see the dataset's schema and also provides a sample value. This is very useful to act as a quick reference to the data when creating CSS rules that filter or manipulate features based on the value of one or more properties. The final tab is the **CSS Reference** tab, and it is effectively an IFRAME into which the CSS reference documentation is loaded. This allows us to check on CSS styling rules and syntax without having to leave the editor.

The basics of CSS styles

CSS-based styles work in the same way as SLD-based styles, using rules to match features and then applying a style to the matched set. A CSS-based style rule follows this pattern:

```
Selector {
    Property_name : property_value
}
```

Those of you familiar with CSS will immediately recognize this structure. The `selector` element is what GeoServer will use to select features to apply the styling to. To select all the features, use an asterisk (*) as the selector; to select features based on properties, use a valid ECQL filter as the selector.

> For more information on how to use filters to select features by properties, take a look at the GeoServer documentation at `http://docs.geoserver.org/stable/en/user/extensions/css/filters.html`. Further information on ECQL can be found at `http://docs.geoserver.org/stable/en/user/tutorials/cql/cql_tutorial.html`.

It is important to know that by default, a CSS style will not render anything. When using CSS styles, you must have a minimum of one rule; otherwise, nothing will be styled, and blank maps will be rendered. You can use the * filter to apply a basic style to all features.

Within the curly braces, there are the styling properties that can be applied to the selected feature(s). These are expressed as name/value pairs separated by a colon (`:`); they are almost the same as in standard CSS.

> The GeoServer documentation provides a list of valid properties to use in styling at `http://docs.geoserver.org/stable/en/user/extensions/css/properties.html`.

As we can see, the basic structure of a CSS style rule is pretty simple and easy to understand. Consider the following example rule:

```
* {
  fill: #FF0000;
  stroke-width: 0.5;
}
```

Looking at this rule, we will expect to see all the features given a fill color of red (`fill: #FF0000`) with a border width of 0.5 (`stroke-width: 0.5`). However, if we actually apply this rule to a layer, then what we will see are polygons filled with red but without any border. This happened because the CSS styling extension has the concept of a key property for each symbolizer. If a key property is not present in the rule, then all the child properties will be ignored. In the previous example, the key property for the border is `stroke`, and as this is not present, the `stroke-width` property is ignored. Let's rewrite the previous rule to:

```
* {
    fill: #FF0000;
    stroke: #000000;
    stroke-width: 0.5;
}
```

We will now see polygon features with a red fill and black border (`stroke: #000000`) that is 0.5 thick. The following table lists the key properties for each of the symbolizers:

Property name	Symbolizer	Description
`fill`	Polygon	This property specifies whether a polygon fill is applied; the value is either the color or a graphic
`stroke`	Polygon and line	This property specifies whether line or polygon outlines are applied; the value is either the color or a graphic
`mark`	Point	This property specifies whether point marks are applied; the value is a well-known mark or URL to an image
`label`	Text	This property specifies whether the text is drawn on the map as labels; the value is an ECQL expression for the property that contains the value to be used as the label
`Halo-radius`	Text	This property specifies whether to draw a halo around labels or not; the value is the size of the halo

Now that we understand the basics of CSS styling, let's take a look at an example using one of the datasets we loaded in *Chapter 3, Working with Vector Data in Spatial Databases*.

Putting it all together

Now let's take a look at bringing all of this together to create a style for one of the datasets that we loaded into GeoServer. For this example, we are going to use the UK Level Street Crime data that we loaded in *Chapter 3, Working with Vector Data in Spatial Databases*. The objective of this style will be to create a symbol for each point based on the value of its CRIME_TYPE property. The following is the legend for what we are trying to achieve:

```
❋  Vehicle crime
❋  Criminal damage and arson
❋  Other crime
❋  Robbery
❋  Other theft
❋
❋  Burglary
❋  Public disorder and weapons
❋  Shoplifting
❋  Anti-social behaviour
❋  Violent crime
❋  Drugs
```

First, we need to make sure that we are on the **CSS Styles** page by selecting the option from the left-hand side panel of GeoServer's web administration console. Before we create the new style, we need to specify the layer that we want to work with; this will be the layer that appears in the **Map** tab and allows us to preview our style as we create it.

Click on the link called **Choose a different layer** and select the crime data layer that we loaded in *Chapter 3, Working with Vector Data in Spatial Databases*.

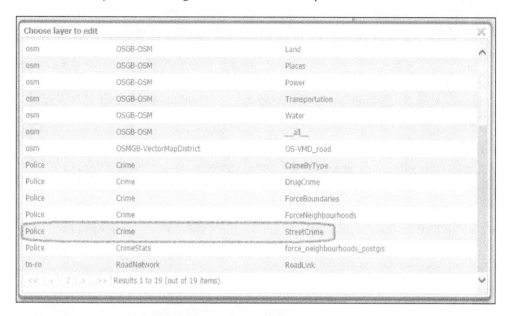

When we click on the layer name, the layer selection dialog will close. The text on the page will change to indicate that we are now previewing data from the `Police:StreetCrime` layer.

Now, we need to click on the link called **Create a new style** to open a new dialog where we can specify the name and workspace for the new style we that create. The workspace is not a required value, and leaving it blank will not impact the way the style functions.

Click on the **Create** button to dismiss the dialog. The **CSS Styles** page is now set up and ready for us to work on with our CSS style. We can make edits inside the textbox and then click on the **Submit** button to have them committed. The **Map** and **Generated SLD** tab contents will be updated to reflect the changes made to the CSS style.

 The syntax of our style will be checked without the need to press the **Submit** button; however, the **Map** and the **Generated SLD** tab contents are only updated after clicking on **Submit**.

To create the output for this style, we are going to create a CSS style that uses selectors to filter the data based on the CRIME_TYPE property. The complete CSS style file can be downloaded from the website of this book; look for the file called CrimeByType_CSS_Style.css.

Let's take a look at the most important elements of this file, starting with the first rule:

```
* {
  mark: symbol('x');
}
```

The asterisk (*) is a wildcard, which means that it will select all the features; essentially, this rule means that all the features will be given a symbol of an X. The next rule following on from this one is:

```
:mark {
  stroke: #000000;
  stroke-width: 1;
  fill: #C0C0C0;
}
```

This rule uses a pseudo-class selector to select all the symbol elements (points) in the output. This rule is used to provide a common set of styling properties to be applied to all the points, irrespective of their CRIME_TYPE property. In this case, we will apply a black outline (stroke: #000000) with a width of 1 (stroke-width: 1) and a light-gray fill (fill: #C0C0C0). It is beneficial to have this *catch-all* rule, as it means that any points that do not match our following rules will be displayed with a default style.

There are a number of different pseudo-class selectors that can be used to select symbols. Take a look at the **Symbol Selectors** section of the CSS documentation at `http://docs.geoserver.org/2.4.x/en/user/extensions/css/styled-marks.html` for a complete list.

The next set of rules all follow the same structure and provide different colors for the points based on their `CRIME_TYPE` property. For example:

```
/*@title Anti-social behaviour */
[CRIME_TYPE = 'Anti-social behaviour'] :mark {
  fill: #1932ff;
}
```

There are a couple of elements to this rule for us to examine. The first and most important element is the selector itself. This is any valid ECQL filter and is used to select the data to style based on the value of a property, in this case, `CRIME_TYPE`. This particular selector will select all the points whose `CRIME_TYPE` is equal to " anti-social behavior." The rule will then provide a color for the point using the `fill` property. The same rule is then repeated for each of the categories that we need to create, with the selector property as well as the value for the `fill` color changing.

Did you notice that there is a comment at the start of the rule? This provides an element of metadata that GeoServer can use when generating the SLD equivalent of this style. It can also be used within the legend that is output in response to WMS `GetLegendGraphic` requests. There are two elements of metadata that can be included at the start of a rule.

Metadata tag	Description
`@title`	This tag provides the title value to be used when this rule is selected for inclusion in a legend
`@abstract`	This tag provides a description of what the rule is depicting

The two metadata elements can be combined and must always be *before* the rule to which they apply. An example of combining the two will be:

```
/*
 * @title This is the legend label
 * @abstract This is a description of the rule
 */
```

The final set of rules for this style allows us to specify different-sized symbols based on the zoom level of the map:

```
[@scale < 20000] {
    mark-size: 12;
}

[@scale > 20000] [@scale < 100000] {
    mark-size: 8;
}

[@scale > 100000] {
    mark-size: 4;
}
```

These three rules define a range of scales at which different-sized point symbols should be drawn. Anything below a scale of 1:20,000 will be drawn with a size of 12, and anything above 1:100,000 will be drawn with a size of 4. Anything in between will be drawn with a size of 8. The mark-size property specifies the size for the mark, and the @scale selector is a pseudo-attribute that provides the rendering context, in this case based on the scale denominator.

That is all there is to it. Submitting this CSS style will save it to GeoServer, and we can then use it like any other style. Assign it to the UK Street Level Crime data and then have a look at the Layer Preview:

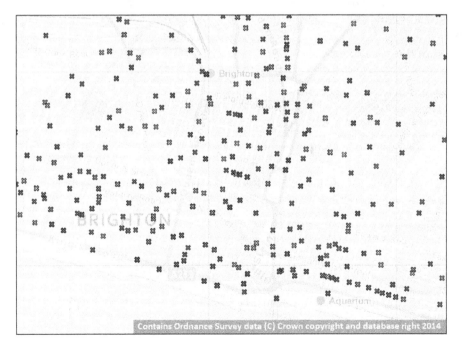

As discussed earlier, one of the reasons we might wish to utilize CSS styles over standard SLDs is because CSS styles can be less verbose than SLD. We already saw this by the way in which we set up the base style properties common to all the points and then simply varied the fill color on each rule. In an SLD, we will have to repeat all the basic style properties on each rule, and then we will have to repeat each rule three times for the different scale denominations. The result is that the SLD file is significantly more verbose. Consider the following fragment:

```
<sld:Rule>
    <sld:Title>Robbery </sld:Title>
    <ogc:Filter>
      <ogc:PropertyIsEqualTo>
        <ogc:PropertyName>CRIME_TYPE</ogc:PropertyName>
        <ogc:Literal>Robbery</ogc:Literal>
      </ogc:PropertyIsEqualTo>
    </ogc:Filter>
    <sld:MaxScaleDenominator>20000.0</sld:MaxScaleDenominator>
    <sld:PointSymbolizer>
      <sld:Graphic>
        <sld:Mark>
          <sld:WellKnownName>x</sld:WellKnownName>
          <sld:Fill>
            <sld:CssParameter name="fill">#27a800</sld:CssParameter>
          </sld:Fill>
          <sld:Stroke/>
        </sld:Mark>
        <sld:Size>12</sld:Size>
      </sld:Graphic>
    </sld:PointSymbolizer>
</sld:Rule>
```

This is 26 lines for one rule to style points based on the CRIME_TYPE property being equal to "Robbery", and this is only for the lowest zoom level. This rule will need to be repeated twice with only the `<sld:MinScaleDenominator>`, `<sld:MaxScaleDenominator>`, and `<sld:Size>` elements varying. Take a look for yourself; I have placed the equivalent SLD style in the same location as the CSS style for download. Look for the file named CrimeByType_SLD_Style.sld and open it up in an editor. If your editor has line numbers, then you will see that this file is 999 lines long, whereas the equivalent CSS file (CrimeByType_CSS_Style.css) is only 65 lines.

One final thing to touch on for CSS styling is the ability to combine styles into a single rule to create a compound style. This is achieved using the multivalued properties capability in CSS styles. This approach is useful for situations where you want to paint a feature multiple times to create an effect; the most common use case for this will be to create cased lines to indicate roads. Consider the following example:

```
[ROAD_TYPE = 'Motorway'] {
    stroke: #0000FF, #000000;
    stroke-width: 5px, 3px;
    stroke-linecap: round;
    z-index: 0, 1;
}
```

This example assumes that the dataset it is being applied to contains a property called ROAD_TYPE, and the dataset uses it to select all the roads that are of type Motorway. It then draws the line feature twice as indicated by the two comma-separated values for the stroke property. In this case, it will draw the line first in blue and then a second time in white, the order being indicated by the comma-separated integers for the z-index property. The effect of casing the line, to create a blue line with a white fill, is done by varying the width of the line using the stroke-width property. The blue line is drawn with a width of 5, and the white line is drawn with a width of 3. This is because the z-index indicates that the blue line is drawn first (because it has the lowest value) and the white line is drawn on top. As it is thinner, the blue line will effectively appear to be the border.

Multivalued properties can be used in this way to create a wide range of styling effects.

Per-request styling of map features

It is possible to ask GeoServer to render features in a style that does not exist within its own catalog. This ability to do per-request styling is also referred to as external styles.

 Per-request styling of map features is part of the OGC WMS standard. Any web mapping software that conforms to the standard will contain a similar capability. As this is a book on GeoServer, we will explore GeoServer's implementation of the WMS standard.

There are three different ways in which an external style can be provided to GeoServer:

- The SLD= parameter can be set on the GetMap GET request to point at an Internet-accessible SLD file

- The SLD_BODY= parameter can be set on the GetMap GET request to provide the SLD document as a URL-encoded XML

- The SLD can be provided in the XML GetMap POST request body

The mode in which GeoServer works to apply the styling depends on whether or not the LAYERS parameter is included in the GetMap request. When the LAYERS parameter is not present, the supplied SLD file defines all of the layers and styles for the map's content. When the LAYERS parameter is present, GeoServer operates in **Library Mode**.

> An external style can also include new layers of data using the SLD <InlineFeature> element. This element can provide feature data within the SLD itself, along with information on how to style these features. This can be very useful, for example, to perform dynamic feature highlighting or provide additional elements of information on the map. The GeoServer documentation at http://docs.geoserver.org/2.4.x/en/user/styling/sld-reference/layers.html#sld-reference-inlinefeature has more details on this topic.

In Library Mode, any styles supplied externally are treated as a style library in their own right, and they extend the built-in GeoServer style catalog. This means that while rendering, the external styles will override the default server styles, based on a selection criteria. The details of the selection criteria that GeoServer uses can be found at http://docs.geoserver.org/2.4.x/en/user/styling/sld-working.html#library-mode.

Let's take a look at an implementation of external styling. In this example, we will take our UK Street Level Crime data and overlay it on an OpenStreetMap base layer. We will then add two versions of the same layer to the map. The first version will be requested without any specific styles so that GeoServer will render using the default style. The second layer will be added with a simple SLD_BODY style that will style all the points as a *circle* with a black outline and a red fill. The code for this example can be downloaded from the Packt Publishing website of this book. To demonstrate this capability, we are going to create a simple OpenLayers application; the code is contained within the Index.html file and links to the OpenLayers.js file in the lib directory.

The first layer is added to the map without any styling information:

```
defaultCrimeLyr = new OpenLayers.Layer.WMS(
    "UK Street Level Crime",
    baseWMSUrl,
    {
    "layers": "Police:StreetCrime",
    "format": "image/png",
    "transparent": "TRUE",
    "version": "1.1.1"
    ,
    {
        isBaseLayer: false
    }
);
```

This code fragment creates an `OpenLayers.Layer.WMS` layer that points to our GeoServer WMS end-point (specified by the `baseWMSUrl` variable) and requests the `Police:StreetCrime` layer. Notice that there is no style requested, which means that GeoServer will render the layer using whatever style we specified as the default. In this case, it is using the CSS style we defined earlier in this chapter. When we use the OpenLayers layer control to switch this layer on, we should see the default style:

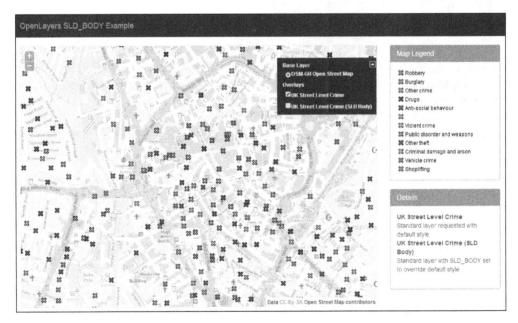

The second layer is added to the map with styling information:

```
sldCrimeLyr = new OpenLayers.Layer.WMS(
  "UK Street Level Crime",
  baseWMSUrl,
  {
    "layers": "Police:StreetCrime",
    "format": "image/png",
    "transparent": "TRUE",
    "version": "1.1.1",
    "SLD_BODY": sldBody
  },
  {
     isBaseLayer: false
  }
);
```

The only difference between this OpenLayers.Layer.WMS definition and the previous one is the addition of the SLD_BODY request parameter, whose value is the sldBody variable. When we use the OpenLayers layer control to switch this layer on, we should see the layer styled using our external style.

The sldBody variable itself is defined as follows:

```
sldBody = '<?xml version="1.0" encoding="utf-
8"?><StyledLayerDescriptor version="1.0.0" xmlns="http://
www.opengis.net/sld" xmlns:gml="http://www.opengis.net/gml"
xmlns:ogc="http://www.opengis.net/ogc" xmlns:xlink="http://www.
w3.org/1999/xlink" xmlns:xsi="http://www.w3.org/2001/XMLSchema-
instance" xsi:schemaLocation="http://www.opengis.net/sld http://
schemas.opengeospatial.net/sld/1.0.0/StyledLayerDescriptor.xsd"
><NamedLayer><Name>Police:StreetCrime</Name><UserStyle><Feature
TypeStyle><Rule><PointSymbolizer><Graphic><Mark><WellKnownName>
circle</WellKnownName><Fill><CssParameter name="fill">#B0B0FF</
CssParameter></Fill><Stroke><CssParameter name="stroke">#0000FF</
CssParameter><CssParameter name="stroke-width">1</CssParameter></
Stroke></Mark><Size>10</Size></Graphic></PointSymbolizer></Rule></
FeatureTypeStyle></UserStyle></NamedLayer></StyledLayerDescriptor>';
```

Simply, it is a valid SLD in XML as a string variable. Notice how the <Name> child element of the <NamedLayer> parent exactly matches the name of the layer that we are applying SLD_BODY to, including its workspace. If we did not make the value a fully qualified name, then the style will not be applied to the layer.

Turning this layer on in the OpenLayers layer switcher and turning the original layer off will show the style to be overridden:

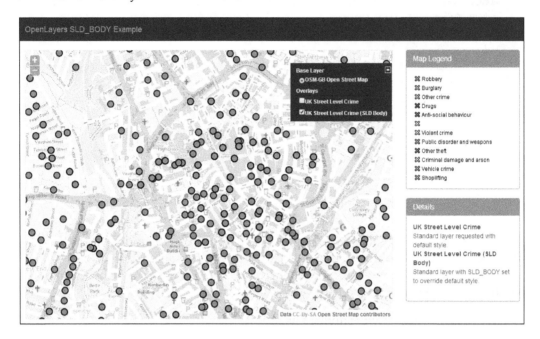

When using SLD_BODY to send external styles, be careful about the size of the SLD itself. There is a limit on the total length of a URL, and adding a complex SLD will likely cause you to reach this limit.

> Remember to always ensure that you provide the content for the SLD_BODY URL encoded to ensure that it is properly handled by web browsers.

If the length of your SLD is an issue, then consider storing it as a web-accessible file. Then, use the SLD request parameter or make your GetMap requests using HTTP POST, with the SLD being defined in the request body.

Per-request filtering of data

The WMS specification allows the use of vendor parameters in requests. Vendor parameters are non-standard (that is; the parameter is not part of the OGC specification) request parameters that have been implemented by a vendor to provide enhanced capabilities. While vendor parameters are useful to provide enhanced capabilities, care must be taken when using them in your own client-side implementations. If you are making a generic client application that can target multiple WMS servers, then it is quite likely that they will be from a range of vendors. If you use a vendor-specific request parameter to a server that is not aware of it, you might see errors occurring. However, if you know for sure that you are targeting a GeoServer WMS, then there are a number of vendor-specific request parameters available.

> A complete list of the vendor-specific WMS parameters that GeoServer supports is available at `http://docs.geoserver.org/2.4.x/en/user/services/wms/vendor.html#wms-vendor-parameters`.

We are going to take a look at one vendor-specific parameter in particular, the `CQL_FILTER` parameter. This parameter is of interest because it will allow us to send a filter parameter as part of our request to GeoServer. In response, GeoServer will return the data resulting from the filter. A CQL filter can range in complexity from a simple filter in a dataset attribute through to a compound filter query that contains a mix of attribute and spatial filter queries.

> The `CQL_FILTER` syntax is expressed using ECQL, which is a compact and readable query language. Details of the language can be found at `http://docs.geoserver.org/2.4.x/en/user/filter/ecql_reference.html#filter-ecql-reference`. A tutorial on using the language can be found at `http://docs.geoserver.org/2.4.x/en/user/tutorials/cql/cql_tutorial.html#cql-tutorial`.

To demonstrate how useful the `CQL_FILTER` parameter can be, we are going to create a simple OpenLayers application to apply filters to the UK Street Level Crime data that we loaded in *Chapter 3, Working with Vector Data in Spatial Databases*. The basic application is available in the code bundle of this book.

Have a look at the folder named `PerRequestFiltering` and load the contents into a web server. Most of the code contained within the `Index.html` file is fairly standard HTML and OpenLayers code. The most interesting function for us to discuss is:

```
function changeMapFilter(){
    // Get the selected option from the user
    var crimeTypeSelect = document.getElementById("crimeFilter");
    var crimeOption = crimeTypeSelect.options[crimeTypeSelect.
selectedIndex].value;

    // Apply the filter
    if (crimeOption == 'None') {
      // Clear the filter to get back all data
      crimeLyr.mergeNewParams({ "CQL_FILTER" : null});
    } else {
      // A type has been selected to filter on, apply the filter
      crimeLyr.mergeNewParams({ "CQL_FILTER": "CRIME_TYPE = '" +
crimeOption + "'" });
    }
}
```

This `changeMapFilter` function is triggered when a user changes the value from the drop-down list that contains the different crime type options. When the selection is made, we will first get a reference to the option that was selected, as shown in lines 3 and 4. Once we have the chosen value, we can then react to it. First, we will check to see if the value is `None`; if it is, then the code removes any `CQL_FILTER` parameter values that are set on the layer. Effectively, this means that the filter is no longer applied, so GeoServer will return all of our data. If the value is something other than `None`, then we need to set a value for the `CQL_FILTER` parameter on our layer. OpenLayers has a method on layers called `mergeNewParams`, which allows us to set new parameters (or change the value of the existing ones) on requests for the layer it is called from. In our case, we will change the value for the filter to:

```
CRIME_TYPE = '<value>'
```

Where `<value>` is the value of the option selected from the drop-down list. When we call the `mergeNewParams` method, OpenLayers will apply it and make a new request for the layer. Once a user selects an option from the drop-down list, the layer is immediately refreshed and will show only the crime locations matching the chosen value.

For example, if the user selected `Robbery` as the value, then they would see the following output:

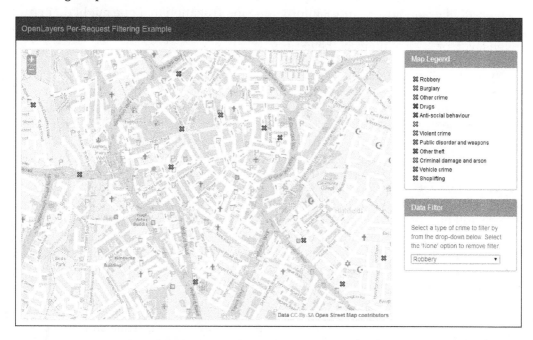

All of the data has been filtered, and only the crimes of type `Robbery` remain, shown by the light-green colored points.

Using Freemarker templates to change WMS responses

Until now, the methods of controlling GeoServer output we have focused on have been concerned with the rendered output. We are going to change the track slightly now and take a look at how we can manipulate the response that GeoServer provides to WMS `GetFeatureInfo` requests.

A `GetFeatureInfo` request is a standard WMS request that returns the feature information for a given location on a map for one or more layers. In essence, it is the equivalent of a standard feature's information interrogation that one might do in a Desktop GIS. GeoServer receives the request and then calculates if any features of the given layer, or layers, intersect the location specified.

If any features are *hit*, then they are included in the response to the request. The format of this response is dependent on the value specified for the `INFO_FORMAT` request parameter. GeoServer has a number of formats that can be output, but in each case, the generated output is fixed. For the majority of cases, this will probably be fine; however, there might be circumstances where it will be good to control the output generated, for example, to create custom JSON output or, perhaps, even XML.

Luckily for us, GeoServer makes use of something called **Freemarker** templates that allow us to create custom outputs when the `INFO_FORMAT` is specified as `text/html`. The default output is to provide a list of features *hit* at the given location in a simple HTML table, with one table for each layer, where one or more features are *hit*. Using Freemarker templates, it is possible to alter the way in which the content is rendered; for example, images can be rendered in place of the attributes where there is a library of images that match feature identifiers.

We learned that output is controlled by Freemarker templates. To learn more about Freemarker templates and how to use them, take a look at *Designer Guide* at `http://freemarker.org/docs/dgui.html` and the GeoServer introduction at `http://docs.geoserver.org/2.4.x/en/user/tutorials/freemarker.html`.

In the context of the `GetFeatureInfo` templates, GeoServer looks in three locations to determine how to respond to a request:

- Inside the `FeatureType` directory for `content.ftl`
- Inside the `DataStore` directory for `content.ftl`
- Inside the `Workspace` directory for `content.ftl`

From this list, we can see that the templates can be used at the feature, data store, and workspace levels. If, for example, we have a template inside the data store directory, then this template will be used for all the feature types that come from this data store. There are also two global overrides in the form of the root of the workspaces folder and also the templates folder in the root of the data directory. What is particularly interesting here though is the ability to create templates inside the FeatureType directory; this means that it is possible for us to be able to define feature-specific templates. This can be very useful for cases where you need to show responses to information requests on specific layers in a certain way.

For example, the default template will display all the attributes from a layer that might not be desirable. Instead, you might need to control the output for specific layers so that not all attributes are output, perhaps, to conceal some data not relevant to general usage of the dataset. A template itself consists of three files:

- The Header.ftl file provides the header or introductory information for the output format and is usually fixed. In the case of an HTML output, this file contains the standard <html>, <head>, and opening <body> tags. Generally speaking, you will not do any feature processing on this file. This file is only ever called once.

- The Content.ftl file is the core of the template, and it is in this file that you will write the logic to process the content of features and feature collections. In the case of the HTML output, this file contains the logic to generate all of the HTML tables that display the attribute name and values of the features. This file is called multiple times, and each time it is supplied with a collection of features, all of which are the same type.

- The Footer.ftl file is the final template file and is used to close off anything to make the output valid. For HTML output, this file will contain the closing </body> and </html> tags. Like the header file, this one is typically static and will not contain any feature-processing logic. This file is only ever called once.

We are now going to take what we have just learned and develop a new output for the `GetFeatureInfo` requests that will be applied globally. This new output will be an XML response that provides a collection of layers and the features found within them. This response format will be useful in situations where we might want to create an application that queries all the layers and shows the response consolidated in a single dialog, such as this example from the Marine Scotland National Marine Plan Interactive available at http://www.scotland.gov.uk/Topics/marine/seamanagement/nmpihome:

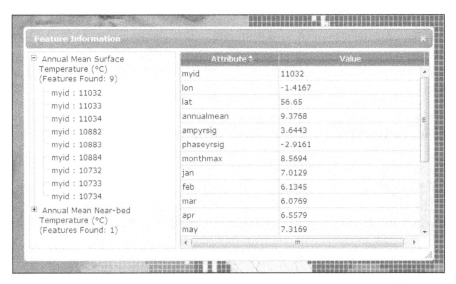

To be able to get a multiple layer response from a `GetFeatureInfo` request, we need to override the templates at a global level. To do this, we need to create a directory called `templates` within our GeoServer data directory; the `templates` directory will contain the three `.ftl` files that we just discussed.

The `header.ftl` file is very simple:

```
<?xml version='1.0' encoding='utf-8'?>
<Features>
```

Here, we are simply defining the fact that the output is XML, and the root element for the document is called `<Features>`. The `footer.ftl` file is even simpler:

```
</Features>
```

It contains a single line that closes off the root element. The meat of the template is contained within the `content.ftl` file:

```
<#list features as feature>
<Feature layerName='${type.name}' fid='${feature.fid}'>
<Attributes>
<#list feature.attributes as attribute>
<#if !attribute.isGeometry>
<Attribute name='${attribute.name}'>${attribute.value}</Attribute>
</#if>
</#list>
</Attributes>
</Feature>
</#list>
```

Once again, this is a fairly simple template file. To start with, we will define that we want to loop through all of the features returned from the query. Remember that the `content.ftl` file is called multiple times, and each call passes a feature collection. We will use the Freemarker template `<#list>` construct to perform a loop over each feature in the collection, and we will create a variable for each feature instance called `feature`. Inside this loop, we will construct our individual feature element by defining its opening element:

```
<Feature layerName='${type.name}' fid='${feature.fid}'>
```

This uses variable substitution to give us the name of the layer the feature belongs to and its unique identifier. Next, we will create an `<Attributes>` element that will contain the details of the attributes for the feature. Once again, this is a loop using the `<#list>` instruction; this time we are looping over the collection of attributes by specifying `feature.attributes` in the loop definition. For each attribute in the collection, we need to check that it is not the geometry of the feature. The `if` statement `!attribute.isGeometry` will return `true` if the attribute is not the geometry of the feature. If the attribute is a normal feature attribute, then we will create an `<Attribute>` element:

```
<Attribute name='${attribute.name}'>${attribute.value}</Attribute>
```

Again, we will use variable substitution to get the name and value of the attribute and then create an appropriate element to represent it. The end result is that we will get a response back from the server similar to the following:

```
<?xml version='1.0' encoding='utf-8'?>
<Features>
<Feature layerName='StreetCrime' fid='StreetCrime.155221'>
<Attributes>
<Attribute name='CRIME_ID'></Attribute>
<Attribute name='MONTH'>2013-12</Attribute>
```

```
<Attribute name='REPORTED_BY'>Lancashire Constabulary</Attribute>
<Attribute name='FALLS_WITHIN'>Lancashire Constabulary</Attribute>
<Attribute name='LONGITUDE'>-3.042373</Attribute>
<Attribute name='LATITUDE'>53.819259</Attribute>
<Attribute name='LOCATION'>On or near Shopping Area</Attribute>
<Attribute name='LSOA_CODE'>E01012675</Attribute>
<Attribute name='LSOA_NAME'>Blackpool 010B</Attribute>
<Attribute name='CRIME_TYPE'>Anti-social behaviour</Attribute>
<Attribute name='LAST_OUTCOME_CATEGORY'></Attribute>
<Attribute name='CONTEXT'></Attribute>
</Attributes>
</Feature>
</Features>
```

This is only a simple example with one feature returned, but in reality, this will be a list of features from multiple layers. Recall how we created this template so that it was global? This means that all the responses for text/html will now actually receive results in our new format, which will show all the attributes. But what if for some layers, we want to override this behavior by only including certain attributes? Well, in this case, we can place a new content.ftl file inside the feature type folder to override the global one inside the templates folder. For example:

```
<#list features as feature>
<Feature layerName='${type.name}' fid='${feature.fid}'>
<Attributes>
<Attribute name='Crime Type'>${feature.CRIME_TYPE.value}</Attribute>
<Attribute name='Month'>${feature.MONTH.value}</Attribute>
<Attribute name='Reported By'>${feature.REPORTED_BY.value}</Attribute>
</Attributes>
</Feature>
</#list>
```

The preceding snippet will generate a response, still using our core structure, but with only three of the attributes actually exposed:

```
<?xml version='1.0' encoding='utf-8'?>
<Features>
<Feature layerName='StreetCrime' fid='StreetCrime.155221'>
<Attributes>
<Attribute name='Crime Type'>Anti-social behaviour</Attribute>
<Attribute name='Month'>2013-12</Attribute>
<Attribute name='Reported By'>Lancashire Constabulary</Attribute>
</Attributes>
</Feature>
```

This will allow us to hide certain attributes that we might not want to make public, through the WMS GetFeatureInfo requests.

Summary

In this chapter, we took a look at some of the different ways in which we can take control of GeoServer. From advanced uses of SLD styles to manipulating the response from a WMS `GetFeatureInfo` request, we saw how powerful and flexible GeoServer can be.

We saw how we can benefit from the presence of the WPS extension when it comes to creating SLD styles to render maps. By making use of the render transformations that the WPS extension provides, we saw how easy it is to create a style that can dynamically generate a response based on our source data. To illustrate this, we saw how we can create a style that can generate heatmaps from any point dataset.

After looking at an advanced SLD, we learned about an alternative means of creating styles for our maps. We learned that the CSS style extension allows us to take a common web standard, Cascading Style Sheets, and use it to describe styling rules for our maps. The benefit of using the CSS style extension is that it opens up the potential for others in our organization to create map styles without having to learn the complexities of SLD.

As it adheres to all the OGC standards for WMS, we saw how it is possible to request a map from GeoServer and tell it how it should be styled. Instead of being stuck with the built-in styles for GeoServer or having to log in to GeoServer to create them, we can actually send the SLD we want GeoServer to use when rendering the map. Along with sending SLD content in requests, we also saw how easy it is to send requests with a filtering query attached. Per-request filtering using the CQL filtering language allows us to *thin* out the data that we get back from GeoServer, based on some form of filtering query.

Finally, we looked at how we can manipulate the output from a WMS `GetFeatureInfo` request through the use of custom Freemarker templates. This is very useful in situations where you might want to create your own custom feature information report control or where you need specific control over the output.

Now we know how to create great-looking maps. In the next chapter, we will learn how to turn them into output that can be printed to hard copies.

7
Using GeoServer to Print Maps

In this chapter, we will take a look at how we can publish our maps in such a way that we will be able to print them. We will explore the capabilities of the community-printing module in GeoServer to output maps using specific templates. Users will expect you to provide print capabilities within your web application. Traditionally, creating print output from a web application has been difficult.

If you have added print capabilities to a web mapping application in the past, you likely implemented this through a specific web page created to fit an A4-size page using various HTML and CSS techniques. Thankfully, things have moved on substantially, and now it is easier than ever to generate an output for printing. To understand how easy it is to add a print capability to your applications, we will explore the following topics:

- What the GeoServer print extension is and how it can be used
- How to install and configure the print extension
- Understand how the configuration is used to define templates
- How to make print requests to generate PDF output

By the end of this chapter, you will have GeoServer set up and ready to accept print requests from your web applications.

The GeoServer print extension

The **GeoServer print** extension is a community module that gives GeoServer the ability to generate output in a number of formats using a template system. The primary output for the extension is PDF; this can then be sent to a printer or other users.

 There are two types of extensions available for GeoServer: official extensions and community extensions. Official extensions form a part of the official release, are maintained, and should be considered stable. Community extensions are not part of the official release and should be considered *experimental* or *pending*. Some community extensions, such as the print extension, have been available for a long time and are reasonably stable.

The print extension itself is a container for the MapFish printing service, which provides an HTTP API interface for printing. The interface can be called from any mapping application that can make web calls, for example, JavaScript mapping applications. More details on MapFish printing can be found on its website at `http://www.mapfish.org/doc/print/`.

 MapFish (`http://www.mapfish.org`) is a web mapping application framework built on the Pylons Python web framework. It provides a number of tools and services for the rapid creation of web mapping applications, including a print service, and is OGC compliant.

Installing the print extension

The method to install the print extension is the same as any other extension in GeoServer. However, since it is a community extension, it won't be found in the usual download location. Community extensions are found in the nightly builds folder of the GeoServer project at `http://ares.boundlessgeo.com/geoserver/2.5.x/community-latest/`. Within this folder, look for the file named `geoserver-2.5-SNAPSHOT-printing-plugin.zip` and click on it to download. At the time of writing this book, the current stable version of GeoServer, and the one we are using, is Version 2.5.2. If you are using a more recent version, then replace the `2.5.x` element of the URL with the version number you are on.

Open a command line in the directory where you downloaded the file and enter the following command:

```
$ unzip geoserver-2.5-SNAPSHOT-printing-plugin.zip *.jar -d <tomcat_
home>/webapps/geoserver/WEB-INF/lib
```

This command will extract the files with a `.jar` extension into the `lib` folder of your GeoServer instance. The following screenshot shows the files that are contained in Version 2.5.x of the plugin:

Name	Type	Compressed size	Password p...	Size	Ratio	Date modified
gs-printing-2.5-SNAPSHOT.jar	Executable Jar File	15 KB	No	18 KB	16%	21/10/2014 15:34
jtsio-1.8.jar	Executable Jar File	27 KB	No	32 KB	14%	21/10/2014 15:34
jyaml-1.3.jar	Executable Jar File	52 KB	No	58 KB	12%	21/10/2014 15:34
mapfish-geo-lib-1.2-20090817094..	Executable Jar File	13 KB	No	14 KB	14%	21/10/2014 15:34
print-lib-1.2-20101018133712.jar	Executable Jar File	238 KB	No	258 KB	8%	21/10/2014 15:34
pvalsecc-0.9.2.jar	Executable Jar File	76 KB	No	84 KB	10%	21/10/2014 15:34
xercesImpl-2.7.1.jar	Executable Jar File	1,048 KB	No	1,176 KB	11%	21/10/2014 15:34
xml-apis-xerces-2.7.1.jar	Executable Jar File	150 KB	No	190 KB	22%	21/10/2014 15:34

Remember to change `<tomcat_home>` to the folder where your Tomcat instance is installed. Repeat the process for all of your Tomcat instances and then restart them.

Verifying the print extension installed

We have installed the extension into all of our GeoServer instances; we now need to verify whether everything worked. Unlike other extensions, the print extension does not provide any obvious indication that it is installed on the web administration console; for example, it does not place a menu item on the left-hand side panel. Instead, to verify that it is installed, we must check our data directory and look for a folder named `printing`. Within this folder, there should be a file named `config.yaml`. If the file exists, then the extension is installed correctly, and GeoServer has detected its presence.

Although there is no obvious indication from the web administration console that the extension has been installed, there is an area that we can check. The print extension includes a demonstration application that we can use to check whether it installed correctly:

1. On the left-hand side panel of the web administration console, there is a menu option called **Demos**:

2. Click on the link to open the page that lists the demo applications:

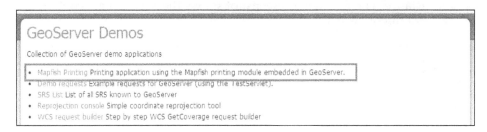

3. Click on the **Mapfish Printing** option to open a page that contains a GeoExt-based application where the test print requests can be made:

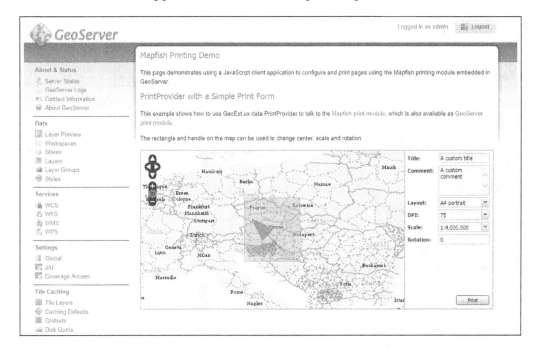

4. If the `printing` folder is present in the data directory, as shown in the following screenshot, and the demonstration the GeoExt application is present, then we have successfully installed the print extension:

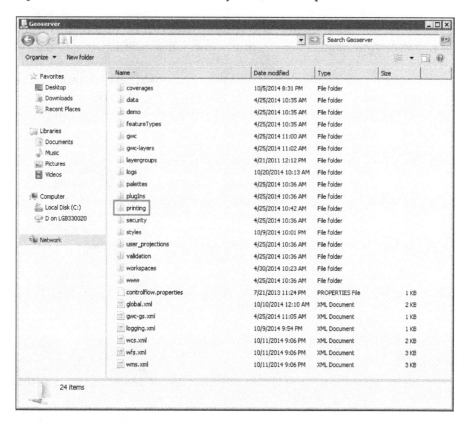

Configuring the print extension

Once installed, the extension provides a default configuration **YAML Ain't Markup Language (YAML)** file that can be used immediately. However, to get the most out of the extension, we need to understand how the configuration file controls the printing capabilities.

The print extension is configured using a configuration script called `config.yaml`; this is stored in the `printing` folder of the data directory. The configuration is written using the **YAML** language, which is a data-serialization standard that can be used in most programming languages.

For more details on the YAML language, visit the project website at http://www.yaml.org.

The configuration is broken up into sections, with each section relating to a specific element of the configuration. When the print extension is installed, it automatically creates a basic configuration that will be useful for most cases; however, we will learn about the structure of the configuration by creating our own custom implementation. The complete file that we will use can be obtained from the code-download website of this book, so it won't be completely replicated here. Instead, we will take a look at the more pertinent elements of the configuration.

 The YAML language uses whitespace to denote its structure, much like Python does. Indentation denotes the structure in YAML, with indentation being defined as one or more space characters at the start of a line. A YAML block is terminated when a new line with indentation less than the previous one is reached. Keep this in mind when editing the config.yaml file. It is a best practice to use space characters for whitespaces instead of tabs, as different systems will interpret the tab character differently. Most text editors can be configured so that tabs are inserted as a number of spaces; if your text editor of choice has this feature, then we recommend that you enable it.

The dpis section

The dpis section provides a list of DPI values that can be used when requesting a print from the service. The configuration that we will use is:

```
dpis: [75, 150, 300]
```

The value selected from this list is sent to GeoServer, using the format_options parameter of a WMS request, so a value of 300 will result in the format_options=dpi:300 parameter being added to the WMS request. The DPI option is a vendor parameter that GeoServer adds to standard WMS requests. It allows for the creation of higher resolution output over the OGC standard. The advice to create higher resolution output is to request an image size that is a factor larger than the intended image size, as well as to set the DPI value. The formula used to calculate the correct image size to request for a higher resolution output is:

```
request_image_size = (target_dpi / 90) * intended_image_size
```

So, if you want to have intended_image_size of 200 x 200 with a resolution of 300 DPI, then request_image_size should be 666 x 666. This is because the OGC standard output resolution is specified as 90 DPI.

The formats section

The formats section is an optional section of the configuration and allows you to specify the output formats that a print can be requested in. If the section is omitted, then only PDF will be allowed as the output format. In our case, we will also allow PNG. The default configuration does not contain the formats section as it is optional; therefore, we need to add it ourselves. Add the following content into the config. yaml file:

```
formats:
    - pdf
    - png
```

You will notice that, like with the DPI section, this is a list of values. However, if you look closely, you will see that we have specified it in two different ways. In the case of the dpis section, we specified it like an array, with values separated by commas inside square brackets. In the formats section, we specified them as individual values, one per line. Either type of list structure is valid, and it is really down to personal preference when choosing which one to use.

The formats that you can specify for the output are dependent on your server configuration; PDF is always available, but image formats rely on having JAI and ImageIO configured on the server. If they are configured, then you can specify any image format supported by these libraries.

 GeoServer makes extensive use of the **Java Advanced Imaging (JAI)** and ImageIO libraries to perform its raster operations. More details on the API can be found at http://www.oracle.com/technetwork/ java/javase/tech/jai-142803.html.

The scales section

The scales section of the configuration allows us to specify the map scales at which the output can be requested. You can specify as many scales as you like; simply add an integer value to the list. For our example, we will just allow a small selection of scales to represent large-scale, mid-scale, and small-scale mapping:

```
scales:
    - 1250
    - 2500
    - 10000
    - 100000
    - 500000
```

When creating your own print configuration, you should consider the type of maps you want your users to be able to generate and set the scales list accordingly.

The fonts section

The fonts section is an optional section of the configuration. By default, the entire PDF output will have access to the following fonts:

- Courier (Bold, Oblique, and BoldOblique)
- Helvetica (Bold, Oblique, and BoldOblique)
- Times (Roman, Bold, Oblique, and BoldOblique)
- Symbol
- ZapfDingbats

However, this is a rather limiting list of fonts, and your system will likely contain a much wider variety of fonts. You might even have your own custom font that you would like to use in the print outputs. That is exactly what the fonts section of the configuration is; therefore, it allows us to specify a location (directory or file) for the font(s) we want to have access to in our layouts. For example, on a Windows system, you might have something like the following section:

```
fonts:
  # Arial
  - 'c:\windows\fonts\arial.ttf'
  # Arial Black
  - 'c:\windows\fonts\ariblk.ttf'
  # Arial Bold
  - 'c:\windows\fonts\arialbd.ttf'
  # Arial Bold Italic
  - 'c:\windows\fonts\arialbi.ttf'
  # Arial Italic
  - 'c:\windows\fonts\ariali.ttf'
  # Verdana
  - 'C:\Windows\Fonts\verdana.ttf'
```

In this particular section, we added the different flavors of the Arial font held in the Windows fonts directory. When specifying a file for the font, we can use any of the following supported formats:

Font format	File extension
TrueType	TTF
OpenType	OTF

Font format	File extension
TrueType Collection	TTC
Adobe Font Metrics	AFM
Printer Font Metric	PFM

Of course, we can also just specify a single directory and then have access to all the fonts available within it, for example:

```
fonts:
  - 'C:\Windows\Fonts'
```

It is worth considering setting the fonts section in your configuration so that you can make better templates for the output. On Linux, we can simply add the system-shared font directory and then have access to all the fonts installed for our layouts. For example, a Linux `config.yaml` might include:

```
fonts:
  - '/usr/share/fonts'
```

The hosts whitelist section

The `hosts` section is mandatory and is there to help protect our servers from being used as a proxy to access internal documents or documents on other servers. The point of this section is to list the hosts that our print templates will contact to get mapping data. As a minimum, we will make sure that we can access `localhost`, since this extension runs within our own GeoServer, and we will need to access it. Each entry in the list can be defined either by specifying a DNS name or an IP address:

```
hosts:
  - !localMatch
    dummy: true
  - !dnsMatch
    host: demo.opengeo.org
  - !ipMatch
    ip: tile.openstreetmap.org
  - !ipMatch
    ip: www.osmgb.org.uk
    port: 80
  - !dnsMatch
    host: www.packtpub.com
  - !ipMatch
    ip: static.geoserver.org
```

In the preceding example, we specified three hosts that we will allow the print server to connect to. The first entry is `localMatch`; this means that we can allow anything on `localhost`. The `dummy` element is required to overcome a shortcoming in the YAML specification, but it does not actually do anything. The second entry is `dnsMatch`, which will allow us to connect to the Open Street Map tile servers. For `dnsMatch`, you specified the address using the `host` element. The third entry is `ipMatch`, which will connect to the Open Street Map GB project server. The IP to connect to is specified using the `ip` element; the eagle-eyed among you might have noticed that we have not actually specified an IP address. The value for `ipMatch` can be either a DNS name that will resolve to an IP address or the actual IP address itself. If necessary, you can also add an element called `port` for `localMatch`, `dnsMatch`, and `ipMatch` to allow you to connect to services exposed on alternative ports; for example, GeoServer instances often run on port `8080`.

The layouts section

The `layouts` section is the part that allows us to define the layouts (or print templates) that we want to make available to our users. We can specify as many layouts as we like; the only condition is that each layout has a unique name. The name will be presented to end users in any client application that reads the print capabilities document. Each layout can be either a single page or multiple pages with a title and end page. All layouts must have a main page defined, but print requests can be made by setting multiple main pages. For example, it will be possible to create an atlas-style output by sending multiple page requests to the print server, with different map configurations on each page.

We will explore the finer points of creating interesting print layouts in the next section of this chapter.

Defining print layouts

The `layouts` section of the `config.yaml` file is where we define the *layouts* we want to make available to our users. Each layout can consist of a title page, main page, and a back page, making it possible to create booklet-style outputs. The main page is where we place our mapping and attribute content that will form the structure for the page. When making a request for output, it is possible to create multiple pages, with the content of each page differing but the layout remaining the same. The server generates each page by repeatedly using the main page definition of the layout but changing the content on each use.

Importantly, we do not have to specify all the three types of pages; it is perfectly valid for a layout to simply define a main page. If the layout does not contain definitions for title and back pages, then these will not be generated. It is important to note that the main page is the only one that can contain a map, so the title and back pages are best used for informational content.

 There are a lot of options available when it comes to creating page layouts, and we will not be able to cover all of them in this chapter. The MapFish project has documented the configuration of the print server, and you can access it at `http://www.mapfish.org/doc/print/configuration.html`.

For our example, we will create two layouts: A4 landscape and A4 portrait. For simplicity, we will only include main page definitions for these layouts, but once you understand the principles of the layout engine, you should consider having a go at adding a title and back page definition too. The A4 landscape portrait will look like the following example:

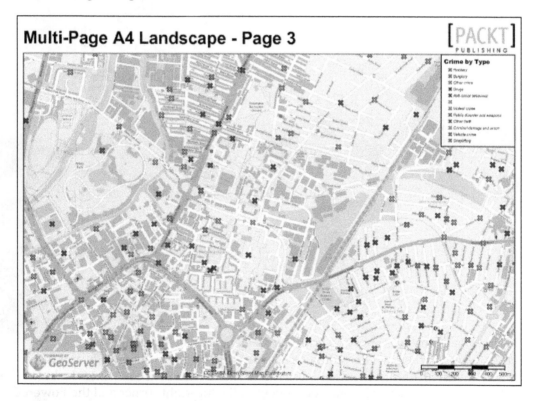

The A4 portrait layout will look like this:

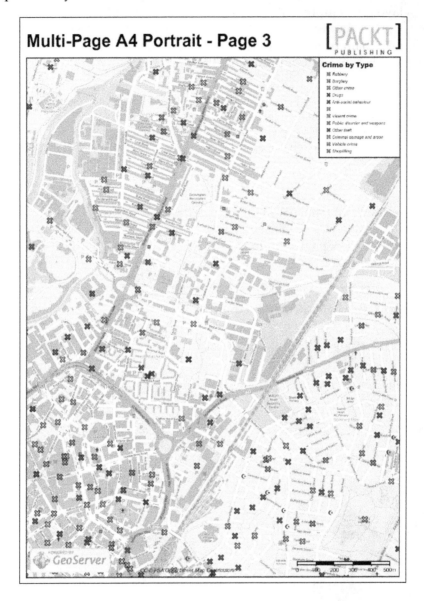

The layouts themselves are straightforward. There is a title element that runs across the top of the page that contains a layout title on the left-hand side and the Packt Publishing logo on the right-hand side. The map element consumes the bulk of the layout space with a legend component in the top-right corner and the **Powered by GeoServer** logo, map copyright notice, and scale bar components at the bottom of the map.

The general structure for the `layouts` section is shown here:

```
layouts:
  {LAYOUT_NAME}:
    metaData:
      {METADATA_DEFINITION}
    titlePage:
      {PAGE_DEFINITION}
    mainPage:
      {PAGE_DEFINITION}
    lastPage:
      {PAGE_DEFINITION}
```

The `metaData`, `titlePage`, and `lastPage` elements are all optional, and the `mainPage` element is mandatory. The `layouts` section can have multiple `{LAYOUT_NAME}` elements, and each one denotes the start of a new layout. All the `{LAYOUT_NAME}` values are compiled into a list in a print capabilities request and form the list of available layouts that can be requested.

Defining the layout metaData element

Although the `metaData` element of a layout is optional, it is worth including it in our layout. This section defines the properties that will be set on the PDF file when it is generated, and they can be very useful in enabling us to tag the output so that others know that it has come from our system. The section is defined in the following way:

```
metaData:
  title: ''
  author: ''
  subject: ''
  keywords: ''
  creator: ''
  supportLegacyReader: false or true
```

Each of the properties are optional; the following table describes the purpose of each one:

Property	Purpose
title	This property is used to specify a title for the PDF document
author	This property is used to identify the author of the layout; this can be passed as a parameter to the service and set as the username

Property	Purpose
subject	This property is used to categorize the layout; this can also be set to a parameter passed to the service
keywords	This property has the keywords to help find this document in systems that support searching PDF document tags
creator	This property is usually used to identify the software used to generate the PDF
supportLegacyReader	This is a property to tell MapFish Print to create a PDF that is compatible with legacy versions of the PDF reader

As mentioned, it is possible to set some of these values to the value of a parameter passed into the service when a print request is made. We will discuss how to pass parameters to the layout when we take a look at making print requests. To set a property to the value of a service parameter, we need to use the ${} notation. For example, to set the author property to the name of the person who makes the print request, we will set the property to:

```
metaData:
    author: ${userName}
```

Here, userName is the parameter passed to the service through the request specification.

> Being able to set the content of the layout using service parameters is very useful in making your layouts user customizable. It is important to note that the name and case of the parameter must be the same in the print request specification and in the configuration.

Defining layout pages

Whether we choose to include the titlePage and lastPage pages along with the mandatory mainPage page definition or not, they are all defined using the same {PAGE_DEFINITION} structure. A {PAGE_DEFINITION} structure has the following elements:

```
pageSize: A4
landscape: false
marginLeft: 40
marginRight: 40
marginTop: 20
marginBottom: 20
backgroundPdf: template.pdf
condition: null
header:
```

```
    height: 50
    items:
      - {BLOCK_DEFINITION}
        {...}
  items:
    - {BLOCK_DEFINITION}
      {...}
  footer:
    height: 50
    items:
      - {BLOCK_DEFINITION}
        {...}
```

All the elements in the definition are optional, except for the ones that have been highlighted; a minimal page definition must contain the `pageSize` and `items` elements. The `pageSize` element can be of any standard-defined page size such as Legal, A4, and A3, or it can be a custom size that specifies the width and height (in points) separated by a space.

> All the widths, heights, and positions in a layout are specified in points, with 72 points being equivalent to 96 pixels or 1 inch. There is a very useful online conversion tool at `http://www.endmemo.com/sconvert/pixelpoint.php` that can help convert to and from points.

Let's take a closer look at the `mainPage` definition for our A4 landscape layout:

```
A4 Landscape:
  metaData:
    author: 'Mastering GeoServer'
    subject: 'Example A4 Landscape Layout'
    keywords: 'map,print,geoserver'
    creator: 'MapFish Print'
```

First of all, we gave the section a name (`A4 Landscape`) that serves a dual purpose: it tells the configuration that this is the start of a new layout section, and it is also the name that will be presented to clients that read the print capabilities response.

> The print module is actually a RESTful service with a complete API. The GeoServer print module effectively wraps this service and provides the runtime environment for the service. As with most other services, the capabilities of the service are published using a capabilities document. This is covered in more detail in the *Making print requests* section later in this chapter.

Next, we will define the metadata element that will populate the generated PDF document properties. We will only define `mainPage` for this particular layout so that it becomes the next element. If we were going to include `titlePage`, then this will be the next section instead:

```
mainPage:
  pageSize: A4
  rotation: false
  landscape: true
  marginLeft: 10
  marginRight: 10
  marginTop: 10
  marginBottom: 10
```

The important properties in this section are `pageSize` and `landscape`, which tell the service that this is an A4 landscape page. To create an A4 portrait page, we will simply set the value of `landscape` to `false`. The various `margin*` properties allow us to create some spacing on our page so that the content does not butt against page edges. In this case, we specified 10 points that will give us a page margin of approximately 13 pixels. The `rotation` property determines whether the map on the page can be rotated. If it is set to `true`, then the print requests can include a rotation value in degrees, and the map on the page will be rotated.

As noted earlier, an `items` element is required for the page element to be valid. The `items` block is where the different components that can be added to a page are defined. For our layout, we have a number of different items, so we will take a look at each one in turn, starting with the `map` element:

```
- !columns
  config:
    borderWidth: 1
    borderColor: black
    cells:
      - row: 0
        paddingTop: 1
        paddingBottom: 1
        paddingLeft: 1
        paddingRight: 1
  absoluteX: 10
  absoluteY: 535
  width: 822
  items:
    - !map
      width: 820
      height: 525
```

To have finer control over the layout, we used table definitions (!columns elements). If we specify the absoluteX and absoluteY values, then the table becomes floating and is affected by layering. To ensure the map does not mask our other page content, we specify it first so that it is the bottom-most layer on the page. We used the config property of the !columns element to specify how we want the table to be created. In our case, we specified a single cell table to hold the map and set a black border for it. The map itself is then defined using the !map element, and we specified the width and height for it as the properties. A !map element can only be added to mainPage; both titlePage and lastPage cannot have map elements added to them.

Following the definition of the map, we will define the top section of the layout, the area of the layout that shows the title and the Packt Publishing logo.

Once again, we will use a !columns element to have greater control over the location of elements:

```
- !columns
    widths: [709, 113]
    width: 822
    absoluteX: 10
    absoluteY: 585
    items:
      - !text
        text: '${mapTitle}'
        font: Arial Bold
        fontSize: 28
        vertAlign: middle
      - !image
        maxWidth: 113
        maxHeight: 49
        align: right
        vertAlign: middle
        url: http://www.packtpub.com/sites/default/files/packt_logo_
small.png
```

The most interesting aspects of this particular code block have been highlighted. The first thing to take a look at is the `widths: [709, 113]` property. This is how we define the number of columns for the table element and also specify their widths In this case, we will have a column that is 709 points wide for the title and another column that is 113 points wide for the logo. The content for the columns is defined inside the `items` block, with the order of the items determining the column in which they are placed. For the layout title, we specified a `!text` element that has the usual properties you would expect, to define the appearance of the text. Note the use of the `Arial Bold` font that we can specify because we defined a `fonts` section in our configuration. Ordinarily, we will not have access to the Arial Bold font as standard. To set the title of the layout dynamically from our client, we make use of the print server's ability to substitute values that it looks for in the print request. In this case, we defined a variable called `mapTitle`, which we can specify inside the print request JSON specification.

The use of `${mapTitle}` in the layout introduces the concept of variable substitution. These are placeholders within our layout; they can be substituted for dynamic text when a print request is made to the service. We will learn more about the print service itself in the *Making print requests* section.

Finally, for this part of the layout, we will specify the logo using an `!image` element. The important part here is the `url` property that should be a link to the location of the image to be inserted; the interesting thing here is that our absolute value can be substituted for a variable. For example, if we specified the `url` property like this, then we can pass the location of the image to insert as part of the print request; this will allow us to have a different logo image for each page request made for the layout:

```
url: ${logoUrl}
```

The layout that we are creating has some elements set at the bottom of the map: a *powered by* GeoServer logo, a map copyright statement, and a scale bar.

Again, we will define these using a !column block and set the absolute position of it such that it will sit neatly at the bottom of the map. The **POWERED BY** GeoServer logo and the map copyright text are defined in much the same way as we defined the top elements of the layout. For the map copyright text, we created a variable called mapCopyright, for which we can send a value dynamically when we request prints. We will take a closer look at the scalebar element, a common and important component for any mapping output. The scalebar element is defined in the following way:

```
- !scalebar
  maxSize: 200
  type: bar_sub
  intervals: 5
  subIntervals: false
  units: m
  barSize: 5
  lineWidth: 1
  labelDistance: 5
  font: Arial
  fontSize: 8
  fontColor: black
  color: #000000
  align: right
  vertAlign: bottom
  barBgColor: white
```

There are a lot of properties that we can define to create scale bars of different types. The type property is where we set the style of the scale bar we want to create; a simple line with graduation marks (line), a thick bar with alternating colors (bar), and a thick bar with alternating colors and little marks for the labels (bar_sub). Examples of these are shown in the following image taken from the MapFish Print documentation:

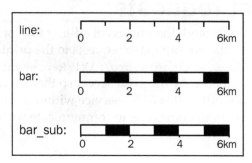

In our layout, we are using the `bar_sub` type of scale bar and have set properties to create the bar with black and white sections. The properties that control the color of the scale bar are `color` for the blocks (in our case, black—`color: #000000`) and `barBgColor` for the background (in our case, white—`barBgColor: white`).

 In a layout, some elements can be provided with color information to affect how they are rendered. All the colors can be specified using the hex code, just like in CSS, or by their *known* name. For example, the color white can be specified using either the hex code #FFFFFF or the known name `white`.

Black and white bars are a very traditional style for a scale bar. We can use these two color properties to change the appearance so that it matches the overall style of our layout or, perhaps, to conform to corporate-branding guidelines. We have also set some properties to control the size of the scale bar and the number of distance elements it displays. The `intervals` property controls how many segments the scale bar will have (five in our case), and the `maxSize` property will make sure the scale bar generated does not exceed the maximum size. The units for the scale bar are specified by the `units` property, and the possible values for this are:

- `m`: This refers to metric units such as mm, cm, m, and km
- `ft`: This refers to imperial units such as in, ft, yd, and mi
- `degrees`: This refers to geographic units such as min, sec, and degree

The engine that generates the scale bar will take the units and select the one that is most appropriate for the size of the bars being generated. For example, if m is set as the value for `units`, then km will be used for large distances, and the scale bar will intelligently select lesser units when the distances decrease.

Making print requests

The whole point of going through the process of editing the configuration and creating the layouts is so that we can make requests to the print server to get an output. A REST (`http://en.wikipedia.org/wiki/Representational_state_transfer`) end-point is exposed by the print server so that we can make requests and receive responses. We can utilize this REST service within our own applications and dynamically configure them to know how to communicate with the print server.

The REST API

Before we get into setting up an application to communicate with the print server, it is worth taking some time out to examine the printing REST API. Understanding the REST API is the key to successfully building applications that can make print requests. The following sequence diagram shows the typical flow when dealing with the print server:

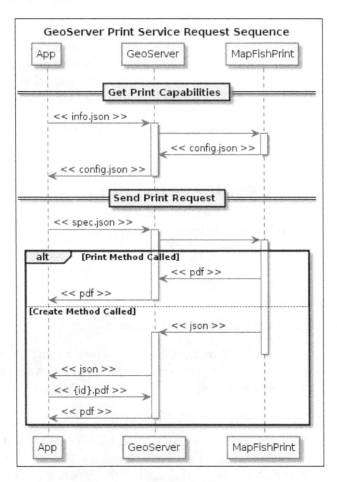

The starting point for any application is to make a call to the info.json REST end-point. This will request the print capabilities information, which is routed through GeoServer as it is acting as the host for the print service. The print service component then responds with a configuration JSON object that GeoServer passes on to the calling application.

The configuration JSON object provides the information that the calling application requires to know what can be printed. We will take a closer look at the print capabilities in the next section. When the calling application needs to request a print from the service, it makes a call either to the `print` or `create` method. Once again, the request is routed through GeoServer as the container for the print service. The print service expects the request to contain a `spec.json` object, which contains the details of what needs to be printed. We will take a closer look at how to generate a `spec.json` object in the *Specifying print requests* section.

The print service reads the `spec.json` object and then creates the requested output. If the `print` method was called, then the print service returns the PDF file directly, routed through GeoServer. The calling application then streams the PDF from GeoServer. If the `create` method is called, the PDF is created and stored in a temporary file location. The print service then responds with a JSON object that contains a `getURL` key. The `getURL` key provides the URL for the generated PDF document.

Getting the print server capabilities

Before we can make print requests, we must first understand the capabilities of the print server. To build an interface to the print server, we need to understand:

- What print layouts are available
- What scales can prints be requested at
- If resolutions can be specified
- What size is the map component for a given layout

Fortunately for us, there is a REST method that will return a structured JSON object that describes the capabilities of the print server. The capabilities are requested by issuing a `HTTP GET` request on the following URL:

```
http://[server name]:[port]/geoserver/pdf/info.json
```

Remember to substitute `[server name]` and `[port]` with values for the GeoServer (or standalone print server) that you want capabilities for. The response from this call will be a structured JSON object that describes the capabilities of the print server. The JSON object has the following structure:

```
{
  "scales" : [
    { name : value }
  ],
```

```
    "dpis" : [
      { name : value }
    ],
    "outputFormats": [
      { name : value }
    ],
    "layouts" : [
      {
        "name" : value,
        "rotation" : true | false,
        "map" : {
          "width" : value,
          "height" : value
        }
      }
    ]
    "printUrl" : value,
    "createUrl" : value
  }
```

The following table lists each of the JSON keys, along with a description of the print capability being exposed:

Key	Description
scales	This is an array of objects with the name and value keys. The name key is a print-friendly name for the scale. The value key is the numeric scale value.
dpis	This is an array of objects with the name and value keys. The name key is a print-friendly name for the DPI. The value key is the numeric value of the DPI. The dpis key will only be present if the config.yaml file has a dpis section.
outputFormats	This is an array of objects with the name and value keys. The name key is a print-friendly name for the format. The value key is the value of the format. The outputFormats key will only be present if the config.yaml file has an outputFormats section.
layouts	This is an array of layout objects. It lists the layouts that are available for printing.
printUrl	This holds the URL to send print requests to. The response will be the output streamed as binary.
createUrl	This holds the URL to send print requests to. The response will be JSON that contains a link to the download URL.

Each item in the `layouts` array is an object that describes the layout. The following table lists the keys along with a description of their purpose:

Key	Description
name	This is the name of the layout. This value needs to be used when making a print request.
rotation	This determines whether the map can be rotated in the generated output or not.
map : width	The map object has a width property to specify what size the map is.
map : height	The map object has a height property to specify what size the map is.

Specifying print requests

Now that we know how to get the print capabilities, we are ready to understand how to make requests for output. In the previous section, we learned that there are two different end-points to request the print output: one streams the output and the other stores it on the server and returns the location as a JSON response. However, irrespective of which method we decide to call, in both cases `spec.json` must be sent either inline as a request parameter for GET or as the body content for POST.

The print specification is a JSON object that tells the print server how and what we want it to print. The basic structure is as follows:

```
{
    "layout" : name,
    <CUSTOM_PARAMETERS>
    "srs" : value,
    "units" : value,
    "geodetic" : true | false,
    "outputFilename" : value,
    "outputFormat" : value,
```

This is the starting section of the specification, and this is where we specify the name of the layout that we want the output to be based on. The <CUSTOM_PARAMETERS> section is where we can enter any of our own custom properties, the values of which will be placed in the sections of our layout where we use variable substitution. Properties defined here are called root properties and are available to all parts of the layout.

The remaining properties allow us to specify the spatial reference system for the maps in the layout, and the `geodetic` property is very useful when we are dealing with geodetic layers that need to consider the curvature of the Earth in calculations:

```
"layers" : [
  {
    <LAYER_DEFINITION>
  }
],
```

The `layers` property is an array of layer-definition objects that the print server will use to compose the maps. The order of layers is important as it determines the layering on the output map. The first item in the array will be the bottom-most layer with all subsequent layers being drawn on top in order.

 Layer ordering is an important factor to consider when creating applications that will call the print services. You should always ensure the first layer definition in the array is your base-mapping layer.

The composition of the layer definition itself depends on the type of layer that is being sent to the server. The current version of the extension supports the following map layer types:

- Vector (as GeoJSON)
- WMS
- WMTS
- TMS
- XYZ
- **Open Street Map (OSM)**
- TileCache
- Image
- MapServer
- KaMap
- KaMapCache
- Google

The MapFish documentation at `http://www.mapfish.org/doc/print/protocol.html#layers-params` describes each of the layer types and the properties that can be set on them. Different types of layers can be specified in the same spec request so that you are not constrained to only supplying one particular type of layer. A typical application will loop through the collection of visible layers on the map, encode each layer into a definition object, and then add them to the `layers` array in the spec.

The format of the definition object will vary according to the type of layer. For example, the following definition is for a WMS layer:

```
{
    "baseUrl": "http://<server>:<port>/geoserver/wms",
    "opacity": 1,
    "singleTile": false,
    "type": "WMS",
    "layers": [<layer names>],
    "format": "image/png",
    "styles": [<style names>],
    "customParams": { <custom parameters> }
}
```

We can see that the definition object describes the parameters required to construct a valid WMS GetMap request. The print service will combine these parameters along with details of the map bounds to construct a valid WMS request.

The following will be the definition required for an OpenStreetMap layer:

```
{
    "baseUrl": "http://a.tile.openstreetmap.org",
    "extension": "png",
    "opacity": 1,
    "singleTile": false,
    "type": "OSM",
    "maxExtent": [-20037508.34, -20037508.34, 20037508.34, 20037508.34],
    "tileSize": [256, 256],
    "resolutions": [156543.03390625,78271.516953125,39135.7584765625,195
67.87923828125,9783.939619140625,4891.9698095703125,2445.9849047851562
,1222.9924523925781,611.4962261962891,305.74811309814453,152.87405654
907226,76.43702827453613,38.218514137268066,19.109257068634033,9.55462
8534317017,4.777314267158508,2.388657133579254,1.194328566789627,0.597
1642833948135]
}
```

This is very similar in nature to the WMS request, except that it has some specific elements for OpenStreetMap servers. In the *An example OpenLayers application* section, we will take a look at some code that converts a WMS layer into a `spec.json` representation. For a more complete example of encoding the different layer types supported by MapFish Print, take a look at the source code of the GeoExt project for its print provider at `http://trac.geoext.org/browser/core/trunk/geoext/lib/GeoExt/data/PrintProvider.js`.

With layer encoding handled, we can take a look at the `pages` element that is used to define the content for the pages that we want to have output for:

```
"pages" : [
  {
    <PAGE_DEFINITION>
  }
],
```

The `pages` property is an array of `<PAGE_DEFINITION>` objects that describe the pages to be added to the output. A page-definition object has the following structure:

```
{
    "center" : [x, y] | "bbox" : [x1, y1, x2, y2],
    "scale" : value,
    "dpi" : value,
    "geodetic" : true | false,
    <CUSTOM_PARAMETERS>
}
```

The location of the map to show on the page can be specified either by setting the center and scale properties or by just setting the bbox property. The dpi property is used to set the output resolution for the map, and the print server will take it into account when generating requests to the layers specified in the request. The geodetic property is *false* by default and can be set to true when the data you are dealing with is based on a spherical system, for example, Google layers. The `<CUSTOM_PARAMETERS>` element is where we can specify the values for substitution on the output; for our example, that is, for the layouts element/layer, we defined two values: `mapTitle` and `mapCopyright`. Parameters set at the page level are only available within the context of a page. Multiple page definitions in the array will result in the output having the same number of pages. This feature allows us to create a multipage PDF, with each page showing a different part of the map.

It is important to note that all the pages will have a map with the same layer composition; the only variability across pages can be the location of the map. The `layers` array is global to the specification, so it applies to all the maps.

The final section of the spec is an array of legend definitions:

```
"legends" : [
  {
    <LEGEND_DEFINITION>
  }
 ]
}
```

Each `<LEGEND_DEFINITION>` provides the composition for a legend to appear on the layout, if a `!legend` element has been defined in the layout. If a `!legend` element has been defined in the layout and the legends array is not empty, then the legend will be drawn according to its configuration. If a `!legend` element has been defined in the layout but the legends array of the spec is empty, then the legend will not be drawn.

The code of this book includes some example print request specs that you can use to call the configuration we created earlier in this chapter.

An example OpenLayers application

So, we installed and configured the print extension inside our GeoServer instance. We created a nice A4 landscape and portrait layout and learned how to communicate with the print server. All that remains is to bring it all together into an application that we can use to test our layouts and actually get some example output.

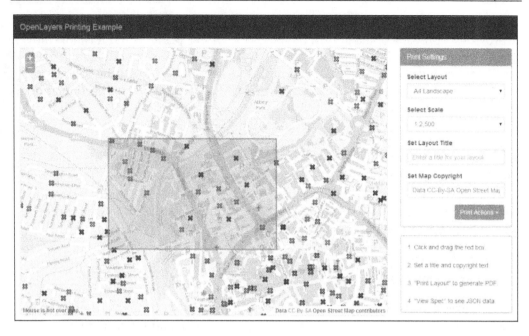

A sample OpenLayers application has been provided in the code of this book; this sample application applies all the concepts that we have learned.

In this section, we will not cover the complete code for the sample application; the code accompanies this book and is well commented. We will discuss some of the key points of the code in this section to aid our understanding of what is happening.

The application itself presents an OpenLayers map that has a WMS layer and OpenStreetMap layer loaded into it. The base layer is the built-in OpenLayers OpenStreetMap layer, and it has an opacity level applied to it to tone down the map. The second layer is our WMS layer of the UK Street Level Crime data, styled by the type of crime. There is also an `OpenLayers.Vector` layer on the map; it is used to hold the red print-extent boundary.

The red print-extent box is actually the core component of the printing application. It provides a preview of the area of the map that will be printed, and it can be moved around and positioned using a click-and-drag action. To the right of the map, there is a **Print Settings** box that contains controls that can be used to set the content for print. The red print-extent is dynamically updated according to the selection of items in the drop-down lists.

Initializing the application

The first thing that the application needs to do is set itself up when the page is loaded. To do this, we will use jQuery (http://www.jquery.org) and place some code inside the $(document).ready() event handler. The first thing we want to do is read the available layouts from the print server:

```
$.each(printCapabilities.layouts, function () {
    $("#selectLayout").append($("<option></option>").val(this.name).
html(this.name));
});
```

We looped over the printCapabilities.layouts array, and for each item, we added an option to the HTML select control with the #selectLayout ID.

The print capabilities for this application are requested in a slightly different way than you might initially expect. Instead of making a GET request to the print server in JavaScript, it has a <script></script> tag in the <head> element of the main page. The src attribute for the <script> tag points to the print server's info.json method and appends the var=printCapabilities parameter. By requesting the information in this way, we will get back a small JavaScript fragment that now sets a global variable called printCapabilities. This global variable is then used in the rest of the application.

Next, we want to do the same thing for the available scales:

```
$.each(printCapabilities.scales, function() {
  $("#selectScale").append($("<option></option>").val(this.value).
html(this.name));
});
```

This time, we looped over the printCapabilities.scales array and added each item to the HTML select control with a #selectScale ID. Once we have the list of scales, we want to order them and then select the scale that is most appropriate for the current zoom level of the map:

```
$("#selectScale > option").sort(function (a, b) { return b.value -
a.value; }).each(function () {
```

```
    var scaleValue = this.value;
    if (scaleValue < mapCtrl.getScale()) {
      $("#selectScale").val(scaleValue);
      return false;
    }
  });
```

Here, we first sorted the array of scale options into descending order and then looped over each item in the array. On each item, we checked against the `scaleValue < mapCtrl.getScale()` condition, which compares the current item value against the map's scale. If the current value is less than the map's scale, then we can be satisfied that it is appropriate to set the print extent to this value.

With the base scale selected for the print extent, the application then needs to create it and add it to the map. The function to handle that is:

```
function createPrintExtent(){
    // Create a feature to represent the print extent and initially
set its geometry to nothing relevant
    printExtent = new OpenLayers.Feature.Vector(OpenLayers.Geometry.
fromWKT("POLYGON((-1 -1,1 -1,1 1,-1 1,-1 -1))"));

    // Add the feature to the map
    printExtentLayer.addFeatures([printExtent]);

    // Get the current selected scale from the drop-down
    var scale = $("#selectScale").val();

    // Calculate the bounds for the feature based on the selected
scale
    var bounds = calculatePrintBounds(scale);

    // Convert the bounds object to a geometry
    var geometry = bounds.toGeometry();

    // Update the geometry of the print extent
    updatePrintExtentGeometry(geometry);

    // Set the centre for the bounds to be the current map centre
    setExtentCentre(mapCtrl.getCenter());

    // Activate the drag print extent control
    dragPrintExtentCtrl.activate();
}
```

The first thing that we did here is set `printExtent` to be a new `OpenLayers.Vector.Feature` feature and initialize it to be a simple polygon. The feature is added to the map, and then its bounds are recalculated using the selected scale and layout values from the drop-down lists. We also attached a handler for the `change` event on both the scale and layout drop-down lists. When the user changes a value in these drop-downs, the print extent feature is updated.

Generating the print SPEC to POST

To be able to request the PDF output, we need to generate the SPEC JSON object that will be sent to the print server. The function to handle the print creates a `printJSON` object that is then sent using jQuery's `$.ajax()` function. The `printJSON` object is constructed as shown here:

```
var printJson = {
    "layout": printCapabilities.layouts[$("#selectLayout").
attr("selectedIndex")].name,
    "title": "Mastering GeoServer - Chapter 7 - Generated PDF",
    "srs": mapCtrl.baseLayer.projection.getCode(),
    "dpi": 300,
    "units": mapCtrl.getUnits(),
    "geodetic": true,
    "outputFilename": "Chapter7Print.pdf",
    "layers": encodedLayers,
    "pages": [{
        center: [printExtentFeature.geometry.getCentroid().x,
printExtentFeature.geometry.getCentroid().y],
        scale: printCapabilities.scales[$("#selectScale").
attr("selectedIndex")].value,
        dpi: 300,
        geodesic: true,
        mapTitle: $("#layoutTitle").val(),
        comment: "",
        mapCopyright: copyrightText
    }],
    "legends": encodedLegends,
    "createURL": printCapabilities.createURL
};
```

Notice that the `layers` key is assigned a variable named `encodedLayers`. The `encodedLayers` variable is an array of encoded layer objects. The following JavaScript code is an example of how a WMS layer can be encoded:

```
function encodeWMSLayer(lyr) {
  var encLyr = {};
```

The function is defined to accept a single parameter that is expected to be an
`OpenLayers.Layer` class. First of all, we will define an object that we will populate
with properties. This object will be the encoded layer definition that will be returned
and added to an array.

The next section considers whether the layer being encoded has a minimum
or maximum scale for display. If this is set in the OpenLayers object, then we
should pass it through to the print server so that unnecessary requesting of
data is not performed:

```
if (lyr.options && lyr.options.maxScale) {
    encLyr.minScaleDenominator = lyr.options.maxScale;
}
if (lyr.options && lyr.options.minScale) {
    encLyr.maxScaleDenominator = lyr.options.minScale;
}
```

Next, we will define the base properties of the WMS layer. The `type` property is
used by the print server to determine how it should interpret the encoded layer
information and, ultimately, how to make requests for data against the layer.
The `layers`, `format`, and `styles` properties are standard WMS request parameters
that we need to pass to the print server. We will get the values for these properties
by interrogating the `params` property of the OpenLayers layer object:

```
encLyr.type = "WMS";
encLyr.baseUrl = "http://www.osmgb.org.uk/ogc/wms";
encLyr.layers = [lyr.params.LAYERS].join(",").split(",");
encLyr.format = lyr.params.FORMAT;
encLyr.styles = [lyr.params.STYLES].join(",").split(",");
```

Next, we will enter into a `for` loop to read any custom parameters that we should
be encoding. Custom parameters are added to the encoded layer so that they can be
passed through to the backend server and applied for the printed output:

```
for (var p in lyr.params) {
    param = p.toLowerCase();
    if (!lyr.DEFAULT_PARAMS[param] && "layers,styles,width,height,
srs".indexOf(param) == -1) {
        if (!encLayer.customParams) {
            encLayer.customParams = {};
        }
        encLayer.customParams[p] = lyr.params[p];
    }
}
```

Finally, we will return the constructed encoded layer by returning the `encLyr` variable. This encoded layer object can now be added to the `layers` array of the print specification so that it can be sent to the print server:

```
    return encLyr;
}
```

Sending the print request

With the `printJSON` object created, all that remains is to post it to the print service. The following snippet of code is an implementation of jQuery's `$.ajax()` function to send the `printJSON` object to the print service:

```
$.ajax({
  type: "POST",
  url: printCapabilities.createURL,
  dataType: "json",
  data: printJSON,
  async: true,
  success: function (response) {
     // Open the PDF from the browser from the generated print URL;
this should be handled differently if the browser is Opera
     if ($.browser.opera) {
        // Make sure Opera does not replace the content tab with the PDF
        window.open(response.getURL);
     } else {
        // Avoids popup blockers for all other browsers
        window.location = response.getURL;
     }
  },
  error: function (request, status, error) {
     alert(request.responseText);
  }
});
```

The method sends the `printJSON` object using the POST method to the URL specified by the `createURL` key of the `printCapabilities` object. We can handle a successful response by reading the returned JSON and issuing a command to open the browser on the `getURL` value of the response. Our browser will then download the generated PDF file from the server.

Summary

By now, you should be able to understand what the GeoServer print community module is and how it can be used within your own applications and projects. It is a very capable print server that can generate exceptional output that really does your maps justice.

The layout configuration is straightforward enough to make it easy to create interesting output that is still powerful enough to enable the creation of interesting and compelling layouts. We saw how the simple REST API of the print server can be used to understand the capabilities of the print server and make requests for prints.

Finally, we saw how all the concepts can be brought together into an application using the OpenLayers map library that can make dynamic print requests through an interactive print-extent feature on the map.

In the next chapter, we will take a look at how we can use our GeoServer instance in a real-world scenario and integrate it into an enterprise platform.

8

Integrating GeoServer in a Spatial Data Infrastructure

Up to now, we have spent a lot of time looking at how we can configure GeoServer and control the way it outputs data. Now, it is time for a change in pace. In this chapter, we will examine the role that GeoServer can play in an enterprise environment, specifically within a **Spatial Data Infrastructure**.

We are going to consider what a Spatial Data Infrastructure is and the role that GeoServer can play in it. Through this chapter, we will examine the following concepts:

- What a Spatial Data Infrastructure is
- The technology platform and the role GeoServer plays in it
- A desktop user's perspective of a Spatial Data Infrastructure
- A data consumer's perspective of a Spatial Data Infrastructure

Spatial Data Infrastructures are complex enterprise systems, and we can't possibly begin to discuss the best approach to implement them in this chapter, as this is a subject worthy of its own book. The purpose of this chapter is to attempt to give you some context in which you can consider how GeoServer can fit within an enterprise environment, based on an internationally accepted concept of a spatial data platform.

Definition of a spatial data infrastructure

A Spatial Data Infrastructure, commonly referred to as **SDI**, is in essence a data infrastructure that enables the efficient use and management of spatial information. Although the manifestation of an SDI is ultimately a technology platform of loosely coupled servers and services, at its heart there is a core set of four guiding principles: people, standards, policy, and data.

People are an integral part of any SDI, as they will use it to deliver services and analysis to stakeholders. Within a corporate environment, one can categorize people into three broad types:

- **Data creators / originators**: These are the people who use powerful desktop GIS tools to create, manipulate, and maintain spatial information.

- **Data users**: These are the people concerned with the analysis and interrogation of spatial information to provide answers. They use a combination of web-based and desktop-based tools.

- **Data consumers**: These are the people concerned with the consumption of data (usually from data users) to inform decision making and/or business planning.

A guiding principle for an SDI should be interoperability, that is to say that a policy around the use of spatial tools should not necessarily dictate or advocate the use of any one specific tool. In other words, standardization should not be achieved at the software or tool level but rather at the service level, through the adoption of industry-recognized *standards*, such as those of the OGC.

Of course, this is not to say that any random tool can be used; there must be a *policy* to govern the selection and use of tools within the environment. Policies should also be utilized to govern many other aspects of how the SDI should be used, operated, and maintained.

But of course, ultimately, an SDI is all about making centrally stored spatial *data* available to as wide an audience as possible, with as few barriers as possible. Data should be easy to discover (metadata), easy to access (services), and easy to use (software).

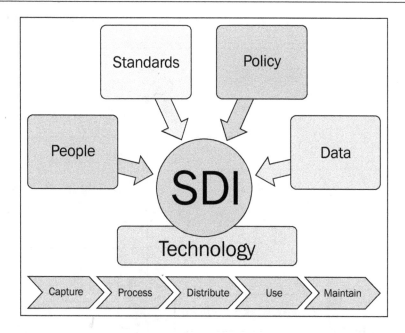

The ultimate aim of any SDI is to support the typical spatial business process of capturing, processing, distributing, using, and maintaining spatial information. The technology platform is the vehicle to provide the tools and services to enable the process, and the four core tenets provide the governance framework to operate under. Collectively, these things can be considered to be the SDI.

The technology platform of a spatial data infrastructure

Given the core tenets of an SDI, the thing to then consider is the technology platform that can deliver them. The core principle for any SDI has to be interoperability through the implementation of open standards and not through the use of proprietary formats or services.

With this in mind, a very simple technology platform for an SDI will at least consist of a database server, a web mapping server, and a metadata server. The web mapping server and the metadata server should publish their data through the WxS range of OGC services with outputs in OGC formats.

The following diagram shows what a typical configuration of servers might look like:

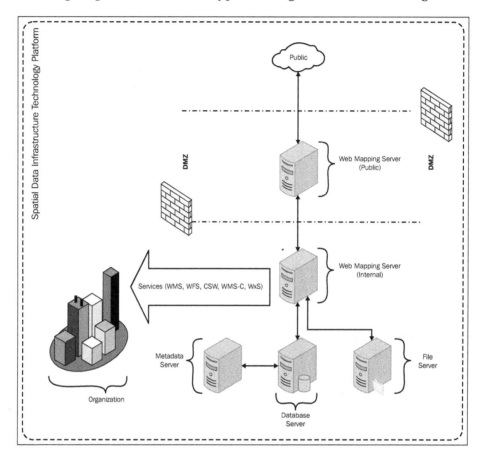

In this very simple configuration, there is a **Web Mapping Server (Internal)** at the core of the platform. This publishes data through OGC standard formats (WMS and WFS). There is a public-facing web mapping server that is used to publish datasets for public consumption. The **Public Web Mapping Server** is isolated from the core system by being placed inside the DMZ network. A **Database Server** and a **File Server** are used to store the spatial information that is being served to the **Organization** and **Public**. A **Metadata Server** exists and allows data to be *discovered* through the use of the **Catalog Service for the Web (CSW)** web service (http://en.wikipedia.org/wiki/Catalog_Service_for_the_Web). In this simple configuration, users can connect to the system with their Desktop GIS packages, using the WxS range of services, and general users will connect to the data through some form of web-based GIS tool that runs on its own web server.

The big question is where does GeoServer fit in this environment. If we reconsider the previous architecture diagram, we could redraw it to show where GeoServer fits. The following diagram is the revised architecture to show GeoServer's role:

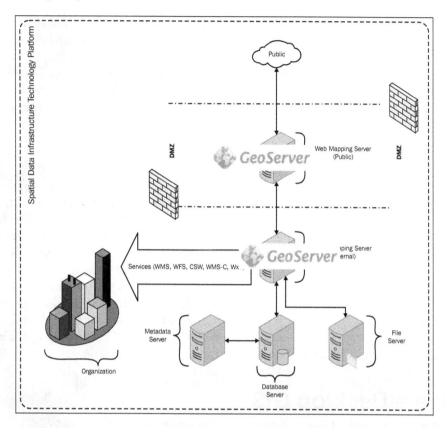

Hopefully, it won't come as much of a surprise to see that GeoServer fits squarely in the web mapping server component of the technology platform. The real power of using GeoServer in this way is that it fully supports the OGC standards for web services. In the context of public-facing services, we can hook the public GeoServer to the internal GeoServer using cascaded services. In other words, we can utilize GeoServer as a reverse proxy server. This will ensure our internal server is protected, and only the datasets we want to be made public are published.

What we have looked at here is a logical view of the technology platform of an SDI. This is to demonstrate the core components required. The reality is that a physical architecture will have a number of servers that perform roles in clusters to handle things such as the required amount of concurrency on service requests, server failover, and disaster recovery as well.

User perspective – editing data through WFS-T

One of the principles of an SDI is that the data contained within it is not managed centrally; it is managed by data owners or originators instead. Data owners or originators can be external third parties, but more likely they will be employees of your organization. These users will require the ability to connect to the SDI with a GIS tool to perform editing operations. Due to the nature of the editing that they will be doing, in most cases these users will use a Desktop GIS. Often, these types of users are known as *power users*.

There are many different Desktop GIS platforms available in the market, ranging from open source tools such as QGIS (http://www.qgis.org) through to proprietary tools such as Esri's ArcGIS for a desktop (http://www.esri.com). Each of these applications will have their own internal data types and will support a different range of formats to read and write spatial data. Where it is possible for you to standardize on a single platform across your organization, these differences in formats will not be an issue. However, in reality, different departments will have different applications. Often, there are valid reasons for this, and ultimately, this should not be discouraged; instead, the central platform should be designed to support multiple tools. The key to supporting different platforms is to ensure the SDI utilizes open standards and that the applications and tools support these standards. This is where utilizing GeoServer as the core of your SDI will really help out. This is because it has built-in support for all the common OGC standards.

Using a Desktop GIS

Now, it is time to look at how a *power user* can connect to GeoServer's **WFS-T** (**WFS Transactions**) using a Desktop GIS application, in this case, QGIS. GeoServer's WFS-T service enables editing of data from any tool that supports the standard. This means that departments can manage their own datasets held in the SDI, irrespective of what desktop application they are using.

To demonstrate this, we will consider a scenario in which a data owner has been tasked with identifying invalid geometries in a dataset that they are responsible for. If they identify any invalid geometry, their task is to delete the record so that the dataset only contains clean and valid geometry. For this example, we will use QGIS, as it has excellent support for OGC standards and is free to use. An in-depth discussion of how to install and use QGIS is beyond the scope of this book, so if you are interested in using QGIS in your environment, I highly recommend that you read the book, *Learning QGIS 2.0, Anita Graser, Packt Publishing*.

Connecting QGIS to GeoServer's WFS-T service

The first thing to do is create a connection to our central GeoServer that is being used to share spatial information across the organization. Since this task will require us to edit spatial data, we will need to create a WFS-T connection to GeoServer so that we get the vector data that we can manipulate in QGIS. Look for the toolbar that contains the new layer options:

Alternatively, you can navigate to **Layer | Add WFS Layer...** if you do not have the toolbar active. This will open the **Add WFS Layer from a Server** dialog box where we can choose which layer we would like to add to the map to work with:

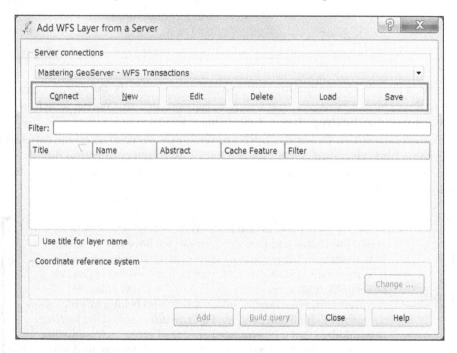

QGIS has a built-in connection manager that allows us to create and store connections to different services such as WMS, WFS, and databases. If we already created a connection to GeoServer, then we can simply select it from the drop-down list and then click on the **Connect** button.

If we do not have a connection, then we can create one using the **New** button.

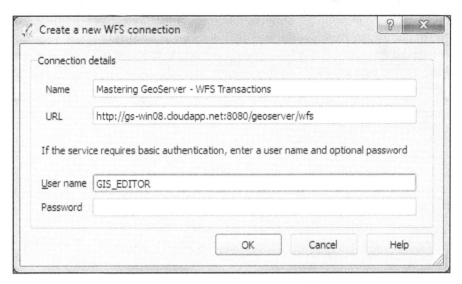

The **Create a new WFS connection** dialog allows us to specify the connection details to the central GeoServer. We will give the connection a name, which is what will appear in the drop-down list in future, and then we will specify the URL to the WFS end-point of the server. If the connection is secured, then we can specify the username and password. When we are happy with the connection details, we can click on the **OK** button, and the connection entry will now appear in the drop-down list.

> When creating a connection to the WFS, we have an option to enter a username and password. So far, we have not discussed how to secure GeoServer in an enterprise environment; however, it is important to note that your production GeoServer should be secured, with users given access based on their roles and requirements. For example, power users who belong to a highways department will likely need read and write access on the highway network data, but they will need only read access to information about the authority's land ownership. We will take an in-depth look at security in *Chapter 10, Enterprise Security and GeoServer*.

With the connection created and stored, we can select it from the drop-down list and then click on the **Connect** button:

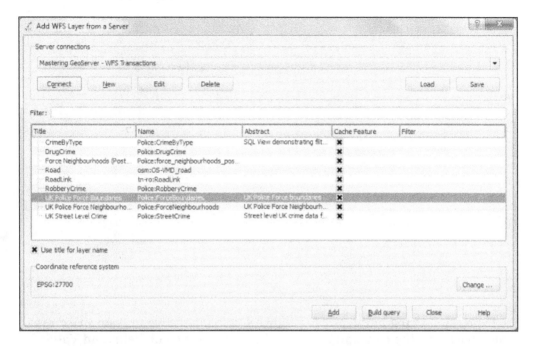

QGIS provides the ability to load and save a list of connections using an XML file. In an enterprise environment, where you potentially need to set up and configure lots of QGIS installations, it is a good practice to create and distribute an XML file to all of your users so that everyone has the same connection properties.

Once we click on the **Connect** button, QGIS will connect to the WFS end point and get the capabilities document; this is processed, and the results are shown in the layer list. The process of fetching and parsing the capabilities document will be transparent. To add a layer to the map, simply select it from the list and then click on the **Add** button.

It is also possible to build a query on the layer to filter results according to an expression; this can be done by clicking on the **Build query** button.

The **Expression string builder** dialog allows you to interactively create an expression to filter the layer. The **Function list** tab will contain a listing of **Fields and Values** read from the selected layer; you can use them in the filter expression. For now, we will just load our layer straight into QGIS:

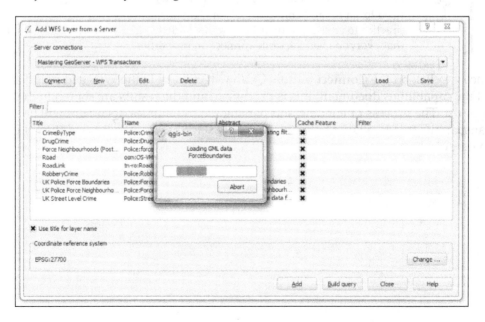

Clicking on the **Add** button will trigger the load process and cause QGIS to start processing the response stream. Ultimately, we will end up with the data layer loaded into the QGIS map window as a vector dataset that is locally stored and that we can manipulate. Depending on the size of the dataset and other settings, this initial download might take a little time. A progress dialog is shown while QGIS is processing the data. Once loaded, the layer will behave like any other layer in QGIS, and all the tools that can be used on the vector data will be available.

Using the QGIS Topology Checker tool

For our use case, we need to check the validity of the feature geometry in the dataset. To do this, we will make use of the **Topology Checker** tool. The QGIS Topology Checker tool allows us to specify some topology rules that we would like to analyze our data against. Any errors found are listed, and we are able to click on an error to zoom to that feature. Launch the **TopologyChecker** option by navigating to **Vector | Topology Checker**.

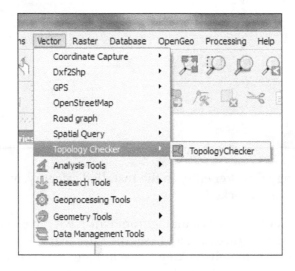

If the menu option is not present in your installation of QGIS, then you need to check whether the plugin is enabled. To do this, navigate to **Plugins | Manage and Install Plugins...** to open the plugin manager.

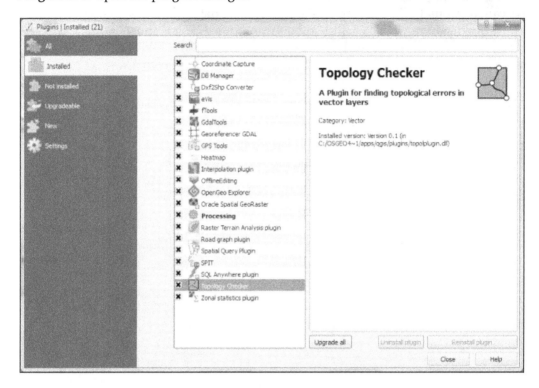

Look for the **Topology Checker** entry in the **Installed** category, and make sure that the checkbox next to it is checked.

The Topology Checker tool opens a dialog from which we can run checks, inspect the errors found, and configure the tool to set the rules that we would like to have checked. In our case, we are only looking to see if there is any invalid feature geometry in our layer, so the rules will be quite simple. However, the Topology Checker tool is a very capable tool, and I recommend that you spend some time getting to know it better.

When the Topology Checker tool initially loads, it will not have any configuration, nor will it list any errors:

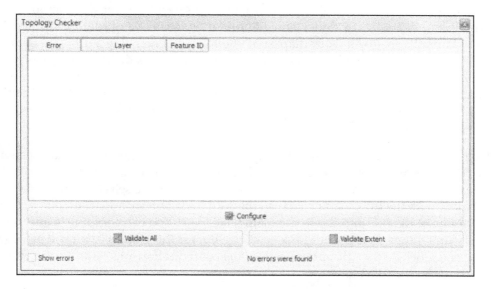

To define some rules, we need to click on the **Configure** button to open the rules editor:

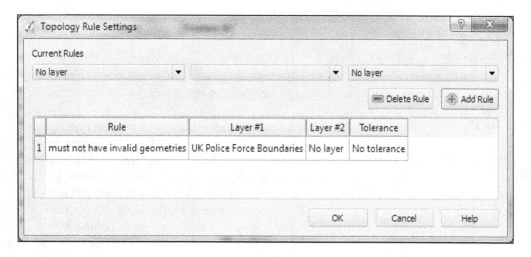

Defining the rules to use is as simple as selecting options from drop-down lists and then adding them. To create our simple geometry-validation rule, we need to make some selections. From the first drop-down, we will select the layer we want to check; in this example, this is **UK Police Force Boundaries**. The list will contain the layer names currently loaded in your map, so if you follow along using a different dataset, then select that one instead. The second drop-down contains the rule that we want to apply to the layer we selected in the first drop-down. There are a number of rules available, and the list will change based on the geometry type of the layer selected. As we are looking at a polygon dataset, the rule that we are interested in is called **must not have invalid geometries**.

The third drop-down is another list of layers and is only relevant when the selected rule compares one layer against another. In our case, the rule only applies to the target layer, so the third drop-down disappears when we select it. Once we are happy with the rule, we can click on the **Add Rule** button, and a summary description of the rule appears in the main table view. You can continue to add rules for as many things as you would like to check, but for this example, we will just stick to the one. Click on the **OK** button to close the configuration and return to the main Topology Checker dialog.

The Topology Checker tool is executed using the buttons along the bottom of the dialog.

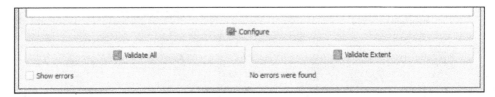

There are two options available: **Validate All** and **Validate Extent**. The first option will check all the rules against all the features in the layers referenced by the rules. The second one will check all the rules against the features that intersect the current view extents in the layers referenced by the rules. For our scenario, we want to check all the features in the dataset, so we need to click on the **Validate All** button. Depending on the number of rules, the complexity of the rules, and the amount of data in each layer, the Topology Checker tool might take a while to complete.

Once it has completed processing, it populates the main table view on the dialog with a summary of any errors found:

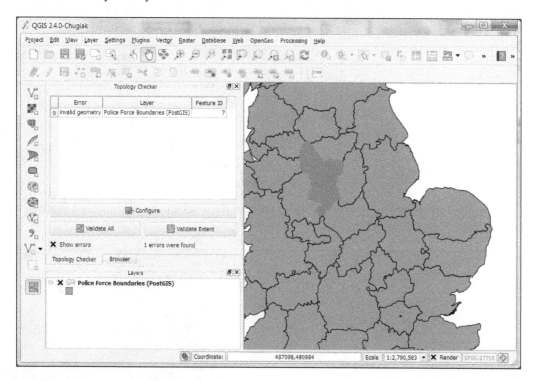

At the bottom of the dialog, there is a checkbox called **Show errors**. If this is checked, then the layer on the map will have all the features that break a rule highlighted in red; clicking on an error in the table will zoom the map to the feature responsible for breaking the rule. This provides a convenient way for us to navigate around the issues and perform any corrective operations.

For our example, the task is to simply delete the feature that contains the invalid geometry. To do this, we first need to place our layer into the edit mode by ensuring the layer is selected in the **Layers** tree view and then clicking on the edit button on the toolbar:

Toggle editing

Once we have the layer in the edit mode, we can then select the highlighted feature on the map with the selection tool:

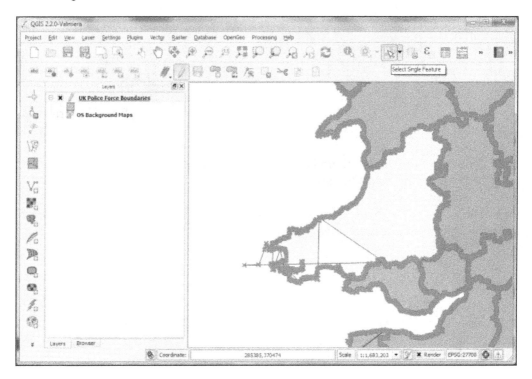

With the feature selected, we just need to click on the **Delete Selected** edit tool button to have the feature removed:

With the feature deleted, we can continue working through our list of errors until we are satisfied that we have corrected everything we need to.

Using the WFS-T service to save results

All that remains is to post our changes to the layer back to GeoServer using the WFS-T service. The **WFS-T** service allows us to edit data in our client and then inform the layer of the changes made so that they can be stored in the central repository. If the user who connects to WFS has write access to the layer, QGIS will automatically save the changes to our layer using WFS-T. To save the changes to the layer, we can use the editing toolbar menu:

QGIS has a clever way of remembering the state of your layer prior to editing, so if you make a mistake during edits, you can simply click on the **Rollback for Selected Layer(s)** or **Rollback for All Layers** option. For now though, we are happy with the edits, so we just want to save them by clicking on the **Save for Selected Layer(s)** option. QGIS will post the changes back to GeoServer as a WFS transaction seamlessly in the background. Depending on security, we might get asked for a password, but other than that, there will be no further interaction with us from QGIS—it just works!

This was a very simple example of using QGIS with GeoServer to do some editing using the WFS-T service; however, it demonstrates a very important concept within the context of an SDI. The ability to read, analyze, and manipulate data should not be dictated by the client tool or application. Instead, the SDI services should be standards-based, providing a common service interface that the client tools and applications can support.

User perspective – consuming data

By far the most common type of user who will access data from an SDI will be *data consumers*. This is a broad term that can be used to describe anyone within an organization who will take and use data that has been captured, created, or generated for the purpose of decision making or informing other business processes. These users will not typically create spatial information, though the spatial information they consume might contribute to some other form of output. For example, a *data consumer* within a department might take the results of spatial analysis (in the form of a map) and then include it in a report to be delivered to the senior management. The *data consumer* has not done anything to manipulate the data; they have simply consumed it and placed it inside their report.

Within an SDI, you will most likely provide *data consumers* with access to data through a visualization platform; this can be a custom web application, an off-the-shelf web application such as GeoNode (http://www.geonode.org), or something like Google Earth. We will now take a look at a simple example of how you might deliver content to *data consumers* using Google Earth.

Launching Google Earth from GeoServer

The simplest way for *data consumers* to view data in Google Earth from GeoServer is to utilize the **Layer Preview** capability. Depending on the security level of GeoServer, this might or might not be a feasible approach. Each layer in GeoServer has a setting that enables you to define whether it is advertised in the *GetCapabilities* response document. In addition to this, there is a global WMS setting that lets you control whether the protected layers are publicly advertised or only advertised to authenticated users.

If the layers are advertised, then the welcome page for GeoServer will have an option on the left-hand side panel called **Layer Preview**:

Clicking on the link will open the **Layer Preview** page and present a list of all the layers that can be advertised. This page allows users to select a layer and then preview it using one of the different service-output formats that GeoServer supports. All the layers have a link called **OpenLayers** that will create a simple OpenLayers application and display the selected layer in it. There is also a drop-down list of formats, and the format selected determines the service that is used. For example, selecting **GML 3.2** from the list will trigger a WFS request for this layer.

GeoServer supports the export of information through KML using something called the **KML Reflector** (`http://docs.geoserver.org/stable/en/user/googleearth/features/kmlreflector.html`).

 KML is the common format for data in Google Earth and Google Maps.

KML is generated as a network link, which means it embeds the WMS link to the reflector inside the KML file. Google Earth then uses this network link to request data for the layer as the user pans and zooms inside the application.

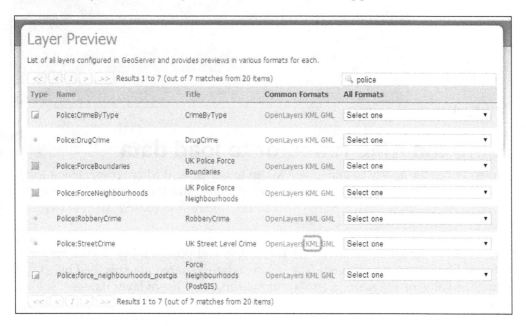

To trigger the creation of KML, simply click on the **KML** link and then choose to open the file returned rather than downloading it. If Google Earth is installed on your system, it will open the KML file and then begin to request data from GeoServer:

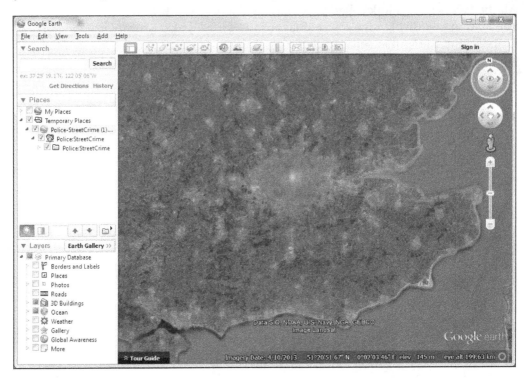

Using the KML reflector to load data

GeoServer has the ability to generate KML in response to WMS requests using the KML reflector. The KML reflector simply takes a URL and then returns KML in response. An example URL is `http://[server address]:[port]/geoserver/wms/kml?layers=[lyername]`.

Here, `[server address]` and `[port]` is the DNS and port number of your server that runs GeoServer, respectively. The layers to be generated are specified by setting the value of `[layername]` to a comma-separated list of layer names present in GeoServer.

The capability of specifying links to data using the KML reflector can be utilized by providing links on a central website or providing links contained in metadata. Users can also share links to data through e-mails.

Using Google Earth network links

A better way of integrating data into Google Earth is using the network link capability to create a direct connection to GeoServer. A Network Link in Google Earth will connect to GeoServer using the KML reflector. This will allow the users to refresh data from within Google Earth without having to go back to layer preview.

A Network Link is created by navigating to **Add** | **Network Link** in Google Earth.

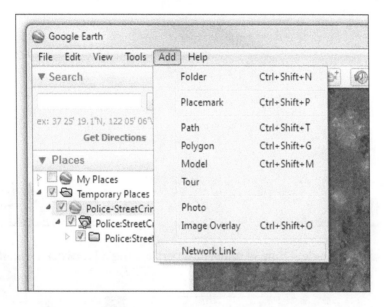

This will open a dialog that will enable us to enter the details for the Network Link to add. Specify the KML reflector URL for the layer or layers you want to add, and specify a name for it. Optionally, set a description, and you can also change the refresh defaults using the **Refresh** tab.

For example, you can have Google Earth refresh the data on a specified interval; this will be useful if you are publishing a layer that links through real-time or near real-time data.

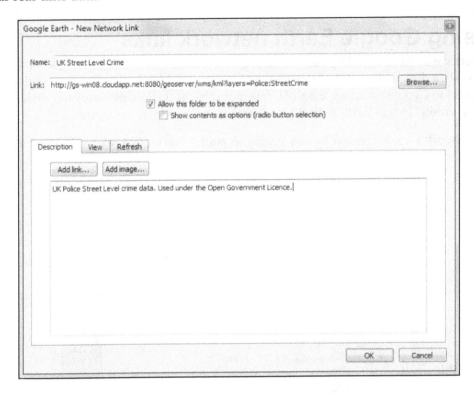

If the **My Places** tree-view item is selected when adding a Network Link, it will be added as a child.

Now, whenever the view in Google Earth is refreshed, the layer will be requested from GeoServer.

Summary

In this chapter, we have taken a high-level look at what an SDI is and the role that GeoServer plays in implementing one. We discussed how an SDI is built on four core tenets of people, policy, standards, and data. An SDI is much more than just an implementation of technology, but the realization of an SDI is through a physical technology platform. By discussing a logical architecture for an SDI, we discovered that its core can be fairly simple, typically consisting of data storage, a metadata server to enable the discovery of data, and an implementation of a web mapping server that supports open standards. We learned that an SDI should be an open platform that a multitude of tools can connect to and consume data from.

To see how a user might interact with an SDI, we considered two different user perspectives: the first was *power user* editing data that is stored centrally, and the second was a *data consumer* who connects to and consumes data from the SDI.

In this chapter, we saw the important role that GeoServer plays in an SDI. In the next chapter, we will look at how GeoServer can be used as a spatial-analysis platform, further demonstrating the core role that it plays in an SDI.

9
GeoServer as a Spatial Analysis Platform

Until now, we have concentrated on GeoServer's ability to serve raster and vector data from file stores and spatial databases. For a large number of use cases, rendering a map for a web application is sufficient. However, there are use cases where one might like to perform server-side spatial analysis and then render the results to the client. As soon as you mention server-side spatial analysis, most people will assume that you need to spend a small fortune to implement a cluster of ArcGIS for server instances to perform Geoprocessing operations. However, GeoServer has a number of tricks up its sleeves that can be used to perform almost any form of spatial analysis you can imagine. With a little bit of effort, GeoServer can challenge any commercial server-side spatial analysis toolkit.

In this chapter, we will look at different approaches to server-side spatial analysis that GeoServer can perform. We will cover the following topics:

- Understanding what a **Web Processing Service (WPS)** is
- How to install and configure WPS
- Using a WPS to perform spatial analysis
- Chaining WPS processes to perform more complex analysis
- Understand what GeoScript is and how it can be used
- How to install and configure GeoScript
- Using GeoScript to create a WPS process
- Using GeoScript to extend GeoServer

Understanding Web Processing Services

A **WPS** is an OGC standard to invoke geospatial processing services across the Web. The standard (http://www.opengeospatial.org/standards/wps) defines a structure that allows for a common interpretation of input and output parameters to processing services. The standard provides an abstract layer to individual vendors' internal processing engines and ensures that clients can call any WPS, irrespective of its backend technology. The standard stipulates three operations that must be exposed:

Operation	Purpose
GetCapabilities	This operation returns an XML document that describes the capabilities of the WPS, the processes on offer, and how they can be called.
DescribeProcess	This operation returns an XML document that provides a detailed description of the process and includes the details required to provide the right inputs and to be able to understand the responses.
Execute	This operation is what a client will call when they want to invoke a specific process.

A WPS process

A WPS process is the atomic unit of a WPS service. This process is the actual geoprocessing code that will be executed on the server when invoked by an **Execute WPS** request. A WPS process can have multiple inputs of different types; these can be passed into the process by value or reference. When passed in by value, the caller is responsible for encoding the input data appropriately, based on the requirements of the process listed in the *DescribeProcess XML* document. Passing values by reference is a more interesting capability of a WPS. In this case, the value for the input parameter will be a reference to another location, typically another web mapping server or possibly even some other web service. For example, the input to a WPS process can be the result of calling another web service or even another WFS server with a Query operation to return a set of features to work on.

A WPS process can return multiple outputs, so a process is not limited to a single output parameter. It is also possible to use the output of one process as the input for another; this is known as **WPS process chaining**.

WPS process chaining

Running a single WPS process to perform some analysis is only going to allow us to achieve a small degree of spatial analysis. If we want to perform a more complex analysis, then we would need to run lots of different WPS processes, each time saving the output in order to use it in the next WPS process. This would be very time-consuming and is not a user-friendly approach to server-side spatial analysis.

WPS process chaining to the rescue!

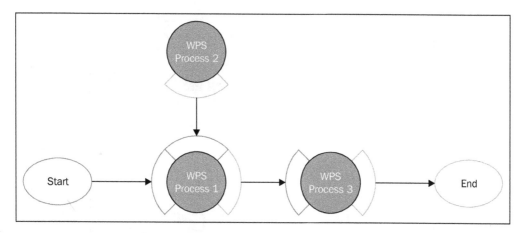

WPS process chaining allows us to take the output of one process and use it as the input to another. The whole set of instructions for all of the WPS processes to be executed is wrapped up into one single WPS process execute operation. We will take a more detailed look at process chaining later in this chapter to see how useful it is when calling multiple, related geoprocessing operations.

Installing the WPS extension

Like all other GeoServer extensions, the WPS extension is straightforward to install. As usual, it is simply a matter of obtaining the correct ZIP file for the extension and then decompressing it to your GeoServer directory. Ensure that you download the correct version of the extension for the GeoServer that you are running. In our case, we are running the current stable version (Version 2.5.2 at the time of writing this book) of GeoServer, so we need to download the extension from `http://www.geoserver.org/release/stable`.

The download page has a section called **Extensions**, as shown in the following screenshot:

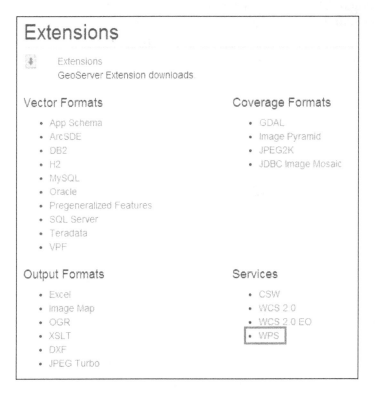

In the **Extensions** section, there is a subgroup named **Services**. Click on the **WPS** link to download a version of the plugin that works with the current stable version of GeoServer. When prompted, save the file to a location on your system, and then open a command line and change the directory to the location. The contents of the ZIP file need to be uncompressed to the WEB-INF/lib folder of your GeoServer installation. This can be achieved by entering the following command in your shell:

```
$ unzip geoserver-2.5.2-wps-plugin.zip *.jar -d <tomcat_home>/WEB-INF/lib
```

This command will extract the files with a .jar extension into the lib folder of your GeoServer instance. Remember to change <tomcat_home> to the folder where your Tomcat instance is installed. Repeat the process for all of your Tomcat instances. For the extension to be recognised by GeoServer, you will need to restart it; do this for all the instances of GeoServer.

Checking whether the extension is installed correctly

There are three ways in which you can check to make sure that the extension is installed correctly. The WPS extension creates a new OGC service end-point in GeoServer. We can use the standard `GetCapabilities` call to request an XML document that describes what our server is capable of doing. From a command line, we can use a tool such as cURL to issue the request:

```
$ curl http://[hostname]:[port]/geoserver/ows?service=wps&version=1.0.0&r
equere=GetCapabilities -o WPSCapabilities.xml
```

 If you are running cURL from a Windows command prompt, the ampersands (&) in the service URL will cause errors, as they have a special meaning in MS-DOS. To prevent this, either replace each single ampersand with double ampersands (&&) or enclose the URL in quotes (" ").

Replace `[hostname]` and `[port]` with the values for your instance of GeoServer. If the WPS extension is properly installed, this command will result in a file called `WPSCapabilities.xml`) being saved to your computer. Opening this file in a text editor will allow you to see a complete description of the capabilities of your WPS service.

If you don't have cURL installed on your computer, then you can check for the service capabilities from the front page of the GeoServer web administration console:

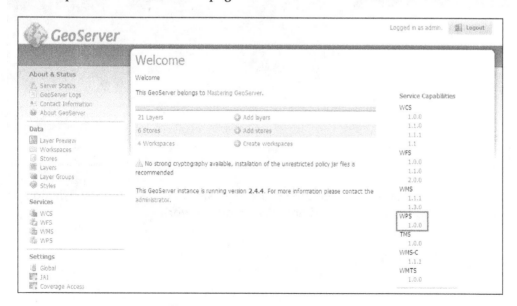

If the extension is installed correctly, there will be a WPS entry in the list of `Service Capabilities` on the right-hand side of the main page. Clicking on the **1.0.0** link will issue the `GetCapabilities` request and return the service capabilities XML file.

The third way to check whether the extension is installed correctly is to check whether the demo app is present in the web administration console. Navigating to `http://[hostname]:[port]/geoserver/ web/?wicket:bookmarkablePage=:o rg.geoserver.web.DemoPage` (change `[hostname]` and `[port]` to your instance) will open the **GeoServer Demos** page:

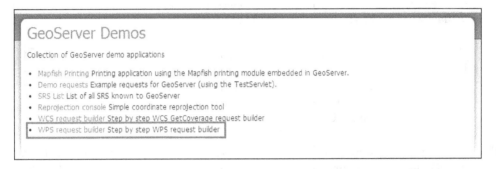

In the list of available demos, there should be one called **WPS request builder Step by step WPS request builder**. Clicking on this link will open the demo app that will guide you through the process of building a WPS service request:

Feel free to play around with building some requests now. We will use the demo app later in this chapter to understand how WPS requests work.

Configuring the extension

The WPS extension creates an OGC-compliant service that GeoServer exposes in the same way as other OGC-compliant services such as WMS and WFS. This means that it is possible to configure how certain elements of the service operate. For example, it is possible to set the service metadata that is published as part of the capabilities XML document. To manage the configuration of the service, you can access its configuration page in the same way you do for other OGC services:

To access the service configuration page, click on the **WPS** link from the **Services** section on the left-hand side menu in the web administration console. The configuration page will be familiar to you if you already accessed one of the other service configuration pages. The service configuration page is divided into sections, with each section affecting a specific part of the service configuration.

The workspace configuration section

As with all other services exposed by GeoServer, it is possible to create local configurations that differ from the global ones. Whether a service has local configurations is determined by the settings for each workspace. Workspaces can be set to have their own local configurations on a per-service basis through the **Edit Workspace** page, accessed by selecting a workspace:

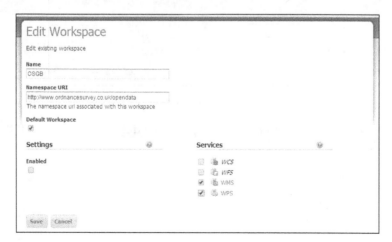

In the preceding example, the OSGB workspace has been configured to have local configurations for the WMS and WPS services. With the WPS service ticked on the **Edit Workspace** page, the OSGB workspace will be populated in the drop-down list, enabling us to define the WPS service options specific to the OSGB workspace.

 This setting demonstrates a capability within GeoServer called virtual services. By default, the contents of all workspaces are published through the various web services (WMS, WFS, WCS, and so on). However, virtual services makes it possible to publish only the content assigned to the workspace that the virtual service is called from. For more information on using virtual services, look at the GeoServer documentation at `http://docs.geoserver.org/2.4.x/en/user/services/virtual-services.html`.

The Service Metadata configuration section

All of the OGC-compliant services must expose their capabilities by publishing a capabilities XML document in response to a `GetCapabilities` request. GeoServer builds the response XML document by combining information from a number of places, depending on the service. There are common contact elements across all of the services, and these are set using the **Contact Information** page of the web administration console:

Contact information

The details set on this page can be used to populate default values for all the capabilities documents that are output.

Possibly, the most important setting in the **Service Metadata** section is the one titled **Enable WPS**. It can be found as the first item in the section, as shown in the following screenshot:

Service Metadata
☑ Enable WPS

☐ Strict CITE compliance

Maintainer
Colin Henderson

Online resource
http://www.example.com

If this checkbox is not checked, the WPS service will be disabled, and therefore unavailable for use.

The service metadata elements that can be set are explained in the following table:

Setting	Description
Maintainer	This is the name of an individual or division that is responsible for maintaining the service to enable users of the service to have a point of contact
Online resource	This is the location of the service online
Title	This is a title to describe the intent of the service
Abstract	This is a brief description of what the service is and what it offers
Fees	This is a description of any fees incurred through use of the service
Access constraints	These are any constraints there are on access to the service
Current keywords	This is a list of keywords to aid in service discovery

The Execution Settings configuration section

The **Execution Settings** section enables us to control how WPS processes will be executed within our environment. There are three settings available to us, as shown in the following screenshot:

Execution Settings

Connection Timeout (seconds, -1 for infinite timeout)

30

Maximum asynchronous executions run parallel

8

Maximum synchronous executions run parallel

8

The settings available are explained in the following table:

Setting name	Description
Connection timeout	This is the amount of time the service should wait before it considers a connection attempt to have failed
Maximum asynchronous executions run parallel	This is the total number of process executions that are allowed to run in parallel when the service is called asynchronously
Maximum synchronous executions run parallel	This is the total number of process executions that are allowed to run in parallel when the service is called synchronously

 Setting the maximum synchronous and asynchronous process executions is important in order to ensure that your server is not over burdened with running WPS processes.

The Process groups configuration section

When the capabilities document is published, it must list all the processes that can be called by a client. A WPS client can present this list of available processes to the end user in some form of selection user interface. GeoServer comes with a number of out-of-the-box WPS processes, and these are collected into process groups. There are a large number of processes available, and depending on our needs, we might not want all of them to be published through the service. The **Process groups** configuration section provides us with a mechanism to control which processes are published:

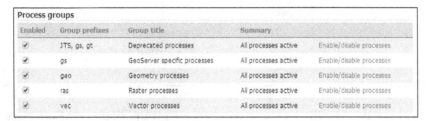

A list of process groups is provided, along with summary information about each one. Any processes without a checked box will be disabled. All the processes belonging to the disabled group will not be published through the capabilities document.

In addition to being able to toggle the enabled state of an entire process group, we can also toggle the state for individual processes within a group. Click on the **Enable/disable processes** link for the **Raster processes** row, as shown in the following screenshot:

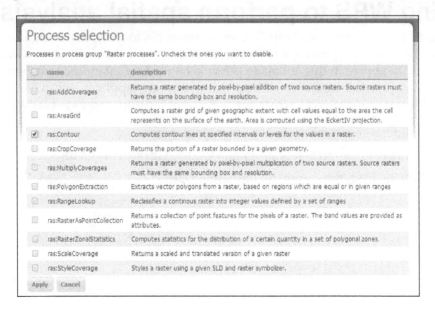

The **Process selection** page allows us to select the processes that we want to enable or disable. By default, all the processes are enabled. Let's disable all the processes, except for ras:Contour, and then click on the **Apply** button. The service configuration page will be loaded, and the **Process groups** table will have changed, as shown in the following screenshot:

Process groups

Enabled	Group prefixes	Group title	Summary	
✔	JTS, gs, gt	Deprecated processes	All processes active	Enable/disable processes
✔	gs	GeoServer specific processes	All processes active	Enable/disable processes
✔	geo	Geometry processes	All processes active	Enable/disable processes
✔	ras	Raster processes	1 active processes out of 11	Enable/disable processes
✔	vec	Vector processes	All processes active	Enable/disable processes

We can now see that the **Raster processes** process group displays a **Summary** value of **1 active processes out of 11**. If we were to perform a capabilities request, only the ras:Contour process will be reported from the **Raster processes** group.

Once we are happy with the configuration of our WPS service, we can click on the **Submit** button to commit the changes to the configuration. Now our GetCapabilities document will reflect the changes that we made to the configuration.

Using WPS to perform spatial analysis

Now that we have configured our GeoServer instances to work as a spatial analysis platform, we can start putting it to work. There are a number of different ways in which we can approach this, all made possible by the OGC standards implemented. Since we are just dealing with a web service, almost any application can be used to send WPS requests and receive responses. Some of the approaches we can take are:

- Build a web mapping client using OpenLayers
- Connect to the WPS service using Desktop GIS such as QGIS
- Execute from the command line using cURL

Regardless of the approach that you want to take, they all have one thing in common: they communicate with the WPS service over HTTP POST using XML. To really learn and understand what is happening, we should interact with the XML directly. Fortunately, GeoServer provides us with a **WPS request builder** application that we can use to interactively build up WPS requests in XML. The request builder was installed as part of the WPS extension and can be accessed by selecting the **Demos** option from the left-hand side menu of the web administration console:

GeoServer Demos

Collection of GeoServer demo applications

* Mapfish Printing Printing application using the Mapfish printing module embedded in GeoServer.
* Demo requests Example requests for GeoServer (using the TestServlet).
* SRS List List of all SRS known to GeoServer
* Reprojection console Simple coordinate reprojection tool
* WCS request builder Step by step WCS GetCoverage request builder
* WPS request builder Step by step WPS request builder

The request builder demo is run by selecting the **WPS request builder** option from the **GeoServer Demos** page. We will use the request builder to try out some different WPS processes.

Executing a WPS process

At its most basic, a WPS service will be used to execute a single process. For example, we might call a `buffer` process to generate a buffer around a given location that we want to show on a map, an exclusion zone, for example. Alternately, we might want to buffer a certain location in order to select other features that are within this zone.

We are now going to execute a simple WPS process to generate a buffer polygon; if we mapped the output from the process, we would get a polygon similar to the one shown in the following screenshot:

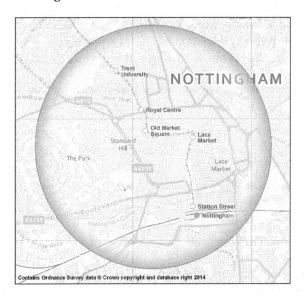

To create this buffer polygon, we will generate a WPS process request and then execute it. We will use the WPS request builder described earlier to build and then execute the request. The first thing we need to do is select the process that we want to execute:

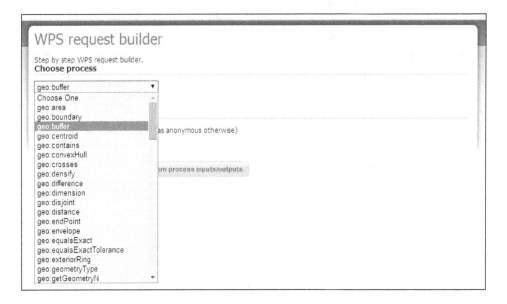

The drop-down list is generated by GeoServer issuing the `GetCapabilities` request on the WPS service. It has parsed the capabilities document and generated a list of processes by extracting the `/wps:Capabilities/wps:ProcessOfferings/wps:Process/ows:Identifier` elements. We are interested in the `geo:buffer` process, so let's select it from the list.

After selecting the `geo:buffer` option from the drop-down, a form is dynamically generated with all the fields that we need to complete. The form itself is divided into sections for process input parameters and process output parameters. GeoServer can dynamically generate this form by reading the contents of an XML response document that describes the process selected. We can look at the contents of such a file by requesting this URL: `http://[server address]:[port]/geoserver/ows?service=WPS&version=1.0.0&request=DescribeProcess&identifier=geo:buffer`.

The response XML document contains all the information that we would need if we were building our own interface to execute WPS processes. GeoServer has made a `DescribeProcess` request and then interpreted the response to generate the correct input and output options.

For process inputs, it has read the collection of elements that match `wps:ProcessDescriptions/ProcessDescription/DataInputs/Input/*`, which results in GeoServer generating the following input form:

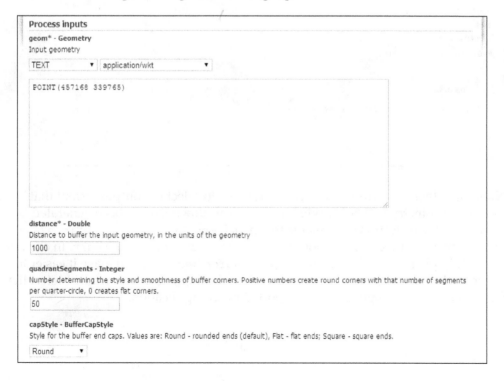

For our purposes, we will specify the location we want to buffer by entering the point as **Well-Known Text (WKT)**. Select the TEXT entry from the first drop-down list for input geometry, and then, in the second drop-down, select the application/ wkt entry. In the text box, enter POINT(457168 339765), which will create a point as the geometry to be buffered. This can just as easily be a polygon or line; we can select this by entering syntactically correct WKT.

The next input that we need to provide is a value for the distance for which we want to buffer our point geometry. This will be in the units of the geometry (in our case, this is meters, as we are dealing with data in the British National Grid coordinate system). Helpfully, there is a little prompt to guide us; this has been read from the ows:Abstract child element of the Input parent. Also, notice how the expected data type is written in the title to the input element on the form.

We will complete the input parameters by specifying the value 50 for quadrantSegments and choosing the Round option from the drop-down list for capStyle.

Wih the process inputs completed, we can now specify the process outputs. For this particular example, the process output will be a geometry object. The generated form provides us with the process output details, including the data type for the output:

Notice that there is a drop-down that enables us to select the output format that the result geometry will be encoded in. This drop-down list has been generated by reading the collection of elements that match wps:ProcessDescriptions/ ProcessDescription/ProcessOutputs/ComplexOutput/Supported/*. In our case, we will simply request the output as application/wkt, as it will make it easier to interpret the output generated. In an actual application, however, we will select the format most appropriate to those supported by the application.

Have you noticed the **Authentication** section? By default, the request builder will attempt to execute the process as an anonymous user. If we enabled security on our GeoServer instance, then we would need to check the **Authenticate** box and provide the username and password details into the fields that appear.

With the form completed, we can now either execute the process and get back a response, or we can ask GeoServer to show us what the generated XML content to post to the WPS service will look like. If we click on the **Generate XML from process inputs/outputs** button, a dialog will be displayed:

```xml
<?xml version="1.0" encoding="UTF-8"?><wps:Execute version="1.0.0" service="WPS"
  <ows:Identifier>geo:buffer</ows:Identifier>
  <wps:DataInputs>
    <wps:Input>
      <ows:Identifier>geom</ows:Identifier>
      <wps:Data>
        <wps:ComplexData mimeType="application/wkt"><![CDATA[POINT(457168 339765
      </wps:Data>
    </wps:Input>
    <wps:Input>
      <ows:Identifier>distance</ows:Identifier>
      <wps:Data>
        <wps:LiteralData>1000</wps:LiteralData>
      </wps:Data>
    </wps:Input>
    <wps:Input>
      <ows:Identifier>quadrantSegments</ows:Identifier>
      <wps:Data>
        <wps:LiteralData>50</wps:LiteralData>
      </wps:Data>
```

The dialog contains the generated XML that will be sent to the WPS service as the body of a POST request.

 Being able to view the generated XML request is a very useful feature of the *WPS request builder*. It provides us with a visual tool to build WPS requests that we can then copy and use in our own applications.

We can go ahead and ask GeoServer to execute the process that we defined by clicking on the **Execute process** button. This will send the process execution request to the WPS service and wait for a response. Depending on the format type selected for the output, our browser will either present us with a **Save As…** dialog to save the generated file to disk or simply display the result inside a pop-up window. Whether the result is displayed or downloaded will depend on the **Multipurpose Internet Mail Extensions (MIME)** type for the format requested as the output. We selected `application/wkt`; the browser will interpret this as a downloadable file type and act accordingly. The XML request and WKT result of this particular request can be found inside the code bundle of this book.

Executing chained WPS processes

In the previous section, we saw how easy it was to build a single WPS request to return a result. However, there will often be times when a single WPS process will not be sufficient to provide us with the answer that we require. For example, we might need to perform several processing steps on our data before we can make the final analysis and obtain a result.

The traditional way to achieve this will be to break the analysis down into smaller steps, saving the output of each step for use in the next, finally arriving at our desired answer and a final dataset. In a desktop environment, this is relatively straightforward, albeit time consuming, to achieve. However, in a server environment, this will be more difficult as we will need to store the intermediate data outputs of each stage and then clean up afterwards. This process can be made easy if we utilize the ability of WPS to perform process chaining, where the outputs of one process can be the inputs to another, with the server cleaning itself as it moves along the process chain.

To demonstrate this, let's consider a simple piece of analysis that we might perform in order to determine the amount of crime, of a particular type, that occurs within a specific Police Force territory. To perform this analysis, we need to determine three different things:

- We need to select the type of crime (user defined) from the police crimes dataset.
- We need to select the polygon that represents the boundary of a specific Police Force (user defined).
- We need to select only the crimes of the specified type that are within the selected Police Force boundary polygon. This will give us the subset of data we want.

To accomplish this, we will use GeoServer's `vec:InclusionFeatureCollection` WPS process and feed it with the data that will be the result of two `vec:Query` WPS processes:

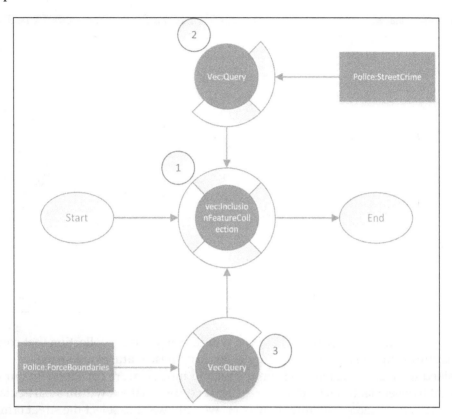

The preceding diagram is a visual representation of what we will attempt; a data-flow diagram. The WPS process that we will call at the start is `vec:InclusionFeatureCollection`. This process has two inputs: the first input **(2)** is the result from a `vec:Query` WPS process, and the second one **(3)** is the result from another `vec:Query` WPS process. The final result of these chained processes will be a feature collection of all the `Police:StreetCrime` features that fall within the selected `Police:ForceBoundaries` feature.

 It is important to remember that the sequence in which you use WPS processes is important. Think carefully about what you want the chained process to achieve. I find it useful to draw out the execution plan first in a data-flow diagram. I find that it helps clarify my thoughts and then build the necessary instructions.

Once again, we will use GeoServer's built-in request builder to assist us in creating the chained process execution XML. From the request builder, select the vec:InclusionFeatureCollection process, as this is our starting process:

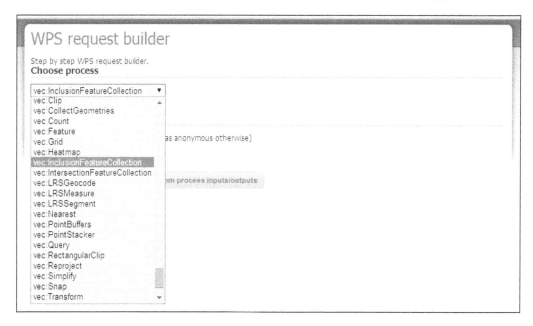

The vec:InclusionFeatureCollection will return a feature collection that contains the features from the first input feature collection; these features are spatially contained in at least one feature from the second input feature collection. In our case, we want to select features from Police:StreetCrime that are within a particular Police:ForceBoundary feature. However, we only want to select the street crime features that have the type of Robbery. To do this, we will use another WPS process called vec:Query.

Selecting the crime type

From the **Process Inputs** section, look for the first input. From the drop-down list, select the **SUBPROCESS** option and then click on the **Define/Edit** link:

This will open another dialog window where we can now specify the `vec:Query` process to execute. This process requires two mandatory inputs that inform it about the feature collection to query and the type of query to perform:

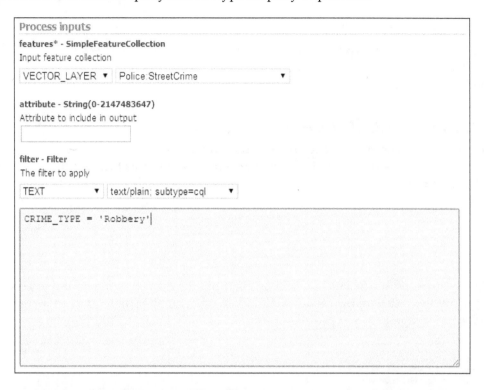

We want the query to be performed on the `Police:StreetCrime` layer, so we chose the **VECTOR_LAYER** option from the drop-down and then selected the **Police:StreetCrime** option from the second drop-down. The list of available vector layers is discovered when GeoServer queries the vector data layers we configured.

Next, we need to specify the query to perform on the features. In this case, a query is created using a WFS filter, so the drop-down contains three types of filter that we can use:

- OGC filter specification 1.0
- OGC filter specification 1.1
- CQL

It doesn't matter which one we choose, as long as the value we enter in the textbox below is valid for the filter type chosen. In this case, we will use CQL. We need to write a valid CQL statement in the box, which, in this case, is very simple:

```
CRIME_TYPE = 'Robbery'
```

When we click on the **Apply** button, GeoServer will inject the correct XML WPS `ExecuteProcess` command into the textbox for the first input to `vec:InclusionFeatureCollection`.

Selecting the Police Force territory

Now we need to do the same for the second input of the process. In this case, we want to perform another `vec:Query` process, but this time, on the `Police:ForceBoundaries` vector layer:

We need to select the **SUBPROCESS** option from the drop-down list for the second input and then click on the **Define/Edit** link to open another dialog where we can define the next `vec:Query` process to run:

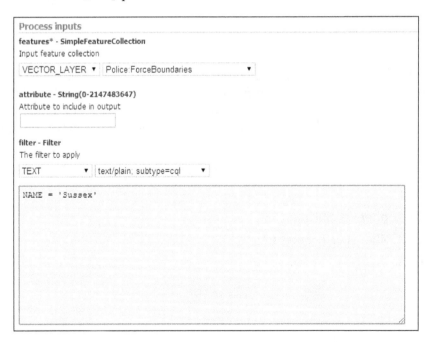

This time we will select `Police:ForceBoundaries` as **VECTOR_LAYER** and set another CQL filter expression to:

```
NAME = 'Sussex'
```

Again, we need to click on the **Apply** button to have the generated XML `ExecuteProcess` injected into the textbox for the second input of the original `vec:InclusionFeatureCollection` process. We will now have a completed form similar to the one shown in the following screenshot:

We will now have both inputs for the `vec:InclusionFeatureCollection` process set as XML `ExecuteProcess` commands.

Executing the WPS process chain

All that remains now is for us to choose the output format for the results and then execute the process:

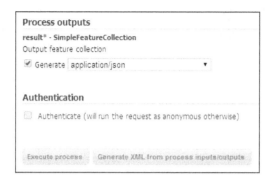

The result output feature collection can be a range of formats that include GML, JSON, and WKT. The most common use case to execute WPS processes will be from the Web, so the best output format to choose will likely be `application/json`. Ultimately, it does not matter what output format we choose as long as the application that will receive the results is capable of reading the output format that we choose.

We can now click on the **Generate XML from process inputs/outputs** button to get a generated XML `ExecuteProcess` request, or we can click on **Execute process** and wait for our results:

```
{"type":"FeatureCollection","features":[{"type":"Feature","geometry":
{"type":"Point","coordinates":[531189.7785,103901.9105]},"properties":
{"CRIME_ID":"96c8fc0265cfdeda39a6612b49343286e4c8c8c6009b38e9a98a242a24c721f4","MONT
H":"2013-12","REPORTED_BY":"Metropolitan Police
Service","FALLS_WITHIN":"Metropolitan Police
Service","LONGITUDE":-0.138962,"LATITUDE":50.81982,"LOCATION":"On or near
Nightclub","LSOA_CODE":"E01016952","LSOA_NAME":"Brighton and Hove
027A","CRIME_TYPE":"Robbery","LAST_OUTCOME_CATEGORY":"Under
investigation","CONTEXT":"
"},"id":"StreetCrime.196799"},{"type":"Feature","geometry":
{"type":"Point","coordinates":[517831.7903,104897.888]},"properties":
{"CRIME_ID":"dcdb211aad1e3747b029b7f96fc6301166a5c2cb22dd5c1a2481b68b8a240399","MONT
H":"2013-12","REPORTED_BY":"Sussex Police","FALLS_WITHIN":"Sussex
Police","LONGITUDE":-0.328186,"LATITUDE":50.831642,"LOCATION":"On or near Lancing
Close","LSOA_CODE":"E01031355","LSOA_NAME":"Adur
003D","CRIME_TYPE":"Robbery","LAST_OUTCOME_CATEGORY":"Under
investigation","CONTEXT":"
"},"id":"StreetCrime.353539"},{"type":"Feature","geometry":
{"type":"Point","coordinates":[493939.7962,99680.9283]},"properties":
{"CRIME_ID":"5fa67d6c7b10e13e35a159eabf979540c2d731ba046a7d3f28204e58b634cba9","MONT
H":"2013-12","REPORTED_BY":"Sussex Police","FALLS_WITHIN":"Sussex
Police","LONGITUDE":-0.668672,"LATITUDE":50.789107,"LOCATION":"On or near Upper
Bognor Road","LSOA_CODE":"E01031431","LSOA_NAME":"Arun
017A","CRIME_TYPE":"Robbery","LAST_OUTCOME_CATEGORY":"Under
investigation","CONTEXT":"
"},"id":"StreetCrime.354383"},{"type":"Feature","geometry":
{"type":"Point","coordinates":[531199.77,108606.9097]},"properties":
{"CRIME_ID":"b529419f9520e3364fe529e844104a744897f592856eba562055ef748b530b01","MONT
```

The generated XML `ExecuteProcess` request for this example is available in the code bundle of this book, along with the `application/json` response.

Understanding GeoScript

The stated goal of the GeoScript project is to provide a geoprocessing library that is easy to use and available in a variety of scripting environments. It uses the same GeoTools library that GeoServer is built on, which means there is a wide range of things that can be accomplished with GeoScript:

- Support for a range of spatial formats
- The ability to render spatial data, including control over styling
- Support for different projections and coordinate systems and the ability to reproject data
- A wide range of geometry manipulation functions

GeoScript itself is a wrapper over the core GeoTools API, providing a layer of abstraction and making the power of the GeoTools library accessible to non-Java developers. GeoScript has its own API to access the core set of functionality from GeoTools; however, due to the way that it is built, it is possible to call any method from the GeoTools API directly. So, if you are a GeoTools developer or can work your way around the documentation, then you can utilize the full power of GeoTools in your own projects through the simplicity of scripting.

At the time of writing this book, GeoScript in GeoServer is available in the following languages:

- Python
- JavaScript
- Groovy
- Beanshell
- Ruby

If you are using a scripting language other than those listed, then it might be possible for you to make use of it by building support into GeoScript. The conditions to build your own scripting language support are:

- The language should have an implementation available on the JVM
- The language runtime should have a JSR-223-compliant script engine

If your scripting language meets these two requirements, then it will be possible to build support for it into GeoScript.

GeoScript is a comprehensive library, and it is not possible to do justice to it in a small section of a chapter. The GeoScript website has a range of examples and documentation to help get you started, and it is recommended that you take a look to really see the power of GeoScript. Visit http://www.geoscript.org for more information.

GeoScript integration with GeoServer

GeoScript has been integrated with GeoServer through some community plugins. These plugins work by creating extension points within the GeoServer subsystem; these extension points are called script hooks. Each script hook has a corresponding directory within the GeoServer data directory into which we can place scripts. As scripting is dynamic, there is no need to restart GeoServer when we add new scripts or modify the existing scripts within a hook directory. The scripting plugin has a filesystem watcher that triggers a dynamic load of a script when it sees something changing.

The available script hooks in GeoServer are:

Hook	Purpose
App	This enables scripts to be run over HTTP, for example, providing a new web service
Function	This provides scripts as functions that can be used in OGC filters for use in WFS queries and SLD styling rules
WPS	This allows the creation of a WPS process
WFSTX	This allows the creation of output formats for WFS transactions

Creating and deploying scripts for these hooks is as simple as writing the script in your favorite text editor or IDE and then saving it into the correct directory. As discussed earlier, scripts are stored in a specific location within the GeoServer data directory, and a file watcher looks for changes in these locations.

The directory structure is shown here:

```
<geoserver_data_directory>
    scripts
        apps
            app-name-1
            app-name-2
            app-name-x
        function
        lib
            py
            js
        process
        wfs
```

The `<geoserver_data_directory>` directory is the location of the root GeoServer data directory. Inside the root is a directory named `scripts`, which is the root directory for the scripting extension.

The `apps` directory is where we can store scripts that will be treated as if they were web pages that can be run over HTTP. Each app that we deploy should have its own folder within the `apps` folder, and the structure will determine the URL needed to call the service. For example, if we stored an app in a folder called `app-name-1`, then we can access that service over HTTP using the `http://<server_name>:<port>/web/scripts/app-name-1` URL, where `<server_name>` is the name or IP address of our server, and `<port>` is the port on which GeoServer is listening.

The `function` directory is where we can store scripts that will be treated as functions by GeoServer. We can then use these functions within WFS queries and SLD styling rules. The heatmap render transformation example shown in *Chapter 6, Controlling the Output of GeoServer*, is an example of a function being used in an SLD rule.

The `lib` folder is a special folder that does not relate to any script extension hooks. It is a common folder location where we can place additional modules/functions that our scripts might need to use. For example, we might want to use the Python Flask micro-web framework module in one of our apps; in this case, we would place the modules in the `py` subdirectory of the `lib` folder. Similarly, for JavaScript, we would place the module/function files in the `js` subdirectory of `lib`.

The `process` folder is where we save scripts that we want to be exposed through the WPS web service.

The `wfs` folder is where we save scripts that we want to be treated as available output formats for WFS requests. These can then be called by specifying the appropriate value for the `OUTPUT_FORMAT` parameter of a WFS request.

With the exception of the `lib/py` and `lib/js` folders, we do not need to worry about having different script files in the same folder. The GeoServer script manager takes care of identifying the type of script from its extension, so files with an extension of `.js` will be interpreted using the JavaScript scripting environment.

Installing the GeoScript extension

This should be very familiar to us now! The scripting extension can be installed in the same way as all other extensions. Download the relevant ZIP file and then unzip its contents to the `geoserver/WEB-INF/lib` folder in the servlet container. However, the scripting extension is a little different in that there is a different extension for each of the supported languages. The following table lists the language and the location to download the corresponding extension; once again it is important to match the version of GeoServer. We are using the current stable version, which, at the time of writing this book, is 2.5.2.

Language	Extension download URL
Python	http://ares.boundlessgeo.com/geoserver/2.5.x/community-latest/geoserver-2.5-SNAPSHOT-python-plugin.zip
Groovy	http://ares.boundlessgeo.com/geoserver/2.5.x/community-latest/geoserver-2.5-SNAPSHOT-groovy-plugin.zip
JavaScript	http://ares.boundlessgeo.com/geoserver/2.5.x/community-latest/geoserver-2.5-SNAPSHOT-javascript-plugin.zip

Select the link that corresponds to the language you would like to use and then download the ZIP file to your system. For the following examples, we will use the Python version of the scripting extension. We will refer to the Python version of the scripting extension simply as the *scripting extension*.

Open a command line on the directory where you downloaded the file to, and enter the following command:

```
$ unzip geoserver-2.5-SNAPSHOT-python-plugin.zip *.jar -d <tomcat_home>/
webapps/geoserver/WEB-INF/lib
```

This command will extract the files with a `.jar` extension into the `lib` folder of your GeoServer instance. Remember to change `<tomcat_home>` to the folder where your Tomcat instance is installed. Repeat the process for all of your Tomcat instances and then restart them.

 The scripting extensions, by their nature, include a lot of additional `.jar` files and classes that will need to be loaded when GeoServer runs. It is important to bear this in mind, as classes are loaded into the PermGen space. Make sure that this memory setting is set to at least 256 Mb to ensure that you do not receive any PermGen space errors. Take a look at `http://docs.geoserver.org/stable/en/user/community/scripting/installation.html` for more details.

If you decide that you would like to script in multiple languages, then by all means, go ahead and install the relevant plugins. In order for each extension to work in its own right, it is necessary to include common `.jar` files across all of them; this means that when you come to unzip the extensions, you may get warning messages about files already existing. You will be asked if you would like to ignore these files or overwrite them; it doesn't matter which option you choose, as all the files are the same.

Checking whether the extension has been installed correctly

In the current version of the scripting extension, there is no web GUI for us to interact with and, therefore, nothing for us to go to in order to check whether the extension has been installed correctly and has been picked up by GeoServer when it restarted. However, the extension does create the scripting hook extension points within the GeoServer data directory when it first runs. Therefore, the best way to check whether the extension has installed correctly is to change directory into the root of our GeoServer data directory. If the extension has been installed correctly, then we will see a folder named `scripts`.

Scripting GeoServer

Now it is time to make GeoServer do something for us through the magic of Python scripts. First, we will see how simple it can be to extend the spatial-analysis capabilities of GeoServer by scripting a WPS process. Then we will follow this up by seeing how simple it is to extend GeoServer's capabilities by creating a new RESTful service to get feature information.

Creating a WPS process

While GeoServer comes with an extensive list of built-in WPS processes, over time it is likely that we will demand more from it. The WPS extension will allow us to add more processes, but to do so will require us to write some Java code to create some JAR files that we will then need to deploy. Once deployed, we will then need to restart our GeoServer instance to ensure that the new process is picked up and loaded. If we do not know how to write Java, then this will be a difficult task to accomplish. However, if we have the scripting extension installed, then we can create a WPS process as a script. The best thing about scripting a WPS process is that it can be deployed simply by copying it into the `scripts` folder.

To demonstrate how easy it is to create a WPS process from a Python script, we will create one to analyze our UK Street Level crime data we loaded in *Chapter 3, Working with Vector Data in Spatial Databases*. The process that we will create will allow us to get a count of all the crimes of a specific type that are within a specified distance of a user-defined location. The logic that we will implement to make this work is:

- Receive the origin location for the search as a point
- Buffer the origin location by the `search_radius` value to constrain the search
- Perform a `WITHIN` spatial filter and attribute-based filter on the UK Street Level Crime dataset to find all the crime locations inside our search radius
- Count the total number found and return the result

The complete Python script for this is available in the code bundle of this chapter. To create the script. We first need to open a text editor or an IDE and create a new Python file; let's call it `CrimeWithinCountByType.py`.

> Think carefully about how you name the Python script file for a WPS process. The name of the file will become the name of the WPS process in the system, with the script type prefixed as the namespace. In our example, this will result in the process being called `py:CrimeWithinCountByType`.

Defining the WPS process

The start of the script includes some essential imports that we need in order for the script to be parsed and run correctly:

```
from geoserver.wps import process
from geoscript.workspace import PostGIS
from geoscript.geom import geom
from geoscript.filter import Filter
```

The first line imports GeoServer's process module, which is used to provide the capabilities for GeoServer to be able to publish the script as a WPS process. The remaining imports are GeoScript-specific imports to allow us to work with PostGIS database, geometry objects, and filters.

The next section of the script is the key to make GeoServer recognize that this script is meant to be a WPS process and to tell it how to register and interpret the script. This is a Python decorator, and it is used by GeoServer to register the script with the WPS service:

```
@process(
    title = 'Crime Within Count by Type',
    description = 'This process will return the number of crimes of a
specified type within distance of the given location',
    inputs = {
        'origin': (Point, 'The location to search within'),
        'crime_type': (str, 'The type of crime to count'),
        'search_radius': (float, 'The maximum radius to search')
    },
    outputs = {
        'count': (int, 'The number of crimes found within the search
distance')
    }
)
```

The keys in this decorator are used by GeoServer when the DescribeProcess WPS request is performed. The name of the decorator that the script extension will look for when it processes a script found in the /scripts/wps directory is @process; without it, an error will be thrown.

The title key is effectively ignored by GeoServer, as the Python scripting extension uses the name of the script file for the WPS process title. The description key, on the other hand, is used; it is the text that will be provided in the DescribeProcess and Capabilities responses. The WPS request builder tool uses the value to provide a description for the selected process:

WPS request builder

Step by step WPS request builder.
Choose process

py:CrimeWithinCountByType ▼

This process will return the number of crimes of a given type within the specified distance of a location (WPS DescribeProcess)

The next keys are `inputs` and `outputs`, and they tell GeoServer what information is required to be able to execute the process and what the user can expect in response. They are specified in the following format:

```
'<parameter_name>' : (type, '<description>')
```

First is the name of the parameter; this is what will be presented to the user on the request builder form, and this is how the parameter will be referred to in the request and response to the service. Following the colon, two pieces of information are required in parenthesis: the type of the parameter and a description for it. The type should be a valid Python type that GeoServer will then convert internally to a format that GeoServer and the underlying GeoTools require. For example, our input parameters are manifested in the request builder interface like this:

We have set the script to expect three inputs: `crime_type` as `String`, the `origin` location as `Point`, and `search_radius` as `Double`. Notice how the double on GeoServer is actually a Python float type in our script. This is GeoServer doing its thing to automatically turn the Python types into valid types that the WPS can use.

Creating the WPS process run method

GeoServer expects our script to have a main method called `run`. This is the entry point to the script that the WPS service will call when it executes. The method will take the same number of parameters that we specify in the decorator. Define the method like this:

```
def run(origin, crime_type, search_radius):
```

The three parameters are the same as we defined in the decorator, and GeoServer will pass the relevant values to our script when it executes. Now we need to start writing the code that will actually execute when the process runs. According to our logic, the first thing we need to do is take the location point and then buffer it. Enter the following into the script:

```
buffer_geom = geom.buffer(origin, search_radius)
```

That's it! One line of code to take the point and then buffer it by the amount specified to form our search radius. There are two reasons why we can achieve so much in such a small amount of code. First, GeoServer has received the input for the location either in WKT or one of the several versions of GML and automatically turned it into a GeoScript `Point` type that we can use straightaway. The second reason is that GeoScript provides us with a lot of convenience methods by abstracting the more complex underpinnings of GeoTools. For example, to create the buffer object that we will use in our spatial query, we just need to call the `geom.buffer` method and pass it the `origin` point object and the value for `search_radius`. We will assign the result of the buffer to a variable called `buffer_geom`.

The next thing we need to do is create a connection to our layer that we want to run the spatial query on. In this case, we will use the UK Street Level Crime data that we loaded into our PostGIS database. First, we need to create a connection to the database, and then we need to get the layer with the data. Now enter the following two lines to the script:

```
pgis_workspace = PostGIS('<db_name>', '<server>', '<port>',
'<schema>', '<username>', '<password>')
crime_lyr = pgis_workspace.get('uk_street_crime')
```

The first line creates a connection to the PostGIS database that holds the data; enter the correct details for your database server, port, schema, and so on. The second line is where we get the UK Street Level Crime as `geoscript.workspace.Layer`. The first line created a connection to what GeoScript calls a `Workspace`.

A workspace is an abstraction for a data connection and contains a list of the tables available in that data source. A table in a database is expressed in `Workspace` as `Layer`. The second line of this code used the `Layer.get()` method to return a layer representation of the table in PostGIS that we are requesting. In this case, the name of our table is `uk_street_crime`.

Now we need to create a `Filter()` object that we can apply to the layer to retrieve only the features that meet the conditions:

```
crime_filter = Filter("crime_type = '%s' AND WITHIN(geom, %s)" %
(crime_type, buffer_geom))
```

One line is all we need to construct the `Filter()` object. A filter in GeoScript is constructed using the CQL language and allows us to use spatial predicates as well as attributes. In our case, we want the filter to do two things for us:

- Only match crime locations where the `crime_type` attribute is equal to the value of the `crime_type` parameter passed in
- Only match crime locations that are inside our search buffer geometry

We build this filtering criteria using the spatial predicate, `WITHIN`, which will return all the geometry objects that are within the second geometry, from the layer the filter is applied to. In this case, the second geometry is dynamically passed in using our `buffer_geom` object.

We now have all the elements of our script in place; all we need to do now is get a count of the crime locations that match the criteria that has been specified. Traditionally, this would have probably take a few lines of code; we would have needed to perform the selection on our layer and then potentially loop through the results to get a count or perform some other tasks. Once again, with GeoScript, this is simplified to one line. In our script, let's enter the following line:

```
return crime_lyr.count(crime_filter)
```

Since we are now at the end of our script, we will return the result. We will return the result from the `count()` method of the `Layer()` object. The `count()` method can take an optional input parameter of type `Filter()` — `Layer.count(filter=None)`. The default value for the filter is `None`, which means that if we simply called `crime_lyr.count()`, then we would return the total number of crime locations in the layer. In other words, it will count all the features on the layer. By specifying a value for `filter`, we are constraining the results to only those matching the filter, which is exactly what we are after.

Testing the Python WPS process

Save the script to `<geoserver_data_directory>/scripts/wps`, and then go to the *WPS request builder* tool that we used earlier in this chapter. We can use this tool to test our WPS process script. From the process drop-down list, notice that there is now a script with a `py` prefix; all processes written in Python will have this prefix. Other scripting languages will have their own prefix, for example, `js` for JavaScript. From the drop-down, select the `py:CrimeWithinCountByType` process. Enter the following values for the input parameters and then click on the **Execute** button:

Parameter name	Value
`crime_type`	Other theft
`origin`	POINT(531088 104498)
`search_radius`	1000

Make sure that the drop-down for the `origin` parameter is set to `application/wkt` so that GeoServer interprets our point correctly; otherwise, an error will occur on execution. The result from this particular execution will be 165.

To make this function slightly more useful in a general context, we can make it more generic. If we removed the hard coding of the layer that we apply the filter to, and provide a means of allowing the user to specify the filter, then it would be generic enough to be used on any vector layer. Why not have a go at doing this? If you get stuck, there is an example script in the code bundle called `FeatureCountWithinRadius.py`.

Creating a RESTful service

Earlier in this chapter, we discussed how the scripting extension creates hooks into different parts of the GeoServer architecture. Exploiting these different hooks means we are able to do different things with our scripts. We just created a WPS process to do some analysis on finding the crimes of a certain type within a given distance of a given location. However, to execute that script, our application(s) will need to know how to talk WPS. In some cases, this will be fine; for example, if QGIS is using the WPS plugin or if we were creating our own web application using OpenLayers, we could use its WPS capabilities. However, how do we integrate this analysis into other business systems that we might have in our enterprise which don't understand how to talk WPS? One answer can be to expose our analysis logic as a RESTful service that nearly any application with a web connection can understand; after all it simply uses the standard HTTP protocol.

A complete discussion of what a RESTful service is, often referred to as REST APIs, is beyond the scope of this book. However, it is a pretty straightforward concept to grasp, and there are plenty of online sources of information. As always, the first place to start is Wikipedia: `http://en.wikipedia.org/wiki/Restful`

We will utilize the app scripting hook to create a REST end-point for our analysis. The idea here is that we can actually use GeoScript to build a full-blown analysis REST API, using the power of GeoServer. For this example, we will only create a single end-point, but it will give us a solid foundation on which we can build a more complete API.

In order to make all of this work nicely in a web service context, we will utilize the Flask micro-web development framework for Python. Flask will provide us with all the necessary plumbing to create URL routes to execute code. Before we get started on the script itself, there is a little configuration that we need to get out of the way first. We need to get all of the Python modules to make Flask work and then copy them into our `scripts` directory. The packages that we need to get are:

- Flask
- Jinja 2
- Werkzeug

These are required for dependencies. You can either download them from the **Python Package Index (PyPI)** at `http://pypi.python.org/pypi`, or you can use the Python `ez_install` command. Irrespective of the approach you decide to take, you will need to place the folders that contain the packages into the `scripts/lib/py` directory so that GeoServer's implementation of Jython can pick them up.

 Jython is an implementation of Python built for the Java platform. It can be used to embed scripting inside Java applications and is what gives GeoScript the ability to run Python code. More details about Jython are available at `http://www.jython.org`.

If you have trouble getting hold of, or compiling, these packages, then I have included the ones I used in the code bundle of this chapter, along with the complete script we are about to create.

Now, with the dependencies resolved, we are ready to create the script to REST-enable our analysis script. Create a new file in your favorite text editor or IDE and call it `main.py`. GeoServer expects to find a file named `main.py` within the directory for an application, which means that we also need to create a folder within the `scripts/apps` folder of the data directory. Let's create a folder called `CrimeAnalysis` within the `scripts/apps` folder and make sure that the `main.py` file is inside it. First of all, we need to add the necessary imports at the start of the script:

```
from geoscript.feature.io import json
from geoscript.geom import geom, Point
from geoscript.workspace import PostGIS
from geoscript.filter import Filter
from StringIO import StringIO
import urllib
from flask import Flask, Response
```

Most of these imports will be familiar from the WPS process script that we created. The last three, however, will be new to us. `StringIO` is a string-creation module that we will use to build up our response to be sent in response to requests. The `urllib` module is necessary so that we can handle URL-encoded strings. Finally, we have the `import` declaration for Flask itself; notice that we are importing the main `Flask` module as well as the `Response` module.

Next, we need to create an instance of the `Flask` class:

```
app = Flask(__name__)
```

The parameter to the Flask class is the name of the application's module or package. As we will be using a single module, we simply need to provide the `__name__` value. Next, we need to create and launch the application:

```
if __name__ == "__main__":
    app.run()
```

We will use the `run()` method of the application to start it. The `if` statement inside which the `run()` call is ensures that the server only runs if the module is called directly from the Python interpreter and not used as a module import.

The next part of the script will define the analysis method itself. At this point, we need to have an idea of how we want people to call our RESTful service, what the structure of the URL will be, and whether we will include any parameters. For the analysis to work, there are four pieces of information that we need to receive: the type of crime, the *x* coordinate of a location, the *y* coordinate of a location, and finally, the search radius. For this example, we will use this URL template: `http://<server-name>:<port>/geoserver/script/apps/CrimeAnalysis/<crime_type>/<api-method>/<parameters>`.

There are a number of elements in this URL template, so let's break it down a little bit:

Element	Purpose	Example
`<server-name>`	This is the server name or IP address of our GeoServer instance	`127.0.0.1`
`<port>`	This is the port number that GeoServer is listening on	`8080`
`<crime_type>`	This is the type of crime we want to analyze	`Drugs`
`<api-method>`	This is an API method to call for analysis	`Within`
`<parameters>`	This is any additional parameters required for the API call to work	

On this structure of a RESTful service, we will create this end-point: `http://<server-name>:<port>/geoserver/script/apps/CrimeAnalysis/<crime_type>/within/<x>/<y>/<radius>`.

This will give us a flexible framework on which we can call the `within` analysis on any type of crime and have flexibility with the location coordinates and search radius. To make this work in our script, we need to add a method and then provide a decorator for it. Enter the following into the script:

```
@app.route("/<crime_type>/within/<x>/<y>/<radius>")
def CrimesByTypeRadius(crime_type, x, y, radius):
```

The `@app.route` decorator is used by the Flask application server to interpret incoming web requests and then route them to the correct method to be handled. You will see that the content is a string for the URL. Notice that some of the elements are enclosed in the opening (<) and closing (>) brackets. These are the tokens that will be replaced by Flask, with the values provided in the URL itself; more important for us though is that these become the parameters for our method. In this case, we can see the four pieces of information that we need to run the analysis.

The first part of the script is very much the same as our WPS process from earlier, so let's copy that:

```
pgis_workspace = PostGIS('<db_name>', '<db_server>', '<port>',
'<schema>', '<username>', '<password>')
crime_lyr = pgis_workspace.get('uk_street_crime')
search_buffer = geom.buffer(Point(num(x), num(y)), num(radius))
crime_filter = Filter("crime_type = '%s' AND WITHIN(geom, %s)" %
(urllib.unquote(crime_type), search_buffer))
```

Though the code is the same as the earlier one, to get a connection to the database, get a reference to the crimes layer and then build the search buffer object; there are some subtle differences. The first and most important one is the use of a method to handle numbers, `num()`. Values are passed to us by Flask as strings unless Flask is instructed otherwise. One way to do this is to provide a type within the opening and closing brackets for a parameter. However, in this scenario, we are constrained to a single type, but our numbers can be whole integers or float values. We don't want to constrain our API to any one type for coordinates and distances, so let's add a new method into the script:

```
def num(s):
    try:
        return int(s)
    except ValueError:
        return float(s)
```

This simple method will first try and parse the supplied string as an integer, and if this fails, then it will try and parse it to a float. Using this method will mean that we can handle values of any type safely.

The other difference is the use of the `urllib.unquote()` method on the `crime_type` parameter. Flask will pass values as URL-encoded strings, so, for example, spaces will be encoded as `%20`; this means that a crime type such as `Other theft` will be passed to us by Flask as `Other%20theft`. The `%20` bit will cause problems on our filter, as the string won't get matched. Using `urllib.unquote()`, we can get back the crime type with spaces (and any other characters) decoded.

Previously, we were simply counting the number of crimes that occurred within the given search radius, but for our API, we will actually return the crimes' locations themselves as GeoJSON.

GeoJSON is a format to encode geographic data such as features, feature collections, or geometry. Features in GeoJSON contain a geometry object and additional properties (attributes). For more details on the specification, look at `http://geojson.rog/geojson-sec.html`.

Back in the body of our method, we need to perform the spatial query:

```
fcursor = crime_lyr.cursor(crime_filter)
```

This line will execute the filter on the crime data layer and then return a feature cursor that contains all the features that were found. We will now construct a response string and then loop over the cursor to build out a GeoJSON FeatureCollection. Enter the following lines of code into the script:

```
buff = StringIO()
buff.write('{\n')
buff.write('    "type": "FeatureCollection",\n')
buff.write('    "features": [\n')

num_features = crime_lyr.count(crime_filter)
i = 1

for f in fcursor:
    if i < num_features:
        buff.write('%s,\n' % json.writeJSON(f))
    else:
        buff.write('%s\n' % json.writeJSON(f))
    i = i + 1

buff.write('    ]\n')
buff.write('}')
```

First, we created a `StringIO` object, and then we called its `write()` method to sequentially build up the response string. Then we got a count of the features that match the filter so that we can control the output as we loop over the features in the cursor. This check is done so that we do not have a trailing comma after the last feature is written out, since this will make our JSON array of features invalid. Instead, if we are on the last feature being written, then we do not bother with the `,`.

That is all there is to it. All that remains now is for us to write the response so that it can be sent back to the caller:

```
return Response(buff.getvalue(), mimetype='application/json')
```

We used the `Response` object to create the response, write out the contents of the buffer object, and then set the MIME type of the response to `application/json`.

To test whether all this works, we can call this URL from a web browser or cURL: `http://<server-name>:<port>/ geoserver/script/apps/CrimeAnalysis/ Robbery/within/531088/104498/1000`.

We will get back a stream of GeoJSON that contains six encoded features. This response can then be parsed, and the data supplied can be analyzed further or displayed on a map.

Summary

In this chapter, we learned that it is possible to use GeoServer as a spatial analysis platform through the use of WPS. We also saw that it is possible to extend the capabilities of GeoServer as a spatial analysis platform by building and adding new WPS processes. Even better, we saw that this can be accomplished using accessible scripting languages such as Python and JavaScript.

We saw how WPS processes can be used to perform a wide variety of analysis, and GeoServer comes with a large selection of processes out of the box. We saw how it is possible to chain processes together so that the result of one process is used as the input to another, thus enabling us to create complex chains of processes that can be executed from a single request. This capability makes GeoServer a great platform for complex server-side spatial analysis.

Extensibility of a platform is the key to its survival. With the inclusion of GeoScript, the ability to extend GeoServer is opened up to a much larger community of users. As we saw, by building a simple RESTful API, users no longer need to know all about Java in order to make meaningful contributions to GeoServer's functionality.

In the next chapter, we will look at how we can secure GeoServer using enterprise-security mechanisms such as LDAP and Active Directory.

10
Enterprise Security and GeoServer

As with any other production system, we must consider how to secure our instances of GeoServer against malicious attacks. Depending on how we anticipate our servers being used, we might also need to implement a security model to prevent unauthorized access to certain datasets or layers. GeoServer has a comprehensive security model enabling us to secure at both the layer and service levels.

In this chapter, we will take a look at how we can implement different strategies to secure GeoServer. The following topics will be covered:

- Authorization and authentication
- Configuring GeoServer to make use of an LDAP server, such as Active Directory, for user authentication
- Configuring GeoServer to make use of the Digest user authentication
- Configuring GeoServer to make use of the HTTP Header proxy authentication
- Understanding user authorization through roles

GeoServer offers a range of approaches for user authentication, including standard HTTP Basic authentication. However, this chapter focuses on integrating with existing enterprise-based authentication servers and schemes. A full discussion of the security subsystem used by GeoServer is out of the scope of this chapter. However, the GeoServer documentation provides a comprehensive run-down of how security is implemented. GeoServer's security documentation can be found at `http://docs.geoserver.org/stable/en/user/security/index.html`.

Authentication and authorization

Any security model that is implemented must gather two pieces of information before granting anybody access to the system. First, it must determine *who* is attempting to access the resource, and once known, *what* this person is allowed to do. The act of determining who requests access to the resource is **user authentication**, and knowing what they are allowed to do is **user authorization**.

To explain the interaction between these two elements, let's consider a standard communication between a client requesting a service from GeoServer and GeoServer sending a response to this service. The following sequence diagram shows the flow across this common transaction:

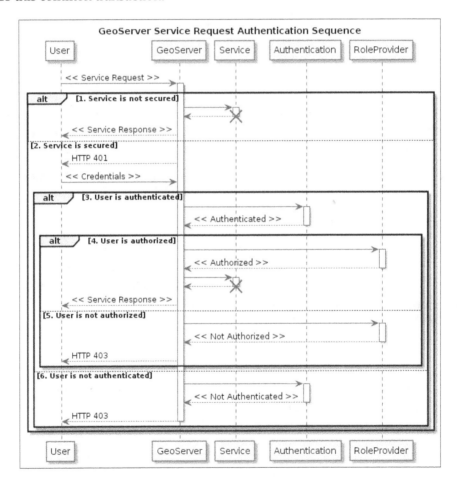

A user makes a request for a service from GeoServer; for example, this might be issuing a WMS GetMap request, or perhaps a WFS-T insert transaction. GeoServer determines whether the service is secured, and then acts accordingly.

If the service is not secured (**1.**), then GeoServer allows the service request to proceed, and it is handled normally. If the service is secured (**2.**) and no credentials are present in the headers, then GeoServer responds with an **HTTP 401** challenge. The client software will then gather the username and password to be used against the service and repeat the request. GeoServer validates the credentials supplied against its configured authentication providers; if there is a match, the user is authenticated (**3.**) and passed on to validate their roles. If the user is authorized (**4.**) to access the service request, then GeoServer will respond to the request in the normal way. However, if the user fails authorization (**5.**) against the service request, then GeoServer will return an **HTTP 403** response. Likewise, if the user is not authenticated (**6.**), an **HTTP 403** response will be returned.

This is a slight simplification of what is actually going on under the hood. However, it serves as a useful outline of the authentication and authorization processes that happen inside GeoServer.

User authentication methods

GeoServer handles authentication using an authentication chain that actually consists of two chains. The first chain is the authentication filter chain, and the second chain is the authentication provider chain. The filter chain is responsible for determining whether authentication of the request is required, and the provider chain provides the mechanisms to perform the authentication.

The following flowchart represents the sequence of events that occur during request processing:

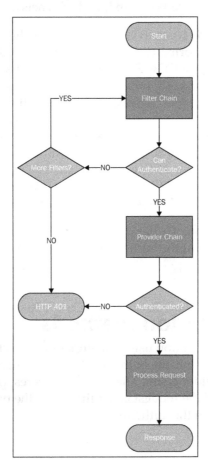

When a request is received by GeoServer, it is passed through the filter chain, where each element of the chain is given a chance to authenticate the request. For example, if the filter chain contains an HTTP Basic authentication filter, it will examine the request headers, looking for an `Authorization` header when it is invoked. If the header is present, the filter will send the request to the *username/ password* authentication provider for authentication. If the request is successfully authenticated, it is sent on for normal processing; otherwise, an HTTP 401 response will be sent. If the filter does not detect an `Authorization` header, the request is passed to the next filter in the chain. The process continues until all the filters have been applied. Often, the last filter in a chain will be the anonymous filter that passes the request on for processing as an anonymous user. Depending on the security settings for the service being requested, it might not be allowed anonymously.

User authorization methods

If user authorization determines what a user is allowed to do, then there must be a mechanism to allow rights to be assigned to users. GeoServer implements a role-based access system to assign roles to users, or groups of users, and determine what they are allowed to do or access.

The role information can be stored in either an XML file, the default service, or in a JDBC database. It is also possible to use the group information contained within a **Lightweight Directory Access Protocol (LDAP)** server. When a user is authenticated, the role service is responsible for calculating the roles that should be assigned to this user. The security subsystem of GeoServer then uses these roles to determine whether a user is allowed to perform a particular operation. In an enterprise environment, the most common form of user authentication and authorization is LDAP.

> It is outside the scope of this book to go into detail of what LDAP is and how it can be implemented. There is a lot of information about this on the Internet, and a good reference point to start at is `http://en.wikipedia.org/wiki/Lightweight_Directory_Access_Protocol`.

Using Active Directory for user authentication and authorization

There is no escaping the fact that a large proportion of enterprise systems are built on top of a Microsoft technology stack. For the management of a domain, and the control of users and access rights, this will more often than not mean the use of **Active Directory**. Love it or hate it, Active Directory is a fact of life in most organizations. If we integrate GeoServer into our enterprise, then we must consider how we can utilize Active Directory to manage access to the mapping data. We can, of course, just utilize the default *username/password* authentication provider, but that will mean users having yet another username and password to remember, or more likely, forget. This can also represent a security risk as the provider uses an HTTP Basic authentication, where the username and password are sent in the clear. Our users will already have a centrally managed username and password, so it will be much better for us to tap into this existing store for authentication and authorization. An additional benefit is that it is likely that Active Directory, and the creation and management of users, will be a centrally managed function, which means that we can focus on managing the map server and let others worry about managing the users.

Configuring Active Directory for authentication

To configure the LDAP authentication provider to connect to Active Directory, we need to select the **Authentication** link from the **Security** group on the left-hand side menu of the web administration console:

We need to scroll down the page until we reach the section named **Authentication Providers**.

This lists all the authentication providers that we configured for GeoServer. By default, there is always a **username/password** authentication provider. To create an LDAP authentication provider, we need to click on the **Add new** link:

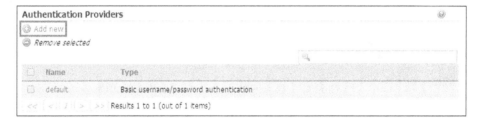

On the **New Authentication Provider** page, we need to select the **LDAP – Authentication via Lightweight Directory Access Protocol server** option:

We can now see the settings form, where we can configure the details for our Active Directory server. First, we must provide a name that this authentication provider will be listed as; it doesn't matter what it is called, but it should be something descriptive. We will call ours `ad-ldap`:

```
Name
ad-ldap

LDAP Settings

Server URL
ldap://ad-server/dc=mastering,dc=geoserver,dc=com

☐ TLS

User lookup pattern


Filter used to lookup user
(|(userPrincipalName={0})(sAMAccountName={1}))

Format used for user login name
{0}@mastering.geoserver.com

Authorization

☑ Use LDAP groups for authorization

☑ Bind user before searching for groups

Group search base
cn=Users

Group search filter
member={0}

Group to use as ADMIN
GEOSERVER_ADMIN

Group to use as GROUP_ADMIN

```

The **Server URL** option will tell the provider where our Active Directory is located. It uses the `ldap` protocol to connect to Active Directory, and the URL should contain the server name or IP address followed by the root of the directory. For our example server, this will be `ldap://ad-server/dc=mastering,dc=geoserver,dc=com`; notice the use of `dc` to describe the root of the directory. The root that we specified will be translated to our domain of `mastering.geoserver.com`.

The **Filter used to lookup user** setting provides the authentication provider with the correct syntax to use when searching the directory for users, for example, when authenticating a login request. Each LDAP implementation will have its own format, but for Active Directory, we need to use `(|(userPrincipalName={0})(sAMAccountName={1}))`. Notice the use of the `0` and `1` tokens, which will be replaced with the value of the username attempting login by GeoServer.

The **Format used for user login name** setting provides the authentication provider with the correct syntax to send user login names. For Active Directory, this should be of the `login-name@domain-name` form. Again, we use a token that will be replaced with the username supplied; for our example, this setting is set to `{0}@mastering.geoserver.com`.

We need to check the box for **Use LDAP groups for authorization** and **Bind user before searching for groups**. The **Bind user before searching for groups** checkbox is very important as Active Directory does not allow anonymous searching of the directory. By checking the box, we tell GeoServer that it must first successfully bind to the directory before searching for groups.

The **Group search base** option tells the authentication provider where to find groups within the directory. Active Directory holds the groups within the users store, so we need to specify the `cn=Users` value. The **Group search filter** option tells the provider how to look for users within groups; for Active Directory, this is set to `member={0}`, where the `0` is replaced with the login name being looked up. Finally, we need to specify **Group to use as ADMIN** so that our administrative users configured in Active Directory can log in as administrators of GeoServer. In our case, this will be set to `GEOSERVER_ADMIN`.

We can test whether the settings are valid using the login controls on the right-hand side of the page. After successfully connecting to Active Directory, we just need to click on the **Save** button. Now, we will be able to log in to the web administration console using our `gis_admin` user from Active Directory.

Configuring Active Directory for authorization

If we use Active Directory to manage our users, then it makes sense that we should use it to manage the groups these users belong to. In this context, we can consider an Active Directory group to be equivalent to a role in GeoServer. Within GeoServer, we have the option of using LDAP as the role service provider. When a user is successfully authenticated, the LDAP role service determines what groups the user is a member of in the directory. Each group is then converted to a role in GeoServer by prefixing the `ROLE_` string to it. So, if we have a group called `GIS_EDITORS` in Active Directory, then this will be translated to a GeoServer role named `ROLE_GIS_EDITORS`. When the LDAP role service is configured, we will be able to select the roles from Active Directory anywhere in GeoServer where roles can be assigned; for example, from the service and layer security.

To enable the LDAP role service, we need to configure it by selecting the **Users, Groups, Roles** option from the **Security** group on the left-hand side menu of the web administration console:

On the **Users, Groups, and Roles** page, we need to scroll down to the **Role Services** section.

Out of the box, GeoServer is configured with the XML role service called *default*. GeoServer allows us to have more than one role service available, so we will keep *default* and configure a new service for LDAP:

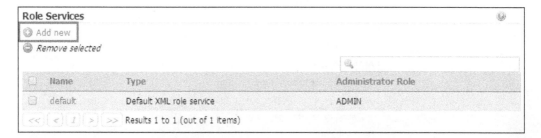

We need to click on the **Add new** button to open the **New Role Service** page. To configure an LDAP role service, we need to select the **LDAP – Role service stored in LDAP repository** option from the list:

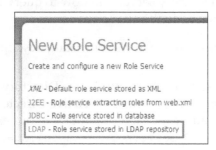

This will load a form underneath the list, where we can configure the role service properties:

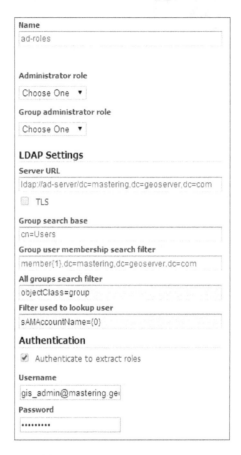

Similar to configuring the LDAP authentication provider, we need to tell GeoServer where to find our Active Directory server and how to query it for user groups. Perform the following steps to do this:

1. Give the role service a name that's something descriptive and meaningful; we shall set it to `ad-roles`.

2. Next, tell the role service where our Active Directory server is located. It uses the `ldap` protocol to connect to Active Directory, just like when we configured the authentication provider. For our example server, this will be `ldap://ad-server/dc=mastering,dc=geoserver,dc=com`.

3. Now, we need to provide details of where the role service should look to find groups within our repository. We need to specify `cn=Users` for the **Group search base** setting, which tells the role service that groups can be found in the `Users` folder of the directory.

4. The **Group user membership search filter** setting tells the role service how to query whether a user belongs to a group. We need to set this to `member{1}, dc=mastering, dc=geoserver, dc=com`, where the token 1 will be replaced with the name of the user being looked up.

5. The **Filter used to lookup user** setting tells the role service how to look for users within the directory; this needs to be set to `sAMAccountName{0}`, where the token 0 will be replaced by the name of the user being looked up.

6. Finally, we need to tick the **Authenticate to extract roles** box since Active Directory only allows querying of the directory by authenticated users. In the username and password boxes, we need to specify an account to use. In our case, we will use our `gis_admin` user account by specifying the `gis_admin@mastering.geoserver.com` value. Notice that the username is in the expected form of `username@domain-name`, just like for the LDAP authentication provider.

7. When we complete the configuration, we need to click on the **Save** button, which will validate our configuration. If there are no errors, the new role service will be created.

8. There is one final change that we need to make before everything is configured. We need to go back into the role service and set up the **Administrator** and **Group administrator** roles:

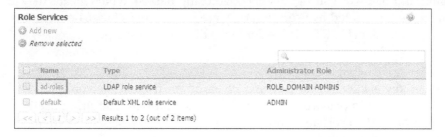

Click on the newly created role service from the list; it should be called **ad-roles**. This will open the same page as before, where we can change the configuration of the role service. As we now have an active role service working against our Active Directory, the two dropdowns at the top of the form will have content listed in them:

Notice how each of the items is an Active Directory group with the ROLE_ prefix added. We need to specify the Active Directory groups that will hold administrators for GeoServer; in this case, we choose the ROLE_DOMAIN ADMINS group.

Now, whenever we configure security for GeoServer, we can choose roles based on groups held in Active Directory.

Using Digest for user authentication

The default security implementation in GeoServer for REST and OGC services is HTTP Basic. The HTTP Basic authentication has the widest adoption, and any client that is OGC compliant will support it. However, there is a downside to the HTTP Basic authentication; it is not very secure. The credentials for an HTTP Basic authentication are sent to the server as a header key in plain text, without any encryption. The username and password strings are encoded using **Base64**, which means they are difficult to be interpreted by users, but they are not secure as Base64-encoded strings can be decoded. An HTTP Basic header looks like the following:

```
Authorization: Basic dXNlcjpwYXNzd29yZA==
```

The header key is Authorization, and its value consists of the word Basic followed by the username and password as Base64-encoded strings. The string itself is a concatenation of the username and password with a colon separator; in the previous example, this will decode to user:password.

So, the HTTP Basic authentication is simple to implement, but not secure. HTTP Digest, on the other hand, is more secure because a cryptographic hash is applied to the password before it is sent with the request.

Setting up an HTTP Digest authentication

To use an HTTP Digest authentication, we need to add a filter into GeoServer's authentication filter chain.

To access the authentication settings, we need to click on the **Authentication** link under the **Security** group on the left-hand side menu of the web administration console. This will take us to the authentication settings page where we can add and configure authentication filters and providers:

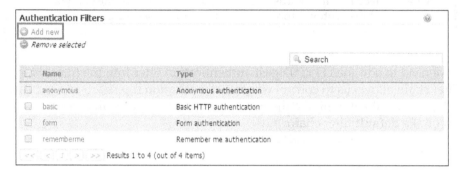

We need to add an authentication filter to the authentication chain. The details required to be entered on this page will change according to the authentication filter option that we choose. In our case, we need **Digest**; clicking on this will show the properties that we need to set to configure the filter:

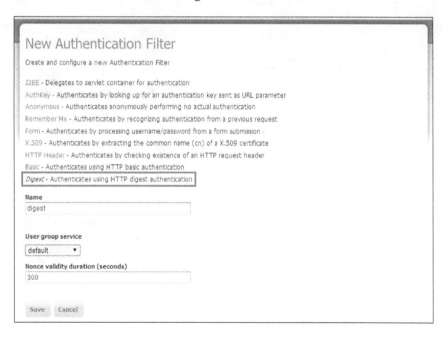

The **Name** property can be anything we like, but it should be descriptive of what the filter is being used for; in this case, we will use digest. The next item, **User group service**, should be set to default, and **Nonce validity duration (seconds)** can also be left at the default value. Click on **Save** to add the new filter into GeoServer.

A **nonce** is a random or pseudo-random number that is generated and used once in cryptographic communications. The validity duration specifies how long the generated nonce value is in effect; in other words, the time span within which the encryption and decryption processes need to occur before the one-time key becomes invalid and can't be used.

Next, we need to add the HTTP Digest authentication filter into the filter chain. The filter chain allows us to control where authentication filters are applied based on URL patterns. We would like the new filter to be applied in all cases, so we need to set it on the **default** filter chain:

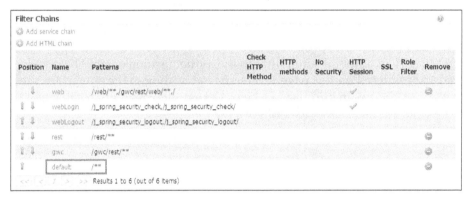

Clicking on the **default** filter chain will open a page where we can specify its properties:

We need to remove **basic** from the **Selected** list and move **digest** into it. We also need to make sure that **anonymous** is the last item in the **Selected** list. Clicking on the **Close** button will store the changes to the filter.

Testing an HTTP Digest authentication

To test whether the HTTP Digest authentication filter is working, we need to make a request to GeoServer, using HTTP Basic followed by HTTP Digest. In the case of the former, we should expect to get an HTTP 403 error, and in the case of the latter, we should see a service response. Before proceeding, make sure that the basic authentication has been removed from the filter chain:

1. We need to secure the services, and for this test, we will apply a default rule to secure all the services. Click on the **Services** link in the **Security** group on the left-hand side menu of the web administration console.

2. Click on **Add new rule** on the **Service access rules list** page to create a new rule:

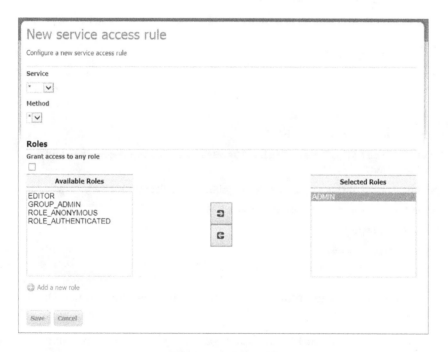

3. Leave the default values for **Service** and **Method**, and then select the **ADMIN** role from the **Available Roles** list and click on the right arrow button to add it to the **Selected Roles** list. This secures all OGC services such that only the users belonging to the **ADMIN** role will be able to access them.

4. To test whether this is the case, we can use cURL to issue a WMS *GetCapabilities* request on our server using basic authentication (the default for cURL):

```
$ curl -v -u admin:password -G "http://localhost:8080/geoserver/wm
s?REQUEST=GetCapabilities&VERSION=1.1.1&SERVICE=WMS"
```

This will make a request for the WMS capabilities basic authentication. The result will be an HTTP 401 unauthorized response similar to this:

```
* timeout on name lookup is not supported
* About to connect() to localhost port 8080 (#0)
*    Trying 127.0.0.1... connected
* Connected to localhost (127.0.0.1) port 8080 (#0)
* Server auth using Basic with user 'admin'
> GET /geoserver/wms?Request=GetCapabilities&Version=1.1.1&Service=WMS
HTTP/1.1
> Authorization: Basic YWRtaW46QXRrMW5zRGV2
> User-Agent: curl/7.21.2 (Windows) libcurl/7.21.2 OpenSSL/1.0.0a
zlib/1.2.3
> Host: localhost:8080
> Accept: */*
>
< HTTP/1.1 401 Unauthorized
< Server: Apache-Coyote/1.1
< WWW-Authenticate: Digest realm="GeoServer Realm", qop="auth",
nonce="MTQxMTAwM

TQ4MTQyNDpiNzM0M2JkODM4Njk3M2ZiYWFiZmNhMjAwOGRiYWI0OA=="
< Content-Type: text/html;charset=utf-8
< Content-Language: en
< Content-Length: 1061
< Date: Thu, 18 Sep 2014 00:46:21 GMT
```

Now, we will issue the same request. However, this time, we will use Digest authentication:

```
$ curl --digest -v -u admin:password -G "http://localhost:8080/geoserver/
wms?REQUEST=GetCapabilities&VERSION=1.1.1&SERVICE=WMS"
```

This will make the request for WMS capabilities again, but this time, cURL will encode the username and password using the digest cryptography. The response from GeoServer will be the capabilities document for WMS.

Using HTTP Header for user authentication

The previous authentication providers that we discussed are widely used in an enterprise environment, and we have seen how we can utilize them in GeoServer. In using these providers, we have been responsible for configuring GeoServer to connect to the providers as well as setting up the security rules against authenticated users. In *n*-tier architectures, it is common that authentication of users occurs in a different tier to that in which GeoServer sits. In other words, the act of authentication and authorization can occur in another system, such as a proxy. This approach makes it possible to integrate with another security system, for example, a system that implements the OGC **Geospatial Digital Rights Management Reference Model (GeoDRM RM)**.

GeoDRM RM provides a mechanism to allow organizations to secure their web mapping servers based on the rights of the user. For example, it is possible to lock down access to specific resources that are constrained to a certain geographic region. Using GeoDRM RM, we can restrict access to a national dataset to a subregion based on what access customers purchased:

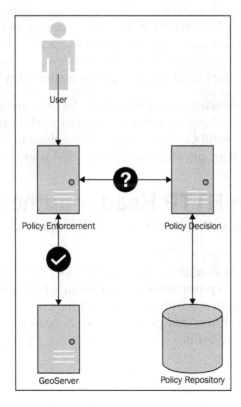

At a high level, there are three components to a GeoDRM RM solution. The **Policy Enforcement** service is used as the gateway to access mapping services. It receives the service request and authenticates the user requesting access. Once the user is authenticated, the **Policy Decision** service is called with the user details along with details of the request being made. The **Policy Decision** service then checks the policy(s) held against the user details and determines whether the request they make is valid, for example, if the area of data they request is within their licensed coverage. Once the **Policy Decision** service validates the request, the decision is sent back to the **Policy Enforcement** service. If the decision is to allow the request, then the **Policy Enforcement** service will pass the request on to GeoServer, and if it is to deny, then a declined response is sent back to the user.

GeoDRM RM is a topic that can fill a book in its own right, and it's certainly beyond the scope of this book. If you are interested in learning more about GeoDRM RM, then you can take a look at the OGC specification at http://www.opengeospatial.org/standards/as/geodrmrm. An implementation of GeoDRM RM is provided by 52 North (http://52north.org/communities/security/).

In this scenario, we will only need to implement a simple level of security on GeoServer. The **Policy Enforcement** service is the gateway so that GeoServer can simply trust any request received from it—much like a proxy server. However, we want to at least put some security on it to try to prevent unauthorized access through back doors. In this case, the HTTP Header authentication provider is perfect.

The HTTP Header authentication provider works by examining the headers of requests coming in and looking for a secret header key. The value of the header key should be the name of a valid GeoServer user. When the authentication provider detects the header key, it grants access to the specified user.

Setting up an HTTP Header authentication

To use an HTTP Header authentication, we need to add the filter into GeoServer's authentication filter chain.

To access the authentication settings, we need to click on the **Authentication** link under the **Security** group on the left-hand side menu of the web administration console. This will take us to the authentication settings page where we can add and configure authentication filters and providers. We need to add an authentication filter to the authentication chain:

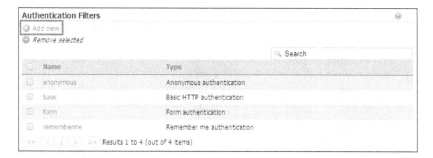

Under the **Authentication Filters** section, we need to click on the **Add new** button to open the **New Authentication Filter** page:

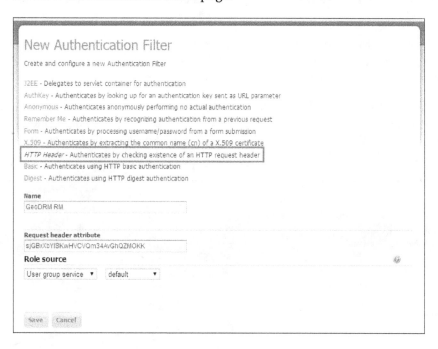

The details required to be entered on this page will change according to the authentication filter option we choose. In our case, we need **HTTP Header**; clicking on this will show the properties we need to set to configure the filter. The **Name** property can be anything we like, but it should be descriptive of what this filter is being used for; in this case, we will use "GeoDRM RM". The next item, **Request header attribute**, is the important setting as this is the HTTP Header attribute that the filter will look for.

The value for the request header attribute should be obscure so that it is not easy to guess; for example, setting the name to the user, and the value being admin, will not be secure. It is best to generate a random sequence of letters and numbers for the name, and potentially, also the username. A string of 20 random characters containing three numbers will offer a strong attribute name. We should also consider securing communication to GeoServer with SSL or place GeoServer behind a firewall for added security.

Specify **User group service** and **default** for the **Role source** settings, and then click on the **Save** button. The filter will be created and added into the authentication filter chain at the top of the list. If you wish, you can change the order in which the filters are applied.

There is no need to set up an authentication provider as the GeoDRM RM system will handle it for us. We can simply accept the value of the header attribute as being a valid user and allow GeoServer to fulfill its service request.

Next, we need to add the HTTP Header authentication filter into the filter chain. The filter chain allows us to control where authentication filters are applied based on URL patterns. We would like the new filter to be applied in all cases, so we need to set it on the *default* filter chain:

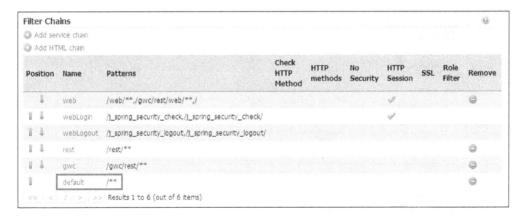

Clicking on the default filter chain will open a page where we can specify
its properties:

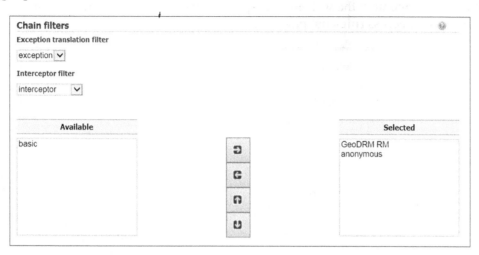

At the bottom of the page, there is a section called **Chain filters**. This is where we
specify which filters apply to this particular filter chain. We want to remove **basic** and
add **GeoDRM RM** in its place, making sure that **anonymous** is the last filter in the list
(anonymous is always required). Click on the **Close** button to store the changes.

Testing the HTTP Header authentication

To test whether the HTTP Header authentication filter works, we will need to make
a request to GeoServer without the header attribute present, and then again with it.
In the case of the former, we should expect to get an HTTP 403 error, and in the case
of the latter, we should see a service response.

First, we need to secure the services; for this test, we will apply a catch-all rule to secure all the services. Click on the **Services** link in the **Security** group on the left-hand side menu of the web administration console. Click on **Add new rule** on the **Service access rules list** page to create a new rule:

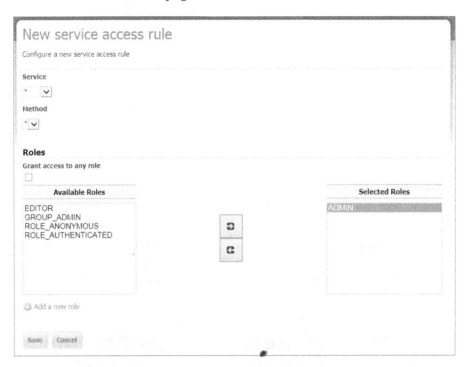

Leave the default values for **Service** and **Method,** and then select the **ADMIN** role from the **Available Roles** list and click on the right arrow button to add it to the **Selected Roles** list. This secures all OGC services such that only the users belonging to the **ADMIN** role will be able to access them.

To test whether this is the case, we can use cURL to issue a WMS *GetCapabilities* request on our server:

```
$ curl -v -G "http://localhost:8080/geoserver/wms?REQUEST=GetCapabilities
&VERSION=1.1.1&SERVICE=WMS"
```

This will make a request for WMS capabilities without supplying a valid user in the header. The result will be an HTTP 403 response similar to this:

```
* timeout on name lookup is not supported
* About to connect() to localhost port 8080 (#0)
*   Trying 127.0.0.1... connected
* Connected to localhost (127.0.0.1) port 8080 (#0)
> GET /geoserver/wms?Request=GetCapabilities&Version=1.1.1&Service=WMS
HTTP/1.1
> User-Agent: curl/7.21.2 (Windows) libcurl/7.21.2 OpenSSL/1.0.0a
zlib/1.2.3
> Host: localhost:8080
> Accept: */*
>
< HTTP/1.1 403 Forbidden
< Server: Apache-Coyote/1.1
< Content-Type: text/html;charset=utf-8
< Content-Language: en
< Content-Length: 987
< Date: Wed, 17 Sep 2014 23:18:00 GMT
```

Now, we will issue the same request, except this time, we will specify the secret header key that we configured:

```
$ curl -v --header "sjGBxXbYISKwHVCVQm34AvGhQZMOKK: admin" -G "http://
localhost:8080/geoserver/wms?REQUEST=GetCapabilities&VERSION=1.1.1&SERVIC
E=WMS"
```

This will make the request for WMS capabilities again, but this time, we provide the `admin` username through the secret header key. The response from GeoServer will be the capabilities document for WMS.

Summary

In this chapter, we covered some of the key concepts behind enterprise security, the concepts of authentication (who) and authorization (what) in particular. Armed with these two distinctions and their relationships, we then explored how each is applied in the context of GeoServer's security subsystem. In particular, we looked at how data and services can be secured.

With Active Directory being the most prevalent enterprise system to manage users and user groups, it seemed like the logical next step to see how easy it is to configure GeoServer to connect to, and utilize, the information stored in the directory. With a connection to Active Directory configured, we have everything in place to integrate GeoServer into our enterprise. This approach now leaves us in a good position to be able to implement single sign-on security.

Finally, we looked at an alternative approach to enterprise security, one in which the authentication and authorization of users is handled through a proxy server. In our example, we considered the concept of utilizing an implementation of the OGC GeoDRM RM model for security. Using the HTTP Header authentication filter, we can trust a *secret key* passed through in the request headers.

We have almost reached the end of our journey. With a well-configured, and secured, GeoServer instance running in production, we now need to see how well it performs. In the next chapter, we will look at how we can monitor the performance of GeoServer.

11

Monitoring the Performance and Health of GeoServer

With our GeoServer instances up, running, and secured, it is now time to consider whether they are performing well, and think about how we can keep an eye on them as they start to get utilized.

In this chapter, we will look at what tools exist within GeoServer to enable us to keep an eye on how things are going. We will understand how to configure them, and then look at how we can interpret the information generated to help us make decisions. We will also look at an approach to stress test our GeoServer instances to understand whether they are performing well.

By the end of this chapter, we will have covered the following topics:

- Understanding the importance of monitoring the health and performance of GeoServer
- Installing and configuring the Monitor extension
- Using JMeter to stress test GeoServer
- Understanding information to help make decisions

The importance of monitoring GeoServer

As with all business systems, it is important to monitor the health and performance of GeoServer. There are many reasons why we should do this, but for the key ones, we need to:

- Understand the amount of sustained load our server can handle
- Benchmark performance to monitor our server

- Understand what factors cause our server(s) to crash

- Know when our server is in danger of being overloaded

- Know when our server has been overloaded

There are numerous tools available that allow us to examine various web logfiles and gather statistics on how our server performs generally, but in a spatial context, we also need to gain some understanding of how well our server delivers map data. There are a number of online services that we can register our GeoServer with to perform this kind of monitoring. Services such as MapMeter from Boundless (`http://boundlessgeo.com/solutions/mapmeter/http://boundlessgeo.com/solutions/mapmeter/`) provide commercial monitoring solutions.

However, there are some open source tools that we can use to test and monitor the health of our GeoServer instances. The monitor extension for GeoServer allows us to track requests against GeoServer and store the results in a database where we can analyze them further. We can also use a test tool such as Apache JMeter™ to simulate different loads on our servers.

The GeoServer monitor extension

Installing the monitor extension is as straightforward as all the other GeoServer extensions. However, we have a choice to make about how we want to utilize the extension in production. The choice is in relation to how the data collected by the monitor extension is stored. There are two options:

Option	Description
Memory (default choice)	Monitor data is persisted in memory, only for the last 100 requests
Hibernate	All the request data is persisted to a database store using Hibernate

The monitor extension configuration controls the storage mechanism; however, we need to consider the options now as it will determine how we install and configure the extension. The choice is a trade-off between having a complete history of the requests made against our GeoServer, but at the expense of storage requirements, versus having a limited history of requests, but without any storage requirement. If we expect our server to get very high volumes of traffic, then we might not want to persist the request information to storage as it will likely fill up very quickly. In a high-transaction environment, we might not be too concerned about historic requests as we will be more interested in how the server performs in real time.

If we want to track the usage of our server over time, then there is no escaping the need to persist the request data to a database. For the purposes of this chapter, we will store the request data in a database and use the `hibernate` option.

Installing the monitor extension

As we will use the `hibernate` option for storage, there are two files that we need to grab to install the monitor extension. The first is the core extension modules for monitor, which provides all the capabilities to log request data. The second is the Hibernate extension, which provides the storage mechanisms using the Hibernate ORM library for Java. To this end, we must download the two files and save them to a location on our server.

As with all other extensions, it is important to download the version of the extension matching the version of GeoServer that you installed. We have been using the stable version of GeoServer, which at the time of writing is Version 2.5.2. To download the monitor extension, go to the GeoServer download page for stable at `http://www.geoserver.org/release/stable`.

Under the **Extensions** section, there is a subgroup named **Miscellaneous**. Within this group, look for the **Monitor (Core, Hibernate)** entry. Click on the **Core** link to download the Monitor extension, and click on the **Hibernate** link to download the Hibernate libraries.

With both the modules downloaded, the method of installation is the same for both. We need to open a command line and enter the following two commands:

```
$ unzip geoserver-2.5.2-monitor-plugin.zip *.jar -d <tomcat-home>/
webapps/geoserver/WEB-INF/lib
```

```
$ unzip geoserver-2.5.2-monitor-hibernate-plugin.zip *.jar -d <tomcat-
home>/webapps/geoserver/WEB-INF/lib
```

These commands will copy all the extension files into our deployed GeoServer directory. We need to repeat the `unzip` commands for all of our instances of GeoServer, and then restart them all to activate the extension. If the extension installs correctly, then we will see a directory called `monitoring` inside our GeoServer data directory. This directory contains the configuration files for the monitor extension.

Configuring the monitor extension

Inside the `monitoring` directory, there will be a number of configuration files that we can edit to set the behavior of the monitor extension to our liking. The following table shows the files and their purposes:

Configuration file	Purpose
`db.properties`	This provides the database connection settings, if using Hibernate
`filter.properties`	This provides the filter patterns the extension will use to select requests, but not to monitor
`hibernate.properties`	This provides the settings to control the behavior of Hibernate
`monitor.properties`	This provides the settings to control the behavior of the extension itself

The GeoServer documentation provides very good coverage of the configuration options, so we won't cover them all here. We'll head on over to `http://docs.geoserver.org/stable/en/user/extensions/monitoring/index.html` for more details. The default configuration files provide a configuration that is good for the vast majority of uses. Therefore, we shall only discuss some of the configuration settings to change how the extension behaves.

The db.properties file

The db.properties file contains the settings to use for database connections. Since we use the hibernate method of storage, we will need to make sure that the configuration settings inside this file are right for our needs. The first choice we need to make is the database that we will use to store the request data. By default, the monitor extension will use a Java H2 database. Hence, it will create some *.db files inside the monitoring directory. For our purposes, we will use a PostgreSQL database to store the request data. We need to change the settings in the file accordingly:

```
Driver=org.postgresql.Driver
url=jdbc:postgresql://<server-name>:<port>/<db-name>
username=<username>
password=<password>
defaultAutoCommit=<true|false>
```

Most of these settings are self-explanatory as they are standard database connection settings. The key thing to notice is that the database connection is constructed using a JDBC connection string; we just need to replace the <server-name>, <port>, and <db-name> elements with our own values.

The filter.properties file

The filter.properties file instructs the monitor extension, which requests *not* to track. By default, it is configured to filter out all the requests to the web administration interface and monitor request API. The settings that control this are:

```
/web/**
/rest/monitor/**
```

Each line of the file should contain a pattern for a URL to be excluded from monitoring. The pattern should be everything in a standard request URL after / geoserver, and up to the ? separator for the start of query parameters. As it is a pattern, it is not necessary to write the entire request URL; for example, the /web/** pattern will filter out any requests with web. In other words, it will filter out all the web administration interface requests. So, if we do not want the monitor extension to log any requests to our WFS service, then we should add a new line to the file and put the value /wfs.

The hibernate.properties file

The `hibernate.properties` file contains the settings for the Hibernate module, and generally speaking, these settings should not really be changed. The default settings are good enough for all users and should only be changed if we have sufficient knowledge of the Hibernate library. However, we do need to change one setting in this file to make sure that the request data is persisted to our PostgreSQL database. The following two lines are required in the file:

```
databasePlatform=org.hibernate.dialect.PostgreSQLDialect
database=POSTGRESQL
```

These two settings instruct the Hibernate library to use the PostgreSQL dialect in its database storage calls.

The monitor.properties file

The `monitor.properties` file contains the properties necessary for the core monitor extension to function. Most of the settings in this file can be left alone, but some should be tweaked. First up, we need to make sure that the storage mode is set to Hibernate:

```
storage=hibernate
```

If we use the memory approach, then we set the value to `memory`. The next setting of interest is the one that controls the mode in which the monitor extension operates. The default configuration is:

```
mode=history
```

The monitor extension can operate in two modes, with the choice determining when the extension persists data to the configured storage. One option is `live`, and the other is `history`. In the `history` mode (the default), the monitor extension persists the information about requests once the processing is complete and the request is fully satisfied. This mode is ideal when real-time information about requests is not necessary. It is worth noting that in this mode, the database is not stressed as much as in the `live` mode as fewer operations are performed. The `live` mode persists information about requests as they happen, which means that it is possible to get a real-time view on what the server does. The trade-off is that this mode will place additional strain on the database as it will perform more operations than in the `history` mode.

Another setting that we might need to consider changing is `maxBodySize`. This determines how much of the request body (in cases of POST requests) is stored. Setting this value too high will cause the storage to fill up quickly, so it is a trade-off between wanting to know details of the request made against how much space is available to store it. It can be useful to unbound this setting (use the value `-1`) when debugging issues with specific requests, but it is highly recommended to set this back to a limit afterwards. It is possible to disable logging of the request body entirely by setting the value to `0`. The value should be the number of characters to capture from the request body; for example, a value of `1024` will capture 1,024 characters.

 It is important to make sure that the database body field has the same size as `bodySize` to ensure the data is stored correctly. This is only necessary when using database persistence.

Checking whether the monitor extension is installed correctly

Once we have the configuration for monitor to our liking, we can go ahead and restart our instances of GeoServer. Once GeoServer restarts, we can check whether everything has been installed and configured correctly by logging in to the web administration console. If everything works as expected, then the left-hand side panel will contain a new section called **Monitor**:

Within the **Monitor** section, we should see two options: **Activity** and **Reports**.

Viewing the monitor extension activity and reports

The monitor extension provides two different views on the request data that it gathers. The first is the **Activity** view that provides a chart of the requests that have been made over a user-defined period. Clicking on the **Activity** link will open the **Activity** page, as shown here:

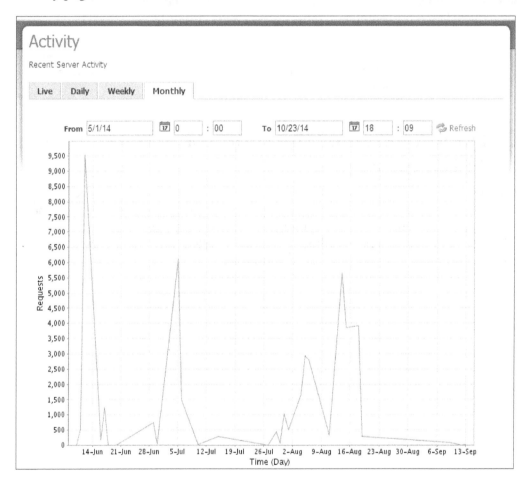

The tabs across the top of the page allow us to look at different aggregates of data. For example, we can use the **Monthly** view to see requests over a period of several months. In the preceding example, we can see that between May 1, 2014 and October 23, 2014, there were three spikes of activity. The biggest spike was in June with peak requests of 9,500.

The second view that is available is **Reports**. Clicking on the **Reports** link will open the **Reports** page where a number of generated charts can be viewed:

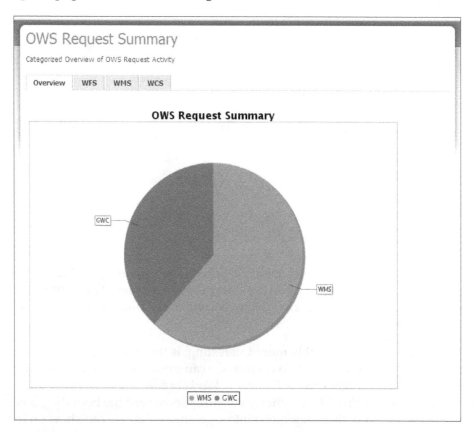

The **OWS Request Summary** report provides a summary of all the requests made against one of the standard OGC services, such as WFS, WMS, and WCS. The **Overview** tab shows the breakdown of requests across the different services. This information is static, but it provides a good overview of the spread of requests across the different OGC services.

Going further with the request data

As useful as the **Activity** and **Reports** views are, they do not tell us the whole story of what goes on with our server. The monitor extension captures a lot of information about each request made to GeoServer. If we use the Hibernate component to store the request data in a database (in our case, we use PostgreSQL), then we can also use standard database and analytics tools to gather more information.

For example, we can use the information captured about requests to find the 10 most popular layers. The following SQL for PostgreSQL will give us the answer:

```
SELECT
    a.name,
    COUNT(*) AS requests
FROM
    request_resources a,
    request b
WHERE
    a.request_id = b.id
    AND
    b.service = 'WMS'
    AND
    b.operation = 'GetMap'
GROUP BY a.name
ORDER BY requests DESC
LIMIT 10;
```

This SELECT statement joins the request table with the request_resources table using the id key, and then groups on name and provides count. The ORDER BY a.name DESC statement puts them into descending order and LIMIT 10 returns us the 10 highest counts.

Another possibility, and arguably more interesting, is the ability to put the extents of each map request onto a map! To do this, we can make use of the SQL View functionality that we discovered in *Chapter 3, Working with Vector Data in Spatial Databases*. We can use PostGIS' geometry constructors to turn the bounding box information captured with each request into a geometry that we can show on the map. The following SQL will generate the geometry for each request:

```
SELECT
    *,
    ST_SetSRID(ST_MakeBox2D(ST_MakePoint(minx, miny), ST_MakePoint(maxx,
maxy))::geometry, trim(leading 'EPSG:' from crs)::integer)
FROM
    request
WHERE
    service = 'WMS' AND operation = 'GetMap'
```

This SELECT statement uses the ST_SetSRID, ST_MakeBox2D, and ST_MakePoint functions to generate polygons representing the bounds of each GetMap request on the WMS service. We can use this SELECT statement in **Edit SQL View**, as shown in the following screenshot:

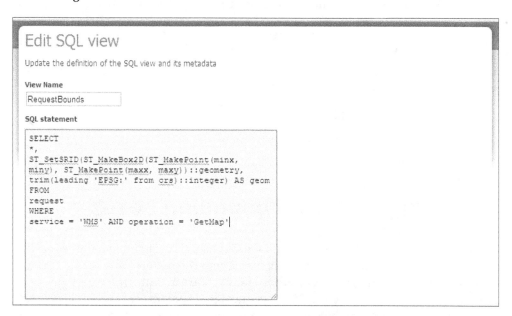

This will create a layer showing us where the requests for our data are being made; we might be able to discern spatial patterns about map requests. When we start to get at the raw monitoring data, we can really learn a lot about the performance of our server as well as the usage pattern over time.

Stress testing GeoServer

With the monitoring extension installed, we now need to consider how we can go about testing the performance of our GeoServer, and then use the logs to analyze the results. To test the performance of our GeoServer instances, we will need a tool that will allow us to send multiple requests to map images and data in different locations and resolutions. We also need to be able to change the flow of requests and simulate multiple concurrent requests.

The web is full of tools that will allow us to simulate different mixes of requests to our servers to test their performance. When it comes to testing the performance of our GeoServer instance, the tool we choose to use is less important than the mix of requests that we decide to send to it. For the purposes of this chapter, we will use the Apache JMeter™ desktop application to simulate a heavy load on our servers.

The Apache JMeter™ software is very capable and has a much broader scope for use than the example that we will use in this book. To learn more about Apache JMeter™, it is highly recommended that you read the documentation at http://jmeter.apache. org/usermanual/index.htmlhttp://jmeter.apache.org/ usermanual/index.html.

To successfully stress test our GeoServer instances, we will have to complete a few configuration tasks first:

1. Generate test WMS bounding box requests.
2. Prepare an Apache JMeter™ workbench.
3. Execute the test.

Generating test WMS bounding boxes

Before we can begin to stress test our GeoServer instances, we need to come up with some WMS request parameters that we can use. If we can make the requests random within a given set of bounds, then so much the better. Fortunately for us, such a script exists in the world of Python. Frank Warmerdam created a Python script that will randomly generate WMS request parameters for random locations within a specified bounding box and at a range of zoom levels. The script itself can be downloaded from http://svn.osgeo.org/osgeo/foss4g/benchmarking/ wms/2010/scripts/wms_request.py. The script accepts a number of parameters to generate the random bounding boxes:

```
$ python wms_request.py [-count n] [-region minx miny maxx maxy] [-minres
minres] [-maxres maxres] [-maxsize width height] [-minsize width height]
[-srs <epsg_code>] [-srs2 <epsg_code>]
```

The command-line options that can be specified are:

Option	Purpose
count	This option specifies the number of requests to randomly generate
region	This option specifies the bounding box of the region to randomly generate requests in
minres	This option specifies the minimum resolution to use for requests
maxres	This option specifies the maximum resolution to use for requests
maxsize	This option specifies the maximum size for a request, expressed as width and height in pixels

Option	Purpose
`minsize`	This option specifies the minimum size for a request, expressed as width and height in pixels
`srs`	This option specifies the source coordinate reference system EPSG code (optional)
`srs2`	This option specifies the output coordinate reference system EPSG code to transform requests to (optional)
`filter_within`	This option specifies the name of the file containing geometries to filter out randomly generated requests

We will generate 100 random WMS requests to give ourselves a good spread of requests. Perform the following steps:

1. Make sure that Python is installed before running this command.

2. Execute the following from a command-line shell:

   ```
   $ python wms_request.py -count 100 -region 0 0 700000 1300000
   -minsize 400 400 -maxsize 800 800 -minres 1 -maxres 15 -srs 27700
   ```

3. This command will generate 100 WMS requests in CSV format inside the bounds of the British National Grid. Here are five examples generated from the command:

   ```
   493;595;126140.02,1241506.4,130761.48,1247084.1
   678;495;400974.82,1089828.8,403242.09,1091484.1
   582;543;633121.29,750590.72,638605.35,755707.28
   652;400;17348.862,386404.58,23686.324,390292.59
   416;481;471897.49,430970.91,472413.77,431567.85
   ```

4. The command will generate the CSV file using the value of `srs` as the filename, so in our case, this will be `27700.csv`. The file is stored in the same location as the command was run.

5. Before we can use this inside Apache JMeter™, we will have to tweak it a little bit. Notice how the first component of CSV contains a string similar to:

   ```
   493;595;126140.02
   ```

6. The first two components are the width and height for the WMS image request. We need to turn these into CSV components by replacing `;` with `,`.

7. Load the CSV file into your favorite text editor and do a find and replace.

8. Save the file.

Creating an Apache JMeter™ test workbench

Before we can get into the nitty-gritty of creating a test workbench for Apache JMeter™, we must download and install it. Apache JMeter™ is a 100 percent Java application, which means that it will run on any platform provided there is a Java 6 or higher runtime environment present. The binaries can be downloaded from `http://jmeter.apache.org/download_jmeter.cgi`, and at the time of writing, the latest version is 2.11. No installation is required; just download the ZIP file and decompress it to a location you can access from a command-line prompt or shell environment.

To launch JMeter on Linux, simply open shell and enter the following command:

```
$ cd <path_to_jmeter>/bin
$ ./jmeter
```

To launch JMeter on Windows, simply open a command prompt and enter the following command:

```
C:> cd <path_to_jmeter>\bin
C:> jmeter
```

After a short time, JMeter GUI should appear, where we can construct our test plan.

> For ease and convenience, consider setting your system's PATH environment variable to the location of the JMeter bin directory. In future, you will be able to launch JMeter from the command line without having to CD first.

The JMeter workbench will open with an empty configuration ready for us to construct our test strategy:

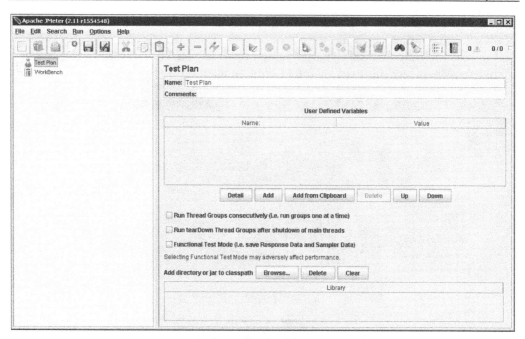

The first thing we need to do is give our test plan a name; for now, let's call it `GeoServer Stress Test`. We can also provide some comments, which is good practice as it will help us remember for what reason we devised the test plan in future.

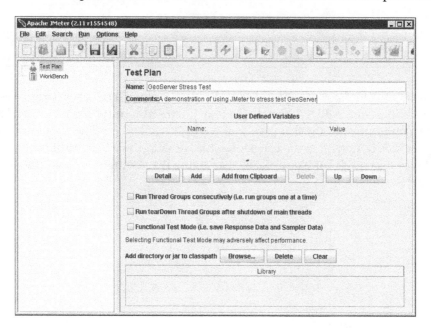

To demonstrate the use of JMeter, we will create a very simple test plan. In this test plan, we will simulate a certain number of users hitting our GeoServer concurrently and requesting maps. To set this up, we first need to add **Thread Group** to our test plan. In a JMeter test, a thread is equivalent to a user:

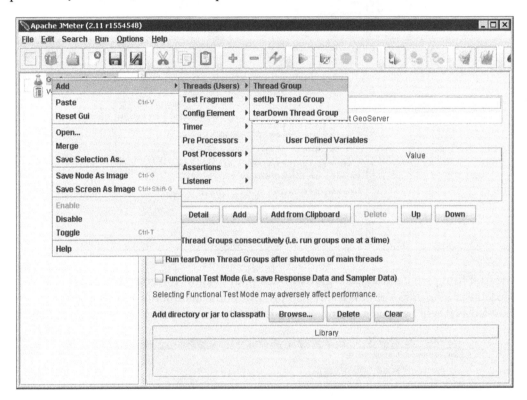

In the left-hand side menu, we need to right-click on the **GeoServer Stress Test** node and choose the **Add | Threads (Users) | Thread Group** menu option. This will add a child node to the test plan that we right-clicked on. The right-hand side panel provides options that we can set for the thread group to control how the user requests are executed. For example, we can name it something meaningful, such as **Web Map Requests**.

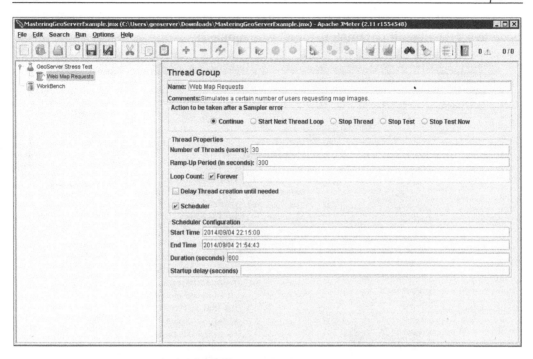

In this test, we will simulate 30 users, making map requests over a total duration of 10 minutes, with a 10-second delay between each user starting. The number of users is set by entering a value for **Number of Threads**; in this case, 30. The **Ramp-Up Period** option controls the delay in starting each user by specifying the duration in which all the threads must start. So, in our case, we enter a duration of 300 seconds, which means all 30 users will be started by the end of 300 seconds. This equates to a 10-second delay between starting threads (*300 / 30 = 10*). Finally, we will set a duration for the test to run over by ticking the box for **Scheduler**, and then specifying a value of 600 seconds for **Duration**. By specifying a duration value, we override the **End Time** setting.

Next, we need to provide some basic configuration elements for our test. First, we need to set the default parameters for all web requests.

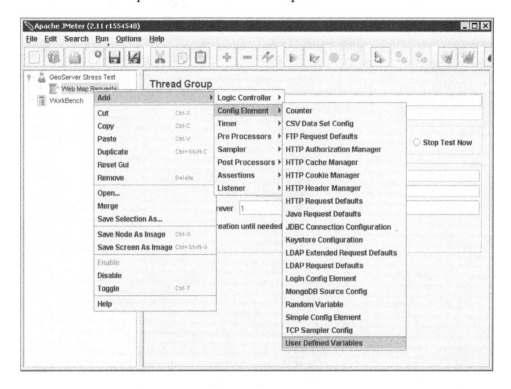

Right-click on the **Web Map Requests** thread group node that we just created, and then navigate to **Add | Config Element | User Defined Variables**. This will add a new node in which we can specify the default HTTP request parameters for our test:

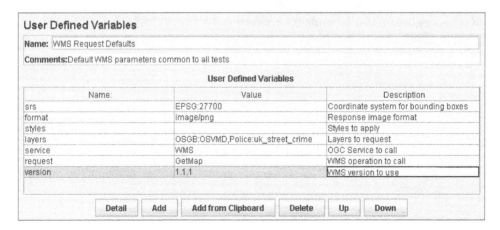

In the right-hand side panel, we can specify any number of variables. We can use these as replacement tokens later when we configure the web requests that will be sent during our test run. In this panel, we specify all the standard WMS query parameters that we don't anticipate changing across requests. Taking this approach is a good practice as it means that we can create a mix of tests using the same values, so if we change one, we don't have to change all the different test elements.

To execute requests, we need to add **Logic Controller**. JMeter contains a lot of different logic controllers, but in this instance, we will use **Simple Controller** to execute a request. To add the controller, right-click on the **Web Map Requests** node and navigate to **Add | Logic Controller | Simple Controller**. A simple controller does not require any configuration; it is merely a container for activities we want to execute. In our case, we want the controller to read some data from our CSV file, and then execute an HTTP request to WMS. To do this, we need to add a CSV dataset configuration. Right-click on the **Simple Controller** node and navigate to **Add | Config Element | CSV Data Set Config**.

CSV Data Set Config

Name: CSV Data Set Config

Comments: Load CSV data containing random WMS request properties

Configure the CSV Data Source

Filename:	27700.csv
File encoding:	
Variable Names (comma-delimited):	width,height,left,bottom,right,top
Delimiter (use 't' for tab):	,
Allow quoted data?:	False
Recycle on EOF ?:	True
Stop thread on EOF ?:	False
Sharing mode:	All threads

The settings for the CSV data are pretty straightforward. The filename is set to the file that we generated previously, containing the random WMS request properties. The path can be specified as relative or absolute. The **Variable Names** property is where we specify the structure of the CSV file. The **Recycle on EOF** option is important as it means that the CSV file will be re-read when the end of the file is reached. Finally, we need to set **Sharing mode** to **All threads** to ensure the data can be used across threads.

Next, we need to add a delay to our requests to simulate user activity; in this case, we will introduce a small delay of five seconds to simulate a user performing a map-pan operation. Right-click on the **Simple Controller** node, and then navigate to **Add | Timer | Constant Timer**:

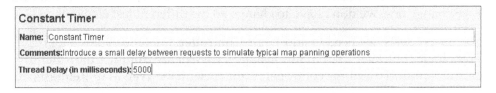

Simply specify the value we want the thread to be paused for in milliseconds. Finally, we need to add a JMeter sampler, which is the unit that will actually perform the HTTP request. Right-click on the **Simple Controller** node and navigate to **Add | Sampler | HTTP Request**. This will add an **HTTP Request** sampler to the test plan:

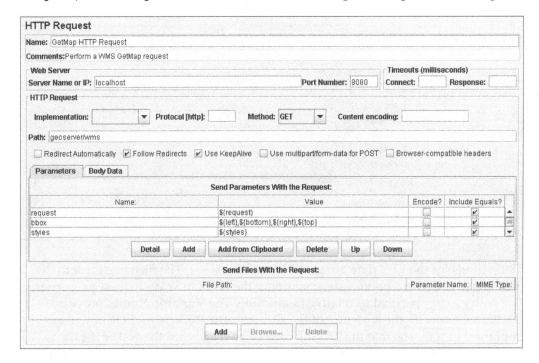

There is a lot of information that goes into this panel; however, all it does is construct an HTTP request that the thread will execute. We specify the server name or IP address along with the HTTP method to use. The important part of this panel is the **Parameters** tab, which is where we need to specify all the WMS request parameters. Notice that we used the tokens that we specified in the **CSV Data Set Config** and **WMS Request Defaults** configuration components. We use the `${token_name}` token, and JMeter replaces the token with the appropriate value of the referenced variable.

We configured our test plan, but before we execute it, we need to add some listeners to the plan. A JMeter listener is the component that will gather the information from all the test runs that occur. We add listeners by right-clicking on the thread group node and then navigating to the **Add | Listeners** menu option. A list of available listeners is displayed, and we can select the one we want to add. For our purposes, we will add the **Graph Results**, **Generate Summary Results**, **Summary Report**, and **Response Time Graph** listeners. Each listener can have its output saved to a datafile for later review. When completed, our test plan structure should look like the following:

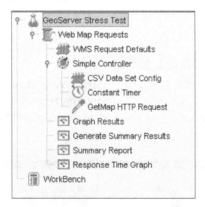

Before executing the plan, we should save it for use later.

Choosing where to execute tests

Before we go ahead and execute our test plan, we must consider from where we will run JMeter. Choosing where to run JMeter is important as it will impact how we interpret the results from the test. Broadly speaking, there are three locations we can choose to run JMeter:

- On the same server as GeoServer
- On a server on the same network as GeoServer
- On a web-connected desktop/laptop/server outside of the GeoServer network

The first option is useful for when we want to simply test our GeoServer's performance at rendering map images; in other words, the *pure* response time from GeoServer. Without the variability of network contention getting in the way (because we will call the local host), we will get a good appreciation of the rendering time of our GeoServer instance.

However, this option is no good if we have GeoServer on a "headless" server that can't display GUI. It is also worth noting that JMeter will itself consume resources, memory and CPU in particular, which can affect the validity of results. In this case, the second option will be the next best thing. By testing on the same network as the GeoServer instance, we will get a realistic reflection of the map image-rendering time of GeoServer, with only a minimal amount of overhead from the network contention.

The third option is the one that we will choose if we want to see how well our GeoServer instance performs in a real-world scenario. By running JMeter from a web-connected client, we will introduce real-world performance issues such as Internet congestion. The results should give us a realistic view of the sort of performance our users can expect to see.

Executing the test profile

Executing the test plan is very straightforward. We just need to hit the big green arrow button on the toolbar. Once we do this, the test will begin its execution, and we can examine the listeners as the test is in progress to see what happens in real time:

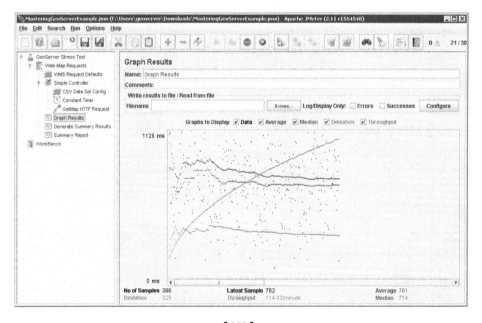

In this case, we can see the **Graph Results** listener plotting the results of the test as it runs. Notice that we didn't yet reach our maximum number of users running on the server. The number on the far right of the toolbar shows us how many threads of the total are running; in this case, there are only 21 out of the maximum 30 threads running. As the test progresses, this number will gradually increase at a rate of one every 10 seconds, as we specified in our **Ramp Up** property.

 We included the **Graph Results** listener in our test plan to demonstrate the visualization of requests. However, in practice, when doing a load test such as this, we will not actually include the **Graph Results** listener, as it is resource intensive.

Analyzing the results of the stress test

Once the test run is complete, we will be left with a range of results to examine. The listeners we add to our test plan will determine the kind of information we can analyze. The key information for us to analyze from our test run are **Summary Report** and **Response Time Graph**.

As its name suggests, **Summary Report** provides us with a summary of the responses received during the test. From it, we can ascertain details such as the average, minimum, and maximum response times for requests as well as an indication of the throughput of our server. Throughput is a good indicator of how well our server will handle the load as it tells us how many requests per second it can handle:

Label	# Samples	Average	Min	Max	Std. Dev.	Error %	Throughput	KB/sec	Avg. Bytes
GetMap HTTP ...	5198	252	35	4046	263.05	0.00%	8.7/sec	659.21	77983.7
TOTAL	5198	252	35	4046	263.05	0.00%	8.7/sec	659.21	77983.7

The summary report gives us a very good baseline measure that we can use to compare results against. For example, the results from this test were performed on a newly configured server without any users accessing it. They show that this particular server can handle a throughput of 8.7 requests per second. We can take this as a baseline indicator of what we can expect our server to do, and we can then do regular monitoring and tests to see if the server starts to deviate from this baseline significantly. If it does, then that will be an indication that there is a potential problem with the server or its configuration.

The **Response Time Graph** output is also a useful indicator of how well our server is processing data, and if we deploy JMeter in a web-connected client, then it will be a good indicator of the real-world response times that we can reasonably expect our server to deliver.

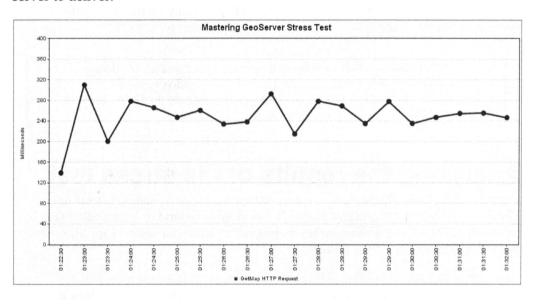

The graph can be structured over specific intervals to see how response times vary. If we make the graph match our ramp-up values, we can expect to see spikes in the response times every 10 seconds as a new user connects to the server. Over time, we can expect to see the server settle down and start to become a little more consistent in its response times. In an ideal world, we would like to see a graph that is relatively flat as that will indicate a server that is optimized well and not susceptible to spikes in load.

Of course, just as JMeter provided us all the information during the stress test, we also logged all the requests through the monitor extension. We can now go back to GeoServer and take a look at the activity and reports, or go direct to the database and run some queries to see how well GeoServer responded to the requests.

Summary

In this chapter, we discussed the reasons why we should monitor the health of our GeoServer instances. We explored how to install and configure GeoServer's monitor extension so that GeoServer logs the map requests made to it. We also looked at how Apache JMeter™ can be used to construct and execute test plans to place loads on our servers so that we can analyze the results and gain an understanding of how well our servers perform.

Performance testing is the key to having an optimized, responsive, and healthy GeoServer implementation. The real art of testing is devising tests in such a way that they are representative of the real-world scenario in which we think our server will be used. For example, it is not much use to simply set the test to create 100 concurrent users immediately and start hammering the server. By gradually introducing the load, and introducing small delays between each request to simulate user habits, we will get a much better reflection of how our server will perform in a real-world setting.

The formula is very simple: *well-performing GeoServer = happy users!*

Now we know how we can run performance tests and monitor the condition of our GeoServer instance, it is time to look at how we can further optimize it. In the next chapter, we will look at some different ways to further optimize our instances.

12
Optimizing GeoServer for Production

Our journey to getting GeoServer deployed and operating in a production environment is almost nearing its end. We now know how to do a wide range of things with our GeoServer instances, so it is time to take a final look at some strategies for how we can ensure our servers operate efficiently and reliably.

There is no point putting in all the effort to create a GeoServer instance packed with capabilities and suited to our needs if we do not consider how well it runs, and more importantly, how robust it is in production. There are numerous things we can do to ensure our instances are performing well, but in this chapter, we will focus on a couple of key elements. By the end of this chapter, we will discover how to:

- Deploy GeoServer as part of a cluster
- Optimize GeoServer by tuning the configuration
- Controlling the throughput of requests using the control-flow module
- Recovering from service failures automatically

Deploying GeoServer in a cluster

To get the most benefit from running GeoServer in a production environment, we should consider running a cluster of GeoServer instances. There are many reasons why we should do this, but the two key reasons are:

- **Performance**: We can spend a lot of time and effort optimizing a single instance of GeoServer to make it perform well, or we can implement several well-configured instances as a cluster. By increasing the number of instances available to service requests, we can clearly increase the number of concurrent requests that we can handle. The important thing, though, is that we spread the increased load across multiple instances rather than a single instance.

- **High availability**: The last thing we want happening, when running in a production environment, is for our server to fail and stop servicing requests. If we have a single instance of GeoServer, then we have a single point of failure within our environment. However, if we have a cluster of instances running, then we can lose a server without impacting our ability to respond to services. This is an important consideration when we design our architecture; we must ask ourselves: "What is the impact on our customers if a server fails?"

So, implementing a cluster of GeoServer appears to make sense, especially if we consider that it costs us nothing in software licensing. There are a number of different strategies for how we can implement a cluster, and we covered a number of these at the end of *Chapter 1, Installing GeoServer for Production*. However, they are all variations of essentially the same architectural design. Let's consider the logical architecture for a moment:

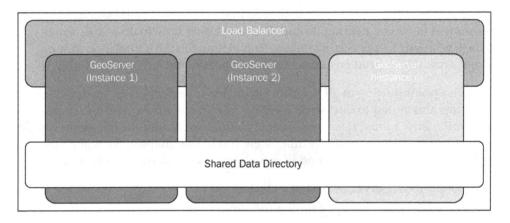

There are, in essence, three core components to any cluster configuration of GeoServer: a **load balancer** to distribute requests across the instances of GeoServer in the cluster, the **GeoServer instances**, and a **shared data directory**. The last component is the most important; without it, managing the cluster will have a significant manual overhead. However, even with a shared data directory, careful management is required to ensure there are no conflicts across the instances in the cluster. The main concern with running GeoServer in a cluster is keeping the individual instances synchronized with changes. To understand why this is a concern, we must first consider the role that the data directory plays.

In normal configurations, GeoServer reads and writes configuration information to and from the data directory. However, the directory is primarily there for persistence of the configuration across server restarts. In a normal operation, most of the configuration is held in memory, where it can be accessed quickly. This means that every time we make a configuration change, such as adding a new datastore or layer, GeoServer persists the configuration to storage and updates the in-memory catalog. If we have a second instance of GeoServer running, it will not be aware that there has been a configuration change triggered on the first. The second instance has its catalog loaded in memory, and it will never go back to the data directory to refresh the catalog unless it is instructed to do so.

Due to this concern, when we run a cluster, we must also consider our strategy to keep all instances in sync. Fortunately, GeoServer provides the ability to trigger a reload of the catalog either through the REST service or through the web administration console.

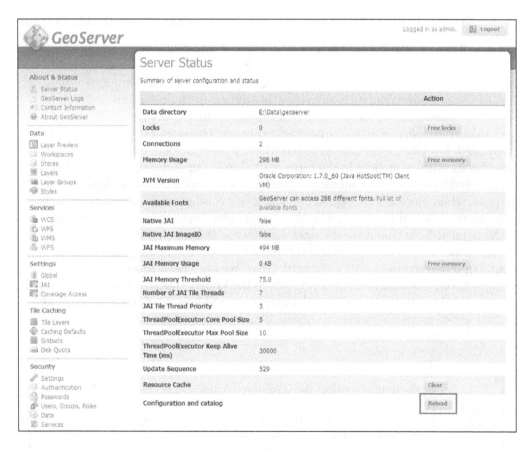

To access the reload function, we need to click on the **Reload** button that is accessible by clicking on the **Server Status** link from the left-hand side menu of the web administration console.

 REST API provides a reload method that we can call from other applications or through management scripts. More details can be found at `http://docs.geoserver.org/stable/en/user/rest/api/reload.html`.

The key is to nominate one of our instances as the *master*, leaving the others as *slaves*. To minimize the chances of configuration changes being made on any of the *slaves*, we can disable the web administration portal. There are two methods to do this:

- Add a Java system property and set it to true: *DGEOSERVER_CONSOLE_DISABLED=true to the JVM options*

- Remove all the JAR files with the prefix web from the `WEB-INF/lib` directory

So, every time we make a change to the configuration of the *master*, we must remember to issue the REST command to all the *slaves* so that they can reload their catalog. For environments where we do not expect much change, or where the change is predictable, such as in monthly data refresh operations, this might not be a big issue. However, if our environment is much more dynamic where the configuration is prone to frequent and sporadic changes, a different approach is required. Luckily for us, this issue has already been tackled, and GeoSolutions provides us with an answer in the form of its GeoServer Active Cluster extension. This extension will actively monitor a cluster of GeoServer instances looking for changes; when there is a change to one instance's configuration, the same change is broadcast to all other instances in the cluster. The clever thing here is that the *master* persisted the change to the data directory and refreshed its in-memory catalog as normal, but the *slaves* did not reload the whole catalog; instead, they simply updated the in-memory element. Now, we only need to worry about making changes to one instance of GeoServer, safe in the knowledge that the extension will take care of the rest. Full details on the extension and how to set it up are available on the GeoSolutions blog at `http://www.geo-solutions.it/blog/advanced-clustering-geoserver/http://www.geo-solutions.it/blog/advanced-clustering-geoserver/`.

 At the time of writing, the GeoServer Active Cluster extension has only just been announced, and as such, it has not been fully tested in production environments. We can support the effort by downloading the extension, using it, and then reporting back any issues. Better yet, if we have Java skills, we can even contribute fixes.

Sharing a data directory in Windows 2008 R2

The key to running a cluster of GeoServer instances is to have the data directory in a location that can be shared with the other servers in the cluster. Typically, on Windows, this means creating a shared directory on a server accessible by all others, and then using a UNC path (`http://en.wikipedia.org/wiki/Path_%28computing%29#UNC_in_Windows`) to access the share from other servers.

The process is straightforward and might be familiar to most Windows users. However, there is a catch that we must be aware of before we can successfully share the directory across the servers, and this is security. By default, the installer for Apache Tomcat will install the service using the Local System account. In most cases, this is fine; however, Local System Account is not able to access network shares due to its restrictions. Therefore, to access a shared data directory residing on another server, we must change the account that the Tomcat service runs under.

To accomplish this task, we can simply create a domain account in Active Directory, perhaps called `SVC_Tomcat`, and then use it across all the servers. However, some domain administrators might not allow domain accounts to be created and used as service accounts. In this case, we will need to implement the same approach using local accounts on the servers; provided we use the same name and password across all the servers, we can accomplish the same objective. Perform the following steps to create a local user account:

1. Launch the *Computer Management* tool:

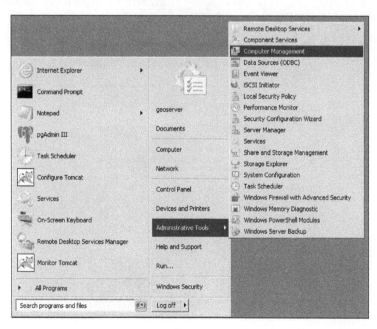

2. Go to **Start** | **Administrative Tools** | **Computer Management** to open the **Computer Management** dialog.

3. Expand the **Local Users and Groups** leaf under the **System Tools** parent:

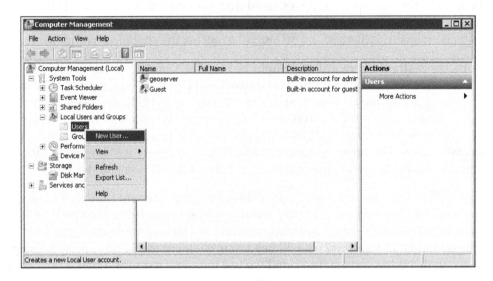

4. Right-click on the **Users** folder, and then select the **New User...** option from the context menu.

5. This will open the **New User** dialog from where we can create a new local user that will be used to run the Tomcat service:

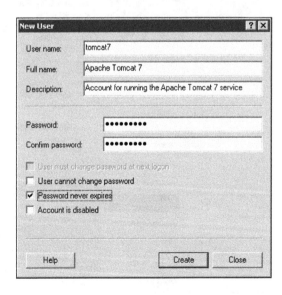

6. We need to give our local user a name, specify the full name, and provide a description so we know what we created the user for. In this example, we will use the name `tomcat7`, but we might consider giving it a prefix of `svc_` so that we can distinguish it as an account to be used for services. For now, though, we will just go with the name `tomcat7`.

7. We need to specify a password for the user, and the important thing is to tick the **Password never expires** box. If we don't tick this box, then we'll find that our local user password will expire, and consequently, the service will stop responding. Click on the **Create** button to create the user, and then close the dialog.

 It is important to remember the username and password we create as we need to repeat these steps on all of our GeoServer instances.

8. With our user created, we can now assign it as the service account for the Tomcat Windows service. To do this, we need to open the **Services** dialog from **Start | Administrative Tools | Services**:

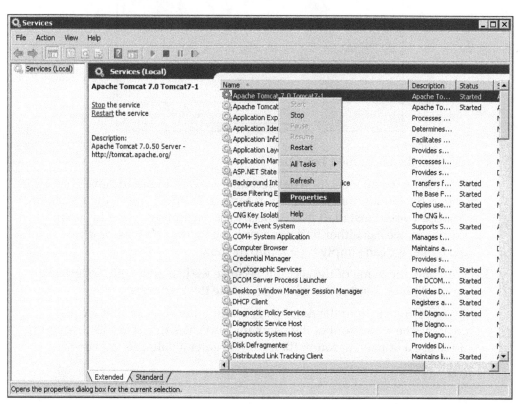

9. Notice that we have two Tomcat services running after the work we did in *Chapter 1, Installing GeoServer for Production*. We need to remember to conduct the same process for both the services.

10. Right-click on the first service, and then select **Properties** from the context menu. This will open the service properties dialog box:

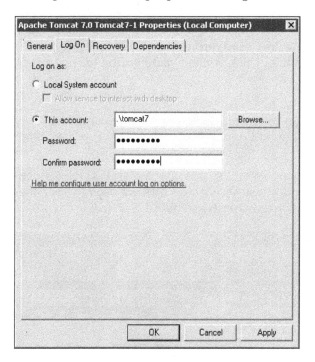

11. Click on the tab named **Log On**.

12. From here, we can specify what account we want to use to run the service under. By default, this will be **Local System account**, following a standard Apache Tomcat installation. To specify the account we want to run the service as, we can either find one using the **Browse** button, or if we know the name, we can simply type it into the box.

13. We know the name of the account because we just created it, so let's click on the **This account** radio button to enable the textboxes.

14. Type `.\tomcat7` into the first box to identify the account that we just created. The `.\` in front of the username indicates that it is a local account. If we use a domain account, then we will enter a value such as `domain-name\user-name`.

15. Click on the **OK** button to accept the changes. It is likely that the following message will appear. This is fine, it is just information, so click on **OK** to close the message:

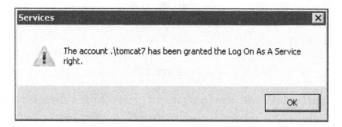

With the service changed so that it will now run under the local account, `tomcat7`, all we need to do is restart the service. We also need to perform the same operation on any other service we have running.

Finally, we need to set sharing on the data directory being used across all the instances in the cluster. To do this, we need to make sure that we also have a local `tomcat7` user created on the server where the data directory resides. Perform the following steps:

1. Right-click on the GeoServer data directory inside Windows Explorer, and select the **Properties** context-menu option:

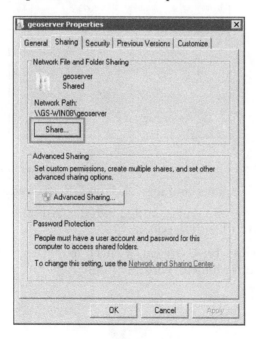

2. Select the **Sharing** tab, and then click on the **Share** button.

3. In the dialog that appears, accept the default properties and click on **OK**.

Our data directory is now shared and will be available for us to connect with any other server. However, when our Tomcat services attempt to write to the directory, an exception will be raised. This is because the directory will have the default security settings applied to it, preventing nonowner users from writing to it. In the same dialog, we need to click on the **Security** tab. Perform the following steps:

1. In the **Security** tab, add the local users group to the directory and ensure they have full control over the directory. We need to click on the **Edit** button:

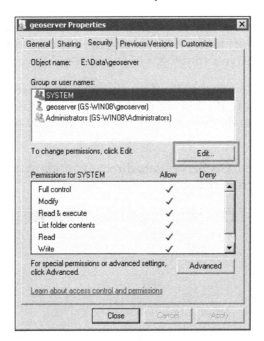

2. Click on the **Add** button, and then enter the value as Users into the textbox.

3. Click on **Check Names**, and then click on **OK** when the name is resolved.

4. The local Users group will be added into the **Group or user names** box; select the newly added **Users** item.

5. In the **Permissions for Users** list, we need to make sure that the box under **Allow** is ticked for the **Full control** option.

6. Click on **OK** to accept the changes and dismiss the dialog:

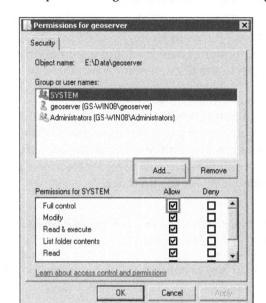

We have now set security on the data directory so that any user belonging to the local Users group will have full control (read and write) on the directory. We use a local account called `tomcat7` belonging to the Users group to run our Tomcat services. This means that any operation requiring the write access to the directory will be allowed, even though the action will be performed on another server. In other words, configuration changes made through the GeoServer web administration console will be written to the shared data directory without any issues.

Once again, this is a very important action to perform in production when you are running Tomcat as a Windows Service and using a shared data directory on another server. Without performing these steps, the Tomcat service will not be able to write configuration changes to the shared data directory.

Optimizing GeoServer

Ensuring your GeoServer instances operate at optimal performance is an important task. There are a number of different strategies used to optimize GeoServer and many different ways of doing it. There is a lot of information available online to optimize GeoServer, both in the documentation and through the community.

The GeoServer documentation contains some very useful information about running GeoServer in a production environment. There is also a white paper available online from Boundless that contains a wealth of information and advice. Rather than replicating all of this information, we will consider the key aspects; after all, the documents can be studied later for the finer details.

> The Boundless white paper, *GeoServer in Production*, is available online at `http://boundlessgeo.com/whitepaper/geoserver-production-2/` and is a very good document to learn about how to optimize GeoServer in production.

Native JAI and JAI image I/O extensions

GeoServer's rendering capabilities for coverages and WMS is provided by the **Java Advanced Imaging (JAI)** API. There is a pure Java version of the API, which is what GeoServer comes with as standard; utilizing pure Java implementations is how GeoServer is able to retain cross-platform compatibility. However, there are native versions of JAI available for Windows and Linux, which have been compiled and optimized specifically for these platforms.

We should give serious consideration for the installation of the native JAI libraries for the platform we run GeoServer on. Tests have shown that a significant increase in rendering performance can be achieved. To install the native libraries for our platform, we just need to follow the instructions at `http://docs.geoserver.org/stable/en/user/production/java.html#install-native-jai-and-jai-image-i-o-extensions`.

> If we deploy to a Windows environment, then the native JAI libraries are only available for 32-bit platforms. If you run a 64-bit Windows OS, then make sure you install 32-bit Java; otherwise, you will not be able to use the native JAI.

Optimizing Java Virtual Machine

Java Virtual Machine (JVM) is where the GeoServer code is run. JVM is the technology that enables Java software to be cross-platform compatible. Each platform that Java has been released for has its own implementation of JVM that converts the compiled Java bytecode into platform-specific instructions. There are numerous settings that control the way in which JVM is executed; we have already seen how we can configure the memory settings for JVM in *Chapter 1, Installing GeoServer for Production*.

Now, we will take a look at some additional settings that we can apply to JVM to optimize it:

Setting	Description
`-server`	This setting enables the server version of JVM that compiles the bytecode faster and with more optimizations.
`-XX:SoftRefLRUPolicyMSPerMB=3600`	This setting controls the lifetime of references in GeoServer, such as references to datastores. Making them live longer improves performance.
`-XX:+UseParallelGC`	This setting enables multithreaded garbage collection when more than one core is present.
`-XX:NewRatio=2`	This setting allows JVM to handle a larger number of short-lived objects.

Setting these options for JVM is platform-specific. On Linux, we can set them with the `JAVA_OPTS` environment variable, which we created in our service script. To edit these scripts, use the following command:

```
$ vi /etc/init.d/tomcat-1
```

Look for the line beginning with `JAVA_OPTS=`, and then add the preceding settings to the line.

On Windows, we can set the parameters inside the properties dialog for the Windows service for Tomcat:

1. Right-click on the service name inside the **Services** dialog, and then click on **Properties**.

2. Click on the **Java** tab, and then enter the settings into the **Java Options** box, one setting per line:

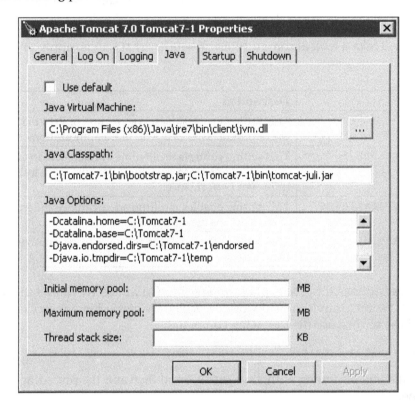

3. Once the settings have been entered, click on **Apply**, go back to the **General** tab, and use the service control buttons to restart the service. Once the service restarts, the new values will take effect.

4. Click on **OK** to accept and close all the changes.

Disabling unused GeoServer services

Each service that GeoServer exposes (WMS, WFS, WCS, and others) consumes resources on the server, primarily memory. Disabling services that we don't intend to use in our implementation is a quick way to reduce the resource requirements, and therefore make them more available for the services that we want to make use of. The services that we want disabled will be dictated by the intended use of our server. For example, if we simply want to serve raster maps for a web-mapping application, we only need to have WMS and read-only WFS services enabled (we need WFS because it can be used to provide vectors for map rendering). Similarly, if we only use the server for feature serving, then we might only enable WFS and WFS-T, and disable everything else.

To disable a service, for example the WCS service, we need to do it from the **Service Metadata** settings. Click on the name of the service from the left-hand side panel of the web administration console:

On the service settings page, we need to find the section called **Service Metadata**:

Notice that there are two options available; the one that we are interested in is called **Enable WCS** and will be ticked by default. We just need to uncheck the box, and then click on the **Save** button.

The WCS service will now be disabled.

Managing request handling with the control-flow extension

By using GeoServer as our web mapping server, we benefit from the many years of experience the community has gained. A lot of this experience has been translated into very useful modules and extensions that are designed to make GeoServer run faster, better, and more reliably. The control-flow module is one such extension. It has been written with the sole purpose of allowing an administrator to control how many requests can run concurrently inside the server.

Controlling the number of concurrent requests executing inside the server is important for a number of reasons, but primarily it is about ensuring the server's memory does not become saturated leading to OutOfMemory errors. There are three main benefits to controlling the number of concurrent requests executing on the server:

- *Performance*: The performance of GeoServer can be optimal when the number of concurrent requests running is no more than double the number of CPU cores. So, if the server contains eight cores, then we should not allow more than 16 GetMap requests to run concurrently.

- *Memory management*: Some requests for data can be very memory intensive, particularly WMS GetMap requests. Servicing WMS requests places much higher demands on memory than servicing WFS requests. Typically, in the case of WFS, the server streams data to respond to requests, but in the case of WMS, the server has to create the response (the image) in memory before sending it in the response. Several large or complex WMS GetMap requests can quickly saturate the server and cause an OutOfMemory exception to occur.

- *Resource contention*: This is reduced when the number of concurrent requests a user is allowed to execute can be controlled. Preventing individual users from flooding the server will allow a fairer distribution of resources across all users.

It is important to note that the control-flow module does not stop requests from being executed. When the configured maximums are reached, additional requests are queued, and then released, by the control-flow module gradually as resources free up. This is an additional benefit to using the module: it allows for a more uniform spread of requests executing inside the server.

Installing the control flow module

The method to install the print extension is the same as any other extension in GeoServer.

1. First, we must download the extension from the GeoServer website. Go to the stable release download page at `http://www.geoserver.org/ release/stable` and scroll to the bottom.

2. Under the **Miscellaneous** section, look for the **Control Flow** link and click to download the module:

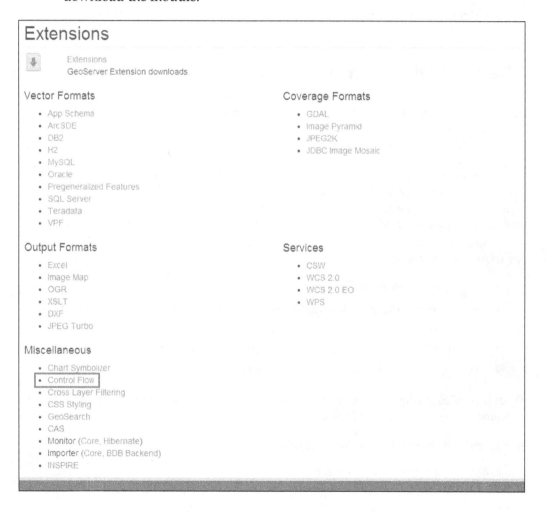

3. Open a command line on the directory where you downloaded the file to and enter the command:

```
$ unzip geoserver-2.5.2-control-flow-plugin.zip *.jar -d <tomcat_
home>/webapps/geoserver/WEB-INF/lib
```

4. This command will extract the files with a `.jar` extension into the `lib` folder of your GeoServer instance.

5. Remember to change `<tomcat_home>` to the folder where your Tomcat instance is installed.

6. Repeat the process for all of your Tomcat instances, but do not restart them yet. First, we must configure rules.

The control-flow module rules configuration

The control-flow module works by processing rules in a configuration file called `controlflow.properties`. This file should be in the GeoServer data directory; it is not created by default. Therefore, we will have to create the file in a text editor, and then save it to our GeoServer data directory.

The rules file is simply a text file, so open your favorite text editor and create a new file. Before being able to create a set of rules, we need to consider how we want to manage requests on our server. The way in which we manage requests will vary across deployments, and will typically depend on the available resources in our server. For the purposes of this book, we will consider the following as our profile for request management:

- The server has eight CPU cores
- We do not want an individual user to have more than four concurrent requests
- We want to blacklist IP addresses to prevent requests
- We want to throttle tile service requests

With this rules configuration, we will ensure we have fair usage for our users as well as manage the throughput in GeoServer.

In the text editor, enter the following lines:

```
# Set a timeout for requests
timeout=60
```

This line will tell the control-flow module to only allow requests to be queued for 60 seconds. If a request sits in the queue longer than this timeout value, then it will not be executed. This is a useful setting to set a value for as it will prevent wasted resources processing a request for which, in all likelihood, the end user has given up waiting for.

 Use # at the start of a line to add a comment. It is important to comment your rules configuration so that you know why you configured it the way you have at a later date.

Next, we will add a global service limit. Enter the following into the editor:

```
# Set a global service limit of 100 requests
ows.global=100
```

This rule means that no more than 100 service requests can run concurrently across all the service types GeoServer exposes. Next, we will configure some specific service controls. Enter the following lines:

```
# Don't allow more than 16 WMS GetMap requests (2 x 8 cores)
ows.wms.getmap=16
```

This will constrain the GetMap WMS requests to only 16 concurrent requests. Now, we will manage the per-user requests with the next lines:

```
# Limit individual users to 4 concurrent requests
user=4
```

The combination of these last two rules means that we should allow four different users to make four concurrent WMS GetMap requests. The GetMap request is throttled to a maximum of 16 requests, and individual users are restricted to only making four concurrent requests; therefore, 16 / 4 = 4 individual users make GetMap requests.

We also want to prevent specific IP addresses from making requests to the server. This can be useful to block servers that create excessive load on our servers, or abuse our service:

```
# Prevent a list of IP addresses from making requests
Ip.blacklist=192.168.1.50,192.168.1.51
```

The blacklist is simply a comma-separated list of IP addresses to block. Any request made from these servers will not be passed through to GeoServer, and instead, the control-flow module will just reject the requests.

Finally, we will throttle the number of WMS-C, WMTS, and TMS requests that can be made. These requests are handled by the built-in GeoWebCache service, and so they can be controlled using the following rule:

```
# Control the number of WMS-C, WMTS, and TMS requests from GWC
ows.gwc=32
```

Testing by the community suggests that GeoWebCache reaches its peak performance when handling four times the number of CPU cores in the server. In this case, a server with eight CPU cores will reach GeoWebCache's peak performance at 32 concurrent requests.

To activate the rules, we just need to save the file with the name `controlflow.properties` to the root of the GeoServer data directory. Once the file is saved, we can restart all of our Tomcat instances to activate the module and enforce the rules.

If at some point we want to disable the rules, then all we need to do is delete the `controlflow.properties` file, or comment out all the lines in the file. When the control-flow module runs, it looks for the rules to enforce; if they don't exist, it will simply do nothing and allow all requests to execute.

Automatic recovery from service failures

When running GeoServer in a production environment, the last thing we want to happen is for an instance to fail, and the first time we hear about it is when a customer complains. In this scenario, what we need is a script that can be executed on a schedule to check that GeoServer is still up and responding to requests.

These types of scripts are commonly referred to as Watchdog scripts. The principle behind the script is very simple: it makes a request to the server, and if it receives a failed response, then it attempts to restart the service.

When running GeoServer in a production environment, we need to create a Watchdog script that executes on a regular schedule and performs the following checks:

- Checks that the Tomcat service is up:
    - If not up, it attempts to restart the service
    - If the service cannot be restarted, an administrator is e-mailed

- If Tomcat is running, then a test request is made to GeoServer:
    - If a 200 response is not received, the service is restarted
    - If the service cannot be restarted, an administrator is e-mailed

Creating a Windows Watchdog script

Following the logic outlined for the Watchdog script is straightforward in Windows. To make the Watchdog script work, we will need to ensure we have *Wget* installed on our server. Wget for Windows can be downloaded from http://gnuwin32. sourceforge.net/packages/wget.htm.

The Watchdog script we will use is included with the code files accompanying this book. The code files are available from the Packt Publishing website.

The first lines of the script are used to set some environment variables for when the script runs; these make the script more configurable as we simply need to change the values once if we want to use the script on other servers:

```
SET WGET={path_to_wget}
SET HTTP_URL=http://localhost:808/geoserver/openlayers/img/west-mini.
png
SET WGET_LOG="WgetLog.txt"
SET TOMCAT_SERVICE={service_name}
SET EMAIL_TO="{email_address}"
SET EMAIL_CC="{email_address}"
SET EMAIL_FROM="{email_address}"
SET EMAIL_NAME="{server_name}"
SET SMTP_SERVER={ip_address}
SET SMTP_PORT=25
SET LOG_FILE=GeoServerWatchdog.log
```

Each SET command specifies an environment variable for the script's execution. When we implement the script in our server, we need to change the {path_to_ wget} values at the location where we installed the wget binaries. The value of {service_name} should be the name of the Tomcat Windows service. The {email_ address} values should be replaced with relevant e-mail addresses appropriate to our organization, as will the {ip_address} and {server_name} values.

Next, we create an entry into the logfile for the Watchdog script:

```
REM Log running of the script
ECHO %DATE% %TIME% - Checking status of Tomcat service >> %LOG_FILE%
```

Then, we get into the core of the script. The script needs to identify whether the Tomcat Windows service is running and act accordingly. This is done by checking the status of the Windows Service using the sc query command:

```
FOR /F "tokens=3 delims=: " %%H IN ('sc query "%TOMCAT_SERVICE%" ^|
findstr "        STATE"') DO (
```

This FOR statement executes the `sc query` command on the Tomcat service, and then examines the response looking for a token with the STATE value in it:

```
IF /I "%%H" NEQ "RUNNING" (
```

If the response is not equal to RUNNING, the script assumes that the Tomcat service has failed:

```
ECHO %DATE% %TIME% - The Tomcat service is not currently running,
attempting to start it... >> %LOG_FILE%


ECHO. >> %LOG_FILE%


net start %TOMCAT_SERVICE% >> %LOG_FILE%


ECHO. >> %LOG_FILE%
```

This block will attempt to start the Tomcat Windows service using the NET START command. The output from the command is written to the logfile to aid in debugging in the case of a failed restart. To determine whether the services have restarted, we perform a similar check as before:

```
FOR /F "tokens=3 delims=: " %%H IN ('sc query "%TOMCAT_SERVICE%" ^|
findstr "        STATE"') DO (
       IF /I "%%H" NEQ "RUNNING" (
          ECHO %DATE% %TIME% - The Tomcat service could not be started,
email alert sent >> %LOG_FILE%
          cscript SendEmail.vbs %SMTP_SERVER% %SMTP_PORT% %EMAIL_NAME%
%EMAIL_FROM% %EMAIL_TO% %EMAIL_CC% "GeoServer Instance Failed"
InstanceFailedMessageBody.txt HTML
       ) ELSE (
          ECHO %DATE% %TIME% - The Tomcat service restarted successfully
>> %LOG_FILE%
          cscript SendEmail.vbs %SMTP_SERVER% %SMTP_PORT% %EMAIL_NAME%
%EMAIL_FROM% %EMAIL_TO% %EMAIL_CC% "GeoServer Instance Restarted"
InstanceRestartedMessageBody.txt HTML
       )
    )
```

If the Tomcat service is successfully restarted, a warning e-mail is sent to the administrator. If the service did not restart, an alert e-mail is sent to the administrator asking them to attempt a manual restart of the service. The method to e-mail is a VBScript file included in the code bundle, and the text of the message bodies are stored in the `InstanceRestartedMessageBody.txt` and `InstanceFailedMessageBody.txt` files.

If the initial check of the Tomcat service shows it to be running, then the script needs to check if GeoServer is servicing requests. Though Tomcat is running fine, it does not mean that GeoServer is alive and responding:

```
) ELSE (
    ECHO %DATE% %TIME% - The Tomcat service is running, checking
GeoServer is responding to requests >> %LOG_FILE%

    %WGET% -t 1 --timeout=20 -o %WGET_LOG% -O NUL %HTTP_URL%

    findstr "200 OK" %WGET_LOG%
```

A wget request is made to a specified URL, and the response is logged to a logfile; the result of the request is actually discarded and not stored. The findstr command is used to inspect the wget logfile, and it specifically looks for a 200 OK response:

```
IF %ERRORLEVEL%==0 (
    ECHO %DATE% %TIME% - GeoServer responded to a download request
>> %LOG_FILE%
    ECHO %DATE% %TIME% - GeoServer is up and running >> %LOG_FILE%
```

The result of the findstr command is stored in an environment variable called ERRORLEVEL. If ERRORLEVEL is equal to 0, then the wget logfile contained a 200 OK response. In this case, we can just log the fact and do nothing further. However, if the response does not contain 200 OK, then we need to attempt to restart the Tomcat service and check its response:

```
) ELSE (
ECHO %DATE% %TIME% - GeoServer did not respond to a download request,
attempting to restart Tomcat service... >> %LOG_FILE%
    ECHO. >> %LOG_FILE%

    net stop %TOMCAT_SERVICE% >> %LOG_FILE%
    net start %TOMCAT_SERVICE% >> %LOG_FILE%

    ECHO. >> %LOG_FILE%

    FOR /F "tokens=3 delims=: " %%H IN ('sc query "%TOMCAT_SERVICE%" ^|
findstr "        STATE"') DO (
IF /I "%%H" NEQ "RUNNING" (
ECHO %DATE% %TIME% - The Tomcat service could not be started, email
alert sent >> %LOG_FILE%
cscript SendEmail.vbs %SMTP_SERVER% %SMTP_PORT% %EMAIL_NAME%
%EMAIL_FROM% %EMAIL_TO% %EMAIL_CC% "GeoServer Instance Failed"
InstanceFailedMessageBody.txt HTML
```

```
        ) ELSE (
            ECHO %DATE% %TIME% - The Tomcat service restarted
successfully >> %LOG_FILE%
            cscript SendEmail.vbs %SMTP_SERVER% %SMTP_PORT% %EMAIL_NAME%
%EMAIL_FROM% %EMAIL_TO% %EMAIL_CC% "GeoServer Instance Restarted"
InstanceRestartedMessageBody.txt HTML
        )
    )
)
```

Finally, we just need to clean up the wget logfile to make it ready for the script to execute again:

```
DEL %WGET_LOG%
```

Scheduling the Watchdog script

Now that we have a script that we can execute periodically, we need a means of executing it on a schedule. This is an ideal use case for the built-in Windows Task Scheduler.

1. To create a schedule, we need to first launch the Task Scheduler from **Administration Tools** in **Control Panel**. The easiest way to do this is to launch it from **Windows** | **Administrative Tools** | **Task Scheduler**:

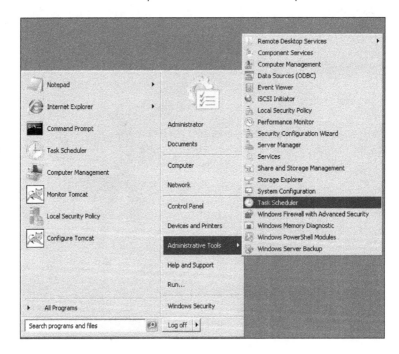

2. To create a new task, we need to click on the **Create Task...** option from the right-hand side panel in **Task Scheduler**:

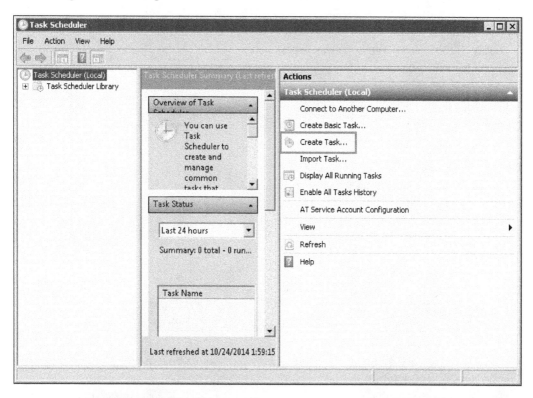

3. This will open the **Create Task** wizard that will guide us through the process of creating the scheduled task.

4. It is a tabbed interface, where we can specify the settings for the task. On the **General** tab, we need to enter a name for our task along with a description of what the task does.

5. The only other setting we need to change on the **General** tab is to make sure the option **Run whether user is logged on or not** is selected:

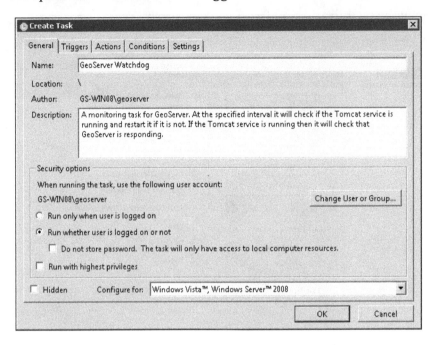

6. Next, we need to specify what causes the task to be executed by clicking on the **Triggers** tab.

7. On the **Triggers** tab, we can specify multiple triggers for the task; however, in our case we will set a very simple time-based trigger. To do this, we need to click on the **New...** button:

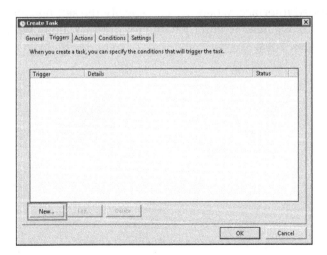

8. Clicking on **New...** should give you the following screen:

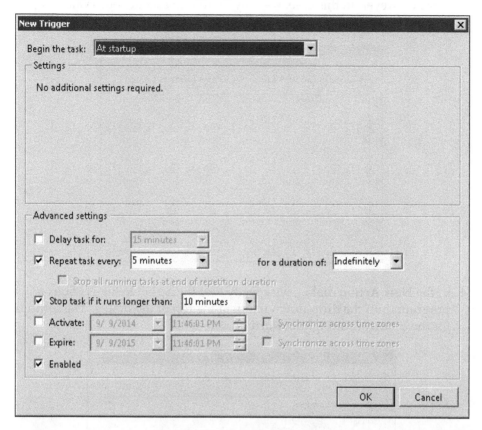

9. We want to make sure that our scheduled task will run every time the server starts up. To do this, we choose the **At startup** option from the drop-down at the top of the dialog.

10. In the **Advanced settings** group box, we want to set the task to repeat every five minutes, and stop the task if it runs for longer than 10 minutes. We also want to make sure that the task is set to run indefinitely.

11. Once we are done with the settings, we need to click on the **OK** button to have the trigger added to the list for the task.

12. Next, we need to specify what we want the task to do when it runs. Click on the **Actions** tab to configure what is executed.

13. Again, this tab allows us to specify multiple actions to take when the task runs. However, in this case, we only want it to execute our Watchdog script, so we click on the **New...** button to create the action:

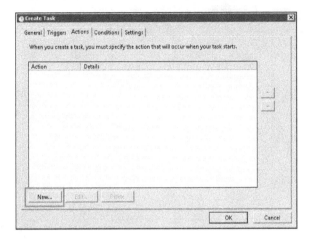

14. In the **New Action** dialog, we specify that the action to take is **Start a program** from the drop-down menu at the top of the dialog. The settings for the action are straightforward:

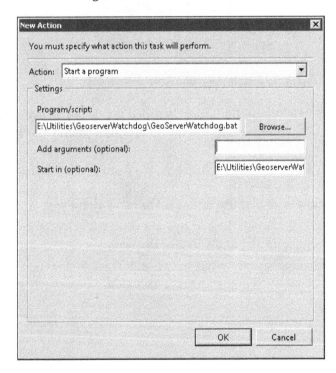

15. We need to specify the location of our `GeoServerWatchdog.bat` script as the program to run.

16. Next, we specify the directory containing the script as the value for the **Start in (optional)** setting to ensure the script executes in the context of its containing directory.

17. When all settings have been defined, we simply click on the **OK** button to add the action to the task.

18. We can leave the default settings for the **Conditions** and **Settings** tabs. We just need to click on the **OK** button to save the task we created.

If you recall, we set our task to run when the server started, but we don't really want to restart the server now just to start the running task.

If we highlight the new task we created, and then click on the **Run** item on the right-hand side panel, our task will start running:

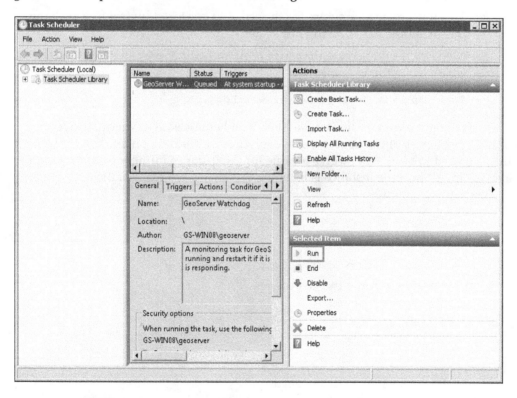

It will continue to execute every five minutes indefinitely, and if the server is ever rebooted, then the task will simply start again on startup.

Creating a Linux Watchdog script

For Linux, we will create a shell script that can be executed as a cron job. There is a complete version of the script in the code bundle accompanying this chapter.

 When you take a look at the script, you will notice that it does not contain any logic to send e-mails. There are several different ways to send e-mails from a shell script, and all require different setups. For the purposes of this book, e-mail sending has not been included. However, it will be a useful learning exercise to research and implement an e-mail-sending capability.

1. First, we need to create a location for the script to go into; from the terminal, enter the following:

    ```
    $ mkdir /opt/watchdog
    ```

2. This will create a directory for the script to be stored in; feel free to change this to another location in your system.

3. Next, we need to create the script itself and edit it; we can do this in one action using the vi text editor:

    ```
    $ vi /opt/watchdog/geoserver-watchdog.sh
    ```

The first thing we want to do is make the script generic so that we can use it on multiple instances of GeoServer that we might have running on our server. To do this, we need to be able to receive a value for the instance number to control, and also the HTTP port the instance is listening on. This is achieved in the first section of the script:

```
# Declare instance related variables
INSTANCE=1
HTTP_PORT=8080

# Check the command-line arguments
if [ ! $# -eq 4 ]; then
  # Insufficient arguments passed to the script
  echo >&2 "usage: $0 -i [instance_number] -p [http_port]"
  exit 1
else
  # Correct number of arguments
  while [ $# -gt 0 ]; do
    case "$1" in
      -i) INSTANCE=$2; shift;;
```

```
        -p) HTTP_PORT=$2; shift;;
        -*) echo >&2 \
          "usage: $0 -i [instance_number] -p [http_port]"
          exit 1;;
        *) break;;
      esac
      shift
    done
  fi
```

We declare some variables to hold the instance number and the HTTP port. Then, we perform a check on the number of arguments passed in to the script. We expect the script to be executed like this:

$ geoserver-watchdog.sh -i 1 -p 8080

Here, -i is the instance number to watch and -p is the HTTP port to query. If the number of arguments is not equal to four, then we break out of the script and print a usage message. If the number of arguments is correct, then we loop through them and populate the variables for the script.

Next, we define some variables that will help us along the way:

```
# Declare other variables
PID_FILE=/var/run/catalina-${INSTANCE}.pid
HTTP_URL=http://localhost:${HTTP_PORT}/geoserver/openlayers/img/west-
mini.png
TOMCAT_SERVICE=tomcat-${INSTANCE}
PID='cat $PID_FILE'
```

The important variables here are HTTP_URL, which we will use when trying to query if GeoServer is responding to web requests. We check the PID_FILE that contains the process ID for the Tomcat service. Finally, we can call the TOMCAT_SERVICE that identifies the Tomcat service control script.

Next, we need to set some logging so that we can record the results of our monitoring:

```
# Set the logfile to stdout if the file does not exist
LOG_FILE=/var/log/geoserver/watchdog-${INSTANCE}.log
if [ ! -e "${LOG_FILE}" ]; then
  LOG_FILE="/dev/stdout"
Fi
```

We create a variable to store the location of our logfile by appending the instance number to a constant string; this means that depending on how we run the script, we will get different logfiles that are generated. In this case, our logfile will be a directory on the host server, but if we save the log to a shared location, we might want to further qualify the name of the logfile using the server hostname. We can change the line to read as the following:

```
SERVER_NAME='hostname'
LOG_FILE=/mnt/share/logs/watchdog-${SERVER_NAME}-geoserver-
${INSTANCE}.log
```

Assuming we have a shared directory (such as an NAS device) mounted on `/mnt/share`, we will store a file into the `logs` directory that will include the server hostname as well as the instance running on this host. The `if` code block will then check that the logfile exists; if it does not, the code block will set the log location to the standard output, which in most cases is the console.

Following the script setup sections, we are ready to get into the core of the script. We first start by checking the status of the process:

```
If [ -d /proc/$PID ]; then
```

This takes PID (process ID) for the Tomcat service, and then performs a check to see if a directory exists with the same ID inside `/proc`. If a process is running, then there will be a directory matching its ID, and if not, then there won't be. We use this fact to determine if the Tomcat instance process is running. If it is, then we need to check that GeoServer responds to the HTTP requests because although the Tomcat service is running, it doesn't mean that GeoServer is responding:

```
# Tomcat is running so we need to check it is responding to requests
  echo "'date' WatchDog Status: Tomcat service ${TOMCAT_SERVICE} is
running" >> "${LOG_FILE}"
  wget $HTTP_URL -T 1 --timeout 20 -O /dev/null &> /dev/null
  if [ $? -ne "0" ]; then
    # HTTP not responding, restart service
    echo "'date' WatchDog Status: Tomcat service ${TOMCAT_SERVICE} is
not responding to HTTP requests" >> "${LOG_FILE}"
    echo "'date' WatchDog Action: Restarting Tomcat service ${TOMCAT_
SERVICE}" >> "${LOG_FILE}"
    service $TOMCAT_SERVICE restart >> "${LOG_FILE}"
  else
    # HTTP is responding
    echo "'date' WatchDog Status: Response OK - Tomcat service
${TOMCAT_SERVICE} is responding to HTTP requests" >> "${LOG_FILE}"
  fi
```

First, we do some logging to keep a record of the actions taken, and their results. Then, we use `wget` to issue a request to GeoServer running on `localhost` to fetch a single image from the OpenLayers directory. The output is piped to the `null` device, so we don't store it, but do check the return value of the command with `[ $? -ne "0" ]`. If the response code is not equal to `0`, then GeoServer failed to respond, so we attempt to restart the service using `service $TOMCAT_SERVICE restart >> "${TOMCAT_SERVICE}`. If we do get a return code of `0`, then we log that the response was `OK`.

If the result of `[ -d /proc/$PID ]` is `false`, then the Tomcat service dies. In this case, we have an `else` block to handle the restart:

```
else
  # Tomcat is not running, restart the service
  echo "'date' WatchDog Status: Tomcat service ${TOMCAT_SERVICE}
process appears to be dead" >> "${LOG_FILE}"
  echo "'date' WatchDog Action: Restarting Tomcat service ${TOMCAT_
SERVICE}" >> "${LOG_FILE}"
  service $TOMCAT_SERVICE restart >> "${LOG_FILE}"
fi
```

In this case, we need to issue the restart command to the Tomcat service using the `service $TOMCAT_SERVICE restart >> "${LOG_FILE}"` command. The result of the command is sent to the logfile.

Before we can use this script in the shell, we need to make it executable:

```
$ chmod +x /opt/watchdog/geoserver-watchdog.sh
```

Scheduling the Watchdog script using cron

Much like Windows, Linux has the ability to run tasks in the background at specific times. Tasks are defined in `crontab` files, and the system `cron` daemon then executes them; this means that we can utilize it to execute our Linux Watchdog script.

To launch `crontab`, we need to open a terminal and enter this command:

```
$ sudo crontab -e
```

This will open the root user's `crontab` file to edit. If an editor environment variable is not set, then you might be asked to select an editor to use; choose the one you are most comfortable with. This command will open the `crontab` file in a text editor so that we can add commands to it. The structure of a command is as follows:

```
minute(0-59) hour(0-23) day(1-31) month(1-12) weekday(0-6) command
```

Notice that the minute, hour, and weekday components are zero-based values, so we need to bear this in mind when we construct our command. Our command will be similar to the one we created for Windows. We will have the Watchdog script execute every 5 minutes. In the text editor, scroll down until the first blank line and then type this line:

```
0,4,9,14,19,24,29,34,39,44,49,54 * * * * {path}/geoserver-watchdog
```

Make sure you replace {path} with the actual path to the location where you saved the Watchdog script. This command lists the minutes at which we want the task to execute, and then sets a wildcard for all other elements. In effect, this is telling cron to run the job every 5 minutes every day of the week, every month of the year, every year; in effect, indefinitely. Save the file, and then exit the editor. On exiting the editor, you will see a crontab: installing new crontab message in the terminal. This means that the crontab file was installed successfully.

Summary

Our long journey through advanced GeoServer configuration has now come to an end. In this chapter, we considered the benefits of implementing a cluster of GeoServer instances and looked at a new extension available to manage it. We also looked at a special case where we have to configure Windows servers in a specific way so that they are able to share a data directory from the network.

Following on from clustering, we examined different approaches to optimize the configuration; we looked at using native JAI libraries, specifying options for JVM, disabling unnecessary services, and managing the flow of requests handled by the server, in particular.

Finally, we looked at how we can implement scripts that can watch and monitor our instances of GeoServer, automatically restarting when failures are detected, checking to ensure the Tomcat service is up and running, but also ensuring it is responding to HTTP web requests. We then saw how to set the Watchdog scripts to run at specific intervals, ensuring our services have minimal disruption.

Index

Symbols

@abstract tag 185
@app.route decorator 300
<geoserver_data_directory> directory
  about 289
  apps directory 289
  function directory 289
  lib folder 289
  process folder 290
  scripts directory 289
  wfs folder 290
@title tag 185
-Xmx512m switch 131

A

Active Directory
  about 309
  configuring, for authentication 310-312
  configuring, for authorization 312-316
  using, for user authentication 309
  using, for user authorization 309
alternatives command 10
Apache JMeter™
  about 340
  reference link 340
  test workbench, creating 342-349
Apache Portable Runtime (APR) 22
Apache Tomcat
  download link 14
  installing 14
**Apache Tomcat 7 installation,
    on CentOS 6.3**
  Apache Tomcat, running as service 16-20
  Apache Tomcat, securing 20, 21
  performing 15

**Apache Tomcat 7 installation, on Windows
    Server 2008 R2 SP1**
  performing 21-24
  Tomcat service, configuring 25-27
  Tomcat service, controlling 24, 25
app-schema extension
  configuring 122
  download link 121
  installing 121
  mapping file 125-127
  WFS service, configuring 123, 124
app-schema mapping file
  about 125
  catalog section 125
  includedTypes section 125
  namespaces section 125
  sourceDataStores section 125
  targetTypes section 126
  typeMappings section 126
ArcGrid
  URL 42
automatic recovery, from service failures
  about 374
  Linux Watchdog script, creating 384-387
  Windows Watchdog script,
    creating 375-378

B

Base64 316
BLOB
  URL 68
Boundless Geo
  URL 44
British National Grid
  reference link 53

C

cascaded services
  defining 143
  using 144
  using, as reverse proxy 146, 147
  WFS-only server, enabling through
      WMS 145, 146
  WMS server capabilities, extending 144
Cascaded Style Sheets. *See* CSS styles
cascaded WFS connection
  configuration options 158
  creating 155
  creating, through proxy 162
  data store, creating 155-160
cascaded WMS connection
  cascaded WMS layer, publishing 151-155
  creating 147
  data store, creating 148-150
catalog section, app-schema
      mapping file 125
Catalogue Service for the Web (CSW)
  URL 242
CentOS 6.3
  Apache Tomcat 7 installation 15
  GeoServer deployment 28, 29
  Java installation 8-10
  multiple GeoServer instances,
      configuring on 34-36
CentOS Linux 6.3
  GDAL binary libraries, installing on 44, 45
chained WPS processes
  crime type, selecting 282-284
  executing 280-282
  Police Force territory, selecting 284, 285
changeMapFilter function 194
command-line options
  count 340
  filter_within 341
  maxres 340
  maxsize 340
  minres 340
  minsize 341
  region 340
  srs 341
  srs2 341

Commercial-Off-The-Shelf (COTS) 30
Common Query Language (CQL)
      expression 138
community extensions
  URL 204
complex features
  about 119, 120
  versus simple features 117
configuration, database connection
      pool 79-81
configuration options, cascaded
      WFS connection
  Character encoding for XML messages 158
  Connection and read timeout (ms) 158
  Favor HTTP POST method over GET 158
  Feature buffer size 158
  Filter compliance level 159
  HTTP Authentication user name 158
  HTTP Authentication user password 158
  Lenient parsing 159
  Maximum number of Features to
      retrieve 159
  usedefaultsrs 159
  Use gzip encoding if server supports it 158
  WFSDataStoreFactory:AXIS_ORDER 159
  WFSDataStoreFactory:
      AXIS_ORDER_FILTER 159
  WFSDataStoreFactory:
      OUTPUTFORMAT 159
  WFS GetCapabilities URL 158
  WFS protocol strategy 159
configuration, print extension
  about 207
  dpis section 208
  fonts section 210, 211
  formats section 209
  hosts whitelist section 211, 212
  layouts section 212
  scales section 209, 210
Content.ftl file 197
control-flow module
  about 370
  download link 371
  installing 371, 372
  rules configuration 372-374
  used, for managing request handling 370

CQL_FILTER parameter
  about 193
  using 193-195
crontab
  about 387
  launching 387
CSS extension
  download link 176
CSS styles
  about 167, 176
  basics 180, 181
  creating 182-188
  extension, installing 176-179
CSS Styling extension 177

D

data
  consuming 256
  editing, WFS-T used 244
  loading, KML reflector used 258
  serving, from Microsoft SQL Server 97
  serving, from Oracle 93
  serving, from PostGIS 90
  serving, from SQL Azure 97
  styling, CSS used 176
  styling, SLD files used 168
database connection pools
  about 78, 79
  configuring 79
  connection timeout option 80, 81
  fetch size option 80, 81
  max connections option 79, 80
  min connections option 80
  validate connections flag 80
database platform, connection pool
  Microsoft SQL Server 83
  MySQL 83
  Oracle 11g R2 83
  PostgreSQL (PostGIS) 83
Database Server 242
database session close-up SQL 89
database session startup SQL 88
database views
  versus GeoServer SQL Views 105

data consumers 240
data creators / originators 240
data directory
  sharing, in Windows 2008 R2 359-365
data publishing, with application schema
  about 128
  application schema mapping file 132-139
  data store, setting up 139-141
  feature type, configuring 139-141
  source data preparation 129-132
data styling, with SLD
  reference link 168
data users 240
db.properties file 333
demilitarized zone. *See* **DMZ**
Desktop GIS
  using 244
Digest
  using, for user authentication 316
DMZ 146, 147
dpis section 208
dynamic heatmap example
  creating, render transformations
    used 170-175

E

ECQL
  reference link 193
Enterprise Linux GIS
  URL 44
Erdas Imagine format 55
European Union INSPIRE Directive
  URL 121
Execute WPS request 264
Execution Settings configuration section,
    WPS extension
  about 272
  connection timeout 272
  maximum asynchronous executions
    run parallel 272
  maximum synchronous executions
    run parallel 272
extensions, GeoServer
  community 204
  official 204

F

Feature Chaining 120
File Server 242
fill property 181
filter.properties file 333
filters, using
   reference link 180
Flask 298
flat representation 119
fonts section 210, 211
Footer.ftl file 197
formats section 209
Freemarker templates
   about 196
   Content.ftl file 197
   Footer.ftl file 197
   Header.ftl file 197
   reference link 196
   used, for changing WMS responses 195-200

G

GDAL 42, 43
GDAL binary libraries
   environment variables, setting 48, 49
   installing 43
   installing, on CentOS Linux 6.3 44, 45
   installing, on Windows Server 2008
       R2 SP1 45-47
   system variables 48, 49
GDAL core
   URL 46
gdalinfo command 51
gdal_merge.py
   reference link 54
GDAL MrSID plugin
   URL 46
GDAL support, adding
   about 43
   GDAL binary libraries, installing 43
   GeoServer GDAL plugin, installing 49
gdal_translate utility 57
general database connection parameters
   about 87
   database session close-up SQL 89
   database session startup SQL 88
   geometry metadata table 89, 90
   primary key metadata table 87
GeoDRM RM 321, 322
Geofabrik
   URL 130
GeoJSON
   about 301
   URL 301
geometry metadata table 89, 90
GeoNode
   URL 256
GeoScript
   about 287
   integrating, with GeoServer 288-290
   URL 288
GeoScript extension
   installation, checking 291
   installing 290, 291
GeoServer
   about 8
   configuring 30
   deploying, in cluster 355-358
   deploying, to Apache Tomcat 27, 28
   GeoScript, integrating with 288-290
   Google Earth, launching from 256-258
   Java requisites 8
   multiple instances, configuring on
       single server 34
   optimizing 366
   Python WPS process, testing 297
   raster formats 42
   RESTful service, creating 297-302
   script hooks 288
   scripting 291
   stress testing 339
   WPS process, creating 292
   WPS process, defining 292-294
   WPS process run method, creating 295, 296
GeoServer application schemas
   using 121
GeoServer configuration
   about 30
   scaling horizontally 32
   scaling vertically 31
   scaling vertically and horizontally 33

GeoServer deployment
about 27, 28
checking 30
on CentOS 28, 29
on Windows Server 2008 R2 SP1 29
GeoServer deployment, in cluster
about 355
data directory, sharing in Windows
 2008 R2 359-365
GeoServer GDAL plugin
installing 49, 50
GeoServer in production
reference link 366
GeoServer monitor extension
about 330
activity, viewing 336
configuring 332
db.properties file 332, 333
download link 331
filter.properties file 332, 333
hibernate.properties file 332, 334
installation, checking 335
installing 331, 332
monitor.properties file 332, 334
OWS Request Summary report 337
reports, viewing 337
request data 337-339
GeoServer monitoring
importance 329, 330
GeoServer, optimizing
control-flow module, installing 371, 372
control-flow module rules
 configuration 372-374
JVM, optimizing 367, 368
native JAI and JAI image I/O
 extensions 366
request handling, managing with
 control-flow extension 370
unused GeoServer services, disabling 369
GeoServer print extension. *See* print
 extension
GeoServer SLD cookbook
reference link 168
GeoServer SQL Views
versus database views 105
GeoServer's security documentation
reference link 305

GeoServer's WFS-T service
QGIS, connecting to 245-249
GeoServer, using as Proxy
about 143
cascaded services, defining 143
cascaded WFS connection, creating 155
cascaded WMS connection, creating 147
server capabilities, extending 162-164
GeoServer WAR (Web Archive) file
about 27
reference link 28
GeoSolutions blog
reference link 358
Geospatial Data Abstraction Library.
 See **GDAL**
Geospatial Digital Rights Management
 Reference Model. *See* **GeoDRM RM**
GeoTIFF
about 55
overviews 55, 56
raster formats, converting to 57, 58
tiles 56
URL 42
GetFeatureInfo request 196
GetFeatureInfo templates 196
Google Earth
launching, from GeoServer 256-258
network links, using 259, 260
granule 59
Groovy 290
Gtopo30
URL 42

H

Halo-radius property 181
Header.ftl file 197
hibernate.properties file 334
hosts whitelist section 211, 212
HTTP Digest authentication
setting up 317-319
testing 319, 320
HTTP Header
using, for user authentication 321, 322
HTTP Header authentication
setting up 322-325
testing 325-327

I

ImageMosaic format
  about 59
  creating, automatically 60-62
  creating, manually 62-66
  index file 59
  projection file 60
  properties file 60
  URL 42
  using 59
ImageMosaic JDBC extension
  configuring 68
  download link 67
  faster searching 67
  features 67
  installing 67, 68
  portability 67
  shared database 67
  using 67
ImageMosaic JDBC extension, using
  extension configuration files, creating 71-73
  GeoServer data store, creating 74, 75
  metadata table, creating 70
  raster data, loading 69
  raster data, preparing 69
includedTypes section, app-schema mapping file 125
index file, ImageMosaic format 59
Infrastructure as a Service (IaaS) 31
INSPIRE Road Transport Network application schema 127
installation
  Apache Tomcat 14
  Apache Tomcat 7, on CentOS 6.3 15
  Apache Tomcat 7, on Windows Server 2008 R2 SP1 21-24
  Java, on CentOS 6.3 8-10
  Java, on Windows Server 2008 R2 SP1 11-14
  Microsoft JDBC drivers, on Linux 98, 99
  Microsoft JDBC drivers, on Windows Server 2008 R2 100-102
  Microsoft SQL Server extension 97
  Oracle extension 94
  print extension 204

J

Java
  download link 9
  installing, on CentOS 6.3 8-10
  installing, on Windows Server 2008 R2 SP1 11-14
Java Advanced Imaging (JAI)
  about 209
  URL 209
Java Development Kit (JDK) 8
Java Naming and Directory Interface. *See* **JNDI**
JAVA_OPTS environment variable
  -server parameter 18
  -Xms512m parameter 18
  -Xmx1024m parameter 18
  -XX:MaxPermSize=128m parameter 18
Java Runtime Environment (JRE) 8
JavaScript 290
Java Virtual Machine. *See* **JVM**
JDBC 82
JDBC ImageMosaic extension. *See* **ImageMosaic JDBC extension**
JMeter
  launching, on Linux 342
  launching, on Windows 342
JNDI
  about 82
  configuring, at servlet container 83-86
JNDI connection 82
JPEG 59
jQuery
  URL 232
JSON keys
  createUrl 225
  dpis 225
  layouts 225
  outputFormats 225
  printUrl 225
  scales 225
JVM
  about 367
  optimizing 367, 368
  settings 367
Jython
  URL 298

K

keys
map : height 226
map : width 226
name 226
rotation 226
KML reflector
URL 257
used, for loading data 258

L

label property 181
layout metaData element
defining 215, 216
layout pages
defining 216-222
layouts section 212
Library Mode 189
Lightweight Directory Access
Protocol (LDAP)
about 309
reference link 309
Linux
Microsoft JDBC drivers, installing on 98, 99
Linux Watchdog script
creating 384-387
scheduling, cron used 387
load balancer 356

M

main connection parameters
database 92, 96, 103
host 91, 96, 103
passwd 92, 96
Password 103
port 91, 96, 103
schema 92, 96, 103
user 92, 96, 103
manager web application
reference link 21
MapFish
about 204
URL 204
URL, for documentation 228

Marine Scotland National Marine Plan
Interactive example
reference link 198
mark property 181
maxOpenPreparedStatements parameter 85
Metadata Server 242
Microsoft JDBC drivers
installation, verifying 102
installing, on Linux 98, 99
installing, on Windows Server
2008 R2 100-102
Microsoft SQL Server
data, serving from 97
extension, installing 97
Microsoft SQL Server table
publishing, as layer 103, 104
monitor.properties file 334
mosaic 59
multiple GeoServer instances
configuring, on CentOS 6.3 34-36
configuring, on single server 34
configuring, on Windows Server 2008
R2 SP1 37-40
Multipurpose Internet Mail Extensions
(MIME) 280

N

namespaces section, app-schema mapping
file 125, 126
Network Attached Storage (NAS) device 32
nonce 318
number of concurrent requests, controlling
benefits 370

O

OGC simple features specification
reference link 118
OGC standard
DescribeProcess operation 264
Execute operation 264
GetCapabilities operation 264
URL 264
ogr2ogr
reference 106
one-to-one mapping 119

OpenLayers application
example 230, 231
initializing 232-234
print request, sending 236
print SPEC to POST, generating 234-236
OpenStreetMap data
downloading, from website 129
using 129
Oracle
data, serving from 93
Oracle extension
installation, validating 95
installing 94
Oracle table
publishing, as layer 96
osm2po
URL 130
OSM-GB project
URL 155
OS StreetView™ 52
OS VectorMap District 69
overviews, GeoTIFF 55, 56

P

parameterized statement 85
per-request filtering of data 193
per-request styling of map features
about 188
implementing 189-192
Library Mode 189
ways 189
PGRASTER
reference link 69
PNG 59
poolPreparedStatements parameter 85
PostGIS
about 90
data, serving from 90
URL 90
PostGIS table
publishing, as layer 90-93
PostgreSQL PGDG 9.3
URL 44
postp.1.class switch 131
prefix=ws argument 131
prepared statement 85

primary key metadata table 87
print extension
about 204
configuring 207
installation, verifying 205-207
installing 204, 205
print layouts
defining 212-215
layout metaData element, defining 215, 216
layout pages, defining 216-222
print requests
making 222
**Process groups configuration section, WPS
extension 273, 274**
projection file, ImageMosaic format 60
properties file, ImageMosaic format
about 60, 65
AbsolutePath property 65
Caching property 65
ExpandToRGB property 65
Heterogenous property 65
LevelsNum property 65
Levels property 65
LocationAttribute property 65
Name property 65
Public Web Mapping Server 242
Python 290
Python Package Index (PyPI)
URL 298

Q

QGIS
about 62
connecting, to GeoServer's WFS-T
service 245-249
reference link 169
Topology Checker tool, using 249-255
URL 62, 169, 244

R

raster2pgsql
reference link 69
raster data optimization
performing 51
single-file, versus multi-file 53, 54
source data 51-53

raster datasets
  serving 58, 59
  serving, ImageMosaic format used 59
  serving, ImageMosaic JDBC extension
    used 67
raster formats
  about 42
  converting, to GeoTIFF 57, 58
raster processing
  reference link 54
regular expressions
  reference link 105
relational representation 119
reload method
  reference link 358
render transformations
  reference link 172
  utilizing 170-175
repository, GDAL library
  Boundless Geo 44
  Enterprise Linux GIS 44
  PostgreSQL PGDG 9.3 44
Response Time Graph output 352
REST API
  about 223, 224
  print requests, specifying 226-230
  print server capabilities, obtaining 224, 225
RESTful service
  reference link 298
results
  saving, WFS-T service used 255

S

scales section 209, 210
scaling out 32
scaling up 31
script hooks, GeoServer
  App 288
  function 288
  WFSTX 288
  WPS 288
SDI
  about 240, 241
  technology platform 241-243

security subsystem
  user authentication 306, 307
  user authorization 306, 307
server capabilities
  extending 162-164
**Service Metadata configuration section,
    WPS extension 270, 271**
service metadata elements
  abstract 271
  access constraints 271
  current keywords 271
  fees 271
  maintainer 271
  online resource 271
  title 271
Service Oriented Architecture (SOA) 145
servlet container
  JNDI, configuring at 83-86
shared data directory 356
simple features
  about 117-119
  versus complex features 117
slaves 358
SLD_BODY= parameter 189
sldBody variable 191
SLD files
  about 167, 168
  creating 168, 169
  render transformations, using 170-175
  used, for styling data 168
SLD= parameter 189
**sourceDatastores section, app-schema
    mapping file 125, 126**
spatial analysis
  performing, WPS used 274, 275
Spatial Data Infrastructure. *See* **SDI**
SQL Azure
  data, serving from 97
SQL injection
  URL 114
SQL View layers
  about 105
  creating 106-115
stress testing, GeoServer
  Apache JMeter™ test workbench,
    creating 342-349

locations, selecting 349, 350
performing 339
results, testing 351, 352
test profile, executing 350, 351
test WMS bounding boxes,
    generating 340, 341
strips, GeoTIFF 55
stroke property 181
Styled Layer Descriptor files. *See* **SLD files**
Summary Report 351
Symbol Selectors section
reference link 185

T

targetTypes section, app-schema mapping
    file 126, 127
TIFF 59
Tile Index tool 63
tiles, GeoTIFF 55, 56
TinyOWS
URL 162
Topology Checker tool, QGIS
using 249-255
typeMappings section, app-schema
    mapping file 126, 128

U

UK Police Data Portal
URL 106
UNC path
reference link 359
URL template
<api-method> element 300
<crime_type> element 300
<parameters> element 300
<port> element 300
<server-name> element 300
user authentication
about 306, 307
Active Directory, configuring for 310-312
Active Directory, using for 309
Digest, using for 316
HTTP Header, using for 321, 322

user authentication methods
about 307, 308
authentication filter chain 307
authentication provider chain 307
user authorization
about 306, 307
Active Directory, configuring for 312-316
Active Directory, using for 309
user authorization methods 309
utilities, by GDAL
reference link 54

V

validationQuery parameter 85
valid properties
reference link 180
variable substitution
reference link 173
vendor-specific WMS parameters
reference link 193
vi command 16
virtual services, using
reference link 270

W

web administration console 50
Web Mapping Server (Internal) 242
Web Processing Service. *See* **WPS**
Well-Known Text (WKT) 278
WFS schema
reference link 124
WFS-Transaction (WFS-T)
about 87
service, using to save results 255
used, for editing data 244
Wget
download link 375
Windows package for JRE
download link 11
Windows Server 2008 R2
data directory, sharing 359-365
Microsoft JDBC drivers,
    installing on 100-102

Windows Server 2008 R2 SP1
Apache Tomcat 7 installation 21-24
GDAL binary libraries, installing on 45-47
GeoServer deployment 29
Java installation 11-14
multiple GeoServer instances,
    configuring on 37-40
Windows Watchdog script
creating 375-378
scheduling 378-383
WMS request parameters
reference link 340
WMS responses
changing, Freemarker templates
    used 195-200
workspace configuration section,
    WPS extension 269, 270
WorldImage
about 59
URL 42
WPS
about 171, 263, 264
processes 264
processes, chaining 265
used, for performing spatial
    analysis 274, 275
WPS extension
configuring 269
download link 265
installation, checking 267, 268
installing 265, 266

WPS extension configuration
about 269
Execution Settings configuration
    section 272
Process groups configuration
    section 273, 274
Service Metadata configuration
    section 270, 271
workspace configuration section 269, 270
WPS process
about 264
chaining 265
executing 275-280
WPS process chain
executing 286, 287
WPS request builder application 275

X

XPath
reference link 139
xsi:schemaLocation attribute 124

Y

YAML Ain't Markup Language (YAML)
about 207, 208
URL 208

Thank you for buying
Mastering GeoServer

About Packt Publishing

Packt, pronounced 'packed', published its first book *"Mastering phpMyAdmin for Effective MySQL Management"* in April 2004 and subsequently continued to specialize in publishing highly focused books on specific technologies and solutions.

Our books and publications share the experiences of your fellow IT professionals in adapting and customizing today's systems, applications, and frameworks. Our solution based books give you the knowledge and power to customize the software and technologies you're using to get the job done. Packt books are more specific and less general than the IT books you have seen in the past. Our unique business model allows us to bring you more focused information, giving you more of what you need to know, and less of what you don't.

Packt is a modern, yet unique publishing company, which focuses on producing quality, cutting-edge books for communities of developers, administrators, and newbies alike. For more information, please visit our website: www.packtpub.com.

About Packt Open Source

In 2010, Packt launched two new brands, Packt Open Source and Packt Enterprise, in order to continue its focus on specialization. This book is part of the Packt Open Source brand, home to books published on software built around Open Source licenses, and offering information to anybody from advanced developers to budding web designers. The Open Source brand also runs Packt's Open Source Royalty Scheme, by which Packt gives a royalty to each Open Source project about whose software a book is sold.

Writing for Packt

We welcome all inquiries from people who are interested in authoring. Book proposals should be sent to author@packtpub.com. If your book idea is still at an early stage and you would like to discuss it first before writing a formal book proposal, contact us; one of our commissioning editors will get in touch with you.

We're not just looking for published authors; if you have strong technical skills but no writing experience, our experienced editors can help you develop a writing career, or simply get some additional reward for your expertise.

Building Websites with ExpressionEngine 2

ISBN: 978-1-84969-050-8   Paperback: 328 pages

A step-by-step guide to ExpressionEngine: the web-publishing system used by top designers and web professionals

1. Learn all the key concepts and terminology of ExpressionEngine: channels, templates, snippets, and more.

2. Use RSS to make your content available in news readers including Google Reader, Outlook, and Thunderbird.

3. Manage your ExpressionEngine website, including backups, restores, and version updates.

GeoServer Beginner's Guide

ISBN: 978-1-84951-668-6   Paperback: 350 pages

Share and edit geospatial data with this open source software server

1. Learn free and open source geospatial mapping without prior GIS experience.

2. Share real-time maps quickly.

3. Learn step-by-step with ample amounts of illustrations and usable code/list.

Please check **www.PacktPub.com** for information on our titles

PostGIS Cookbook

ISBN: 978-1-84951-866-6   Paperback: 484 pages

Over 80 task-based recipes to store, organize, manipulate, and analyze spatial data in a PostGIS database

1. Integrate PostGIS with web frameworks and implement OGC standards such as WMS and WFS using MapServer and GeoServer.

2. Convert 2D and 3D vector data, raster data, and routing data into usable forms.

3. Visualize data from the PostGIS database using a desktop GIS program such as QGIS and OpenJUMP.

Google Maps JavaScript API Cookbook

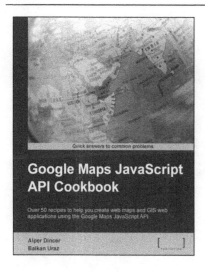

ISBN: 978-1-84969-882-5   Paperback: 316 pages

Over 50 recipes to help you create web maps and GIS web applications using the Google Maps JavaScript API

1. Add to your website's functionality by utilizing Google Maps' power.

2. Full of code examples and screenshots for practical and efficient learning.

3. Empowers you to build your own mapping application from the ground up.

Please check **www.PacktPub.com** for information on our titles